In Common Cause

In Common Cause:

The "Conservative" Frances Trollope and the "Radical" Frances Wright

by

Susan S. Kissel

Bowling Green State University Popular Press
Bowling Green, OH 43403

Women's Studies

General Editor

Jane Bakerman

Library of Congress Catalogue Card No.: 92-75450

ISBN: 0-87972-614-4 Clothbound
       0-87972-617-2 Paperback

Cover design by Gary Dumm

To Michael

Contents

Preface and Acknowledgments

Had I not been a resident of Cincinnati, Ohio, I might never have become interested in either Frances Trollope or Frances Wright. While researching nineteenth century artists who lived in the Cincinnati area, I became immersed in the intertwining, yet separate, lives of these two women. Since neither British writer had been well received in Cincinnati in the early 1800s, it is not surprising, perhaps, that neither is much remembered there today. The former had made Cincinnati notorious during the early nineteenth century in her *Domestic Manners of the Americans* while the latter had made herself notorious throughout the United States, and in Cincinnati, as well, long before she was buried in Cincinnati's Spring Grove Cemetery in 1852.

Cincinnati, in fact, wanted to forget these two women—and so did the rest of mid-nineteenth century American society. What is surprising, however, is the way in which both writers remain virtually unknown throughout America today. Despite the recent, significant work of literary critic Helen Heineman on Frances Trollope's life and fiction, and that of biographer Celia Eckhardt on Frances Wright, few contemporary American women's histories or literary anthologies give more than brief mention to either figure.[1] This remains true despite a virtual outpouring of new publications amidst the last decades of interest in women's writings and in women's historical contributions.[2] Celia Eckhardt theorizes that Frances Wright's nineteenth century radicalism continues today to deter interest in her life: "To be called a Fanny Wrightist in America in the 1830s was no less threatening than being called a communist in the 1950s. No doubt because she was so radical, history has not yet done justice to Fanny Wright" (Eckhardt, "Of Fanny and Camilla Wright" 40). But women's history certainly has begun to deal with other radical women reformers such as Mary Wollstonecraft and Margaret Fuller. Why not Frances Wright? And what about Frances Trollope who was known in her own time, and continues into the twentieth century to be stereotyped, as a Tory conservative, a prudish, class-conscious woman, and an ambitious snob—in other words, as Frances Wright's complete opposite?[3] Surely she is not seen as too radical to be dealt with, as well?

Certainly, both authors have been denigrated as women who failed to know and to honor the proper female sphere—as have many other achieving women who ignored the gender restrictions of their place and period. William Thackeray declared his fellow writer, Frances Trollope, "guilty of a fault which is somewhat too common among them [women authors]; and having very little,

i

except prejudice, on which to found an opinion, she makes up for want of argument by a wonderful fluency of abuse" (Review of *The Vicar of Wrexhill* in Heineman, *Mrs. Trollope* 52). Over a century later, in 1975, C. P. Snow would continue Thackeray's attack, saying of Frances Trollope, as well as of Frances Wright and her sister Camilla: "the total amount of sense possessed by that pair [the Wright sisters] and Mrs. Trollope was not large. Among the three of them they conceived perhaps the scattiest of all Mrs. Trollope's plans [Mrs. Trollope's trip to America]" (25). Eileen Bigland dismissed Frances Wright's life and work virtually in a word, calling her the "fanatical Frances Wright" in 1954 (58), while Lucy Poate Stebbins and Richard Poate Stebbins also stressed Wright's female emotionalism, calling her "the most dangerous member of all the Trollope circle, the ardent and notorious feminist, Frances Wright" (28).

What cannot be denied is that these two women, Frances Trollope and Frances Wright, were two of the most important and most well-known British women of their period. Further, their names were to become virtually household words in Britain and in America for several decades of the 1800s. John Stuart Mill was to call Frances Wright one of the most important women of her time, Elizabeth Cady Stanton was to keep Frances Wright's works on her library table and, together with Susan B. Anthony and Matilda Joslyn Gage, Stanton was to use Frances Wright's portrait as the frontispiece for *The History of Woman Suffrage*. [4] Walt Whitman, as well, borrowed ideas from her and called Frances Wright "one of the best [women] in history though also one of the least understood" (Traubel 2: 204-5). Frances Trollope, too, influenced important figures of her own time in spite of having been as widely misunderstood and criticized as Frances Wright had been. Charles Dickens and Harriet Beecher Stowe were to follow Frances Trollope's literary initiatives with their own popular novels exposing the evils, respectively, of the factory system in England and the institution of slavery in America, in each case a full 15 years after Frances Trollope's controversial works, *The Adventures of Jonathan Jefferson Whitlaw* (1836) and *The Life and Adventures of Michael Armstrong: The Factory Boy* (1840), had gone through several printings each. Further, as Helen Heineman so carefully shows in *Frances Trollope* (1984), Frances Trollope's literary innovations were to change the travel book genre, awaken the British public's interest to fiction based on social realism, and popularize a new kind of female picaresque heroine through the creation of the outlandish Widow Barnaby (139). Finally, Mark Twain came to believe Frances Trollope had understood America better than any other foreign observer of her time despite the vicious attacks which had greeted the publication of her first book, her book on the New World, *Domestic Manners of the Americans* (1832) [Mullen xxviii].

In examining their lives, I wish not only to help recognize the achievements of these two remarkable women—achievements which remain as significant as they are unknown more than a century after their deaths—but to consider, as well, the ways in which Frances Trollope and Frances Wright have continued to be stereotyped and misunderstood up to the present day. Their studies of America, their hopes and concerns for its democratic processes, and their criticisms of the injustices they saw in America, in Great Britain, and elsewhere in the Western World, are important and relevant still. Despite the technological advances that now have changed our lives in the twentieth century, despite an end to the institution of slavery and the advent of suffrage for blacks and for women in America, many of Trollope's and Wright's observations still apply and many of their questions still beg for answers. Further, the pattern of their own individual lives may also suggest the abuses wrought by stereotyping human lives which, in all their complexity, defy easy understanding. The readiness with which we rush to categorize, simplify, judge and dismiss other individuals—women, men and races different from ourselves—is revealed clearly when Frances Trollope's and Frances Wright's lives and works are juxtaposed. It is difficult to understand how these two nineteenth century British women have continued to be seen as so radically different from each other—and yet not only has this been true in the past but it remains so today, as well. For instance, in the introduction to the most recent edition of Frances Trollope's *Domestic Manners of the Americans*, Richard Mullen explains, "Even Fanny Wright, so opposite to Fanny Trollope in almost everything regarding America, agreed with her on [the need for better education for American women]" (Mullen xxv). By continuing this myth of opposition which has served to categorize and dismiss two exceptional women's lives, we not only miss the many similarities in thought and in action between the two writers, but we engage ourselves always in devaluing one life at the expense of the other. The consequence, of course, becomes the devaluation of both authors' lives since, as I hope to show, they overlap and parallel one another to a great extent.

Ironically, both Frances Trollope and Frances Wright spoke often about how such methods of separation and belittlement work to ill ends for everyone. In examining the relationship between the races, and that between the sexes, both writers revealed, as we shall see, how commonality and interdependency can be disregarded only with great cost to the humanity of everyone involved. They would, I believe, regret deeply the way in which their differences have been allowed to overshadow the courageous stands they took and the common struggles they fought for a more just and civilized world.

In the first section of this book, I shall examine the stereotypes by which Frances Trollope and Frances Wright have been known, dismissed, and largely forgotten from their own time until the present day. I will next look at what appear to be the real differences between the two women both in their personal and in their public lives. The third section will examine what history has overlooked or ignored: the many common perspectives and common causes which Frances Trollope and Frances Wright shared in their lifetimes. Part four will consider their influence upon the literature of their times, and, finally, I will look at what their lives and works have to suggest for our own times and our own lives as we near the twenty-first century.

This book would not have been possible, of course, without the recent, ground-breaking scholarship of Helen Heineman on Frances Trollope and Celia Eckhardt on Frances Wright—definitive studies which brought about my own work (without responsibility for its limitations or its conclusions). I am also indebted to my department chair Paul Reichardt for his support of this project and to secretaries Liz Gosney, Vanessa Johnson and Judy Strange for their skillful typing assistance. Nor would this project have come into being without the support of Northern Kentucky University through a project grant and a summer fellowship which enabled me to begin research on these two authors and to visit those places in America and in Great Britain that were most formative and most significant in the lives of these two women. I wish to thank Northern Kentucky University's Media Services and Sharon Taylor who provided invaluable service through Steely Library's Interlibrary Loan department. *Studies in the Novel* has kindly given permission for me to reprint an article on Frances Trollope, published in the summer of 1988, as part of Chapter Six. My children (Greg and Scott) and stepchildren (Davith and Katie) all deserve thanks, as well, for their willingness to accompany me on research trips to study the lives of these two historical figures. And, especially, I must thank my husband and colleague, Michael C.C. Adams, for his major support in this (and in my every other) undertaking and for his companionship on these trips (as on all other journeys significant to me). It is through him—and the difference he has made in my life—that I have come to know the dangers of stereotyping.

Part

❖ 1 ❖

Stereotypes

Stereotypes

The threat of female deviance pervades [America] culture.... History casts [the deviant female] up in the distorted image of Anne Hutchinson, Mary Dyer, and the mostly female victims of the witch hunts; the caricature of Fanny Wright and the spinster symbol Susan B. Anthony; crazy Carrie Nation with her hatchet; bomb-throwing Emma Goldman; and the twentieth-century equivalent of the deviant stereotype, the dyke. (Lerner xxxv)

Both Frances Trollope and Frances Wright experienced vitriolic attacks and constant name-calling in their lifetimes. They had ventured forth, unaccompanied by husbands or guardians, as world travelers and political observers, dared to speak out as writers, and in Frances Wright's case, in public lectures, and had given their opinions on matters of state as well as on matters of family. They received immediate name recognition in their own time after publishing their first books (even though Frances Wright's *Views of Society and Manners in America* was published anonymously) and became acquainted with many of the great thinkers and world leaders of their period. Their lives were not ordinary; neither were their minds nor their contributions to history. Yet these intelligent, active, complicated and inquisitive women were quickly reduced to single-dimensional figures in their own time and beyond.

Unfortunately, little has been passed down to us of the broader scope of their acts, their insights, or their works. In America Frances Trollope is known, when known at all, as the pretentious Englishwoman who wrote *Domestic Manners of the Americans* or as the selfish, neglectful mother of British author Anthony Trollope. Of Frances Wright, even less is known or said. When mentioned in American histories, she is most often given a sentence as a failed female reformer—a woman whose anti-slavery experiment of Nashoba met with almost immediate disaster in the 1820s. For the most part, only these fragments and stereotypes of their lives remain, creating a general impression of each that has distorted our understanding of both Frances Trollope and Frances Wright today and helped to discourage contemporary interest in these two women's lives and writings.

The following two chapters will examine the damaging stereotypes which have served to label each woman, exploring how their separate characterizations arose and how these categorizations have endured over the last century. The first chapter will follow Frances Wright's journey into notoriety (although younger, Frances Wright was to be the elder Frances Trollope's mentor and

3

guide). The second chapter will explore the subsequent, and equally sensational, journey of Frances Trollope into, and then out of, the pages of history where deviant women (the message is clear) do not belong.

Chapter One
Dangerous Radical

It all began rather quietly and sadly for Frances Wright in Dundee, Scotland. In 1798 her parents both died within months of each other, leaving her an orphaned two-year old with a brother three years her senior and an infant sister. The homeless children were separated and parcelled out promptly—the infant Camilla remaining with foster parents in Dundee, the elder Richard being taken in by paternal relations (the Mylne family) in Glasgow, and Frances being sent to London to live with her wealthy maternal grandfather, Major Duncan Campbell of the Royal Marines, and his daughter Frances. Upon receipt of an inheritance for herself and her two young nieces, a decade later Frances Campbell reunited the two orphaned sisters, Frances and Camilla Wright, and took them to live with her in quiet and genteel refinement in Dawlish on the southeast coast of England.

But Frances Wright was neither comfortable nor happy there. Being handed over to strange relatives as a toddler, separated from her brother forever, and abruptly severed from—then reunited with—her sister by adult fiat gave Frances a sense of lifelong hurt. She realized, herself, a connection between her childhood circumstances and her adult sensitivity to cruelty and injustice, speculating in *Views of Society and Manners in America*, "I know not if the circumstances of my own early life have tended to make me sympathize peculiarly with such a situation, but the position of the Indian youth, as an alien and an orphan, among his American guardians and playmates, strikes me as singularly affecting" (112). Growing up in an aristocratic world of wealth and power, she nevertheless had become acutely aware of street beggars in London, outcast peasants in Devonshire and in Scotland, disenfranchised blacks and native Americans in the United States, and the homeless and impoverished everywhere beyond the borders of her proper, privileged world. In her *Biography*, Frances Wright records her youthful—yet lifelong—oath, "to wear ever in her heart the cause of the poor and the helpless; and to aid in all that she could in redressing the grievous wrongs which seemed to prevail in society" (11). An avid reader, Frances Wright chanced upon Carlo Bocca's history of America and rejoiced in her discovery: "There existed a country consecrated to freedom, and in which man might awake to the full knowledge and full exercise of his powers" (11). Her hope and her longing for justice were to increase even further with this knowledge.

Soon after, in 1813, at the age of 17, Frances Wright took her sister Camilla, fled Dawlish society and her Aunt Frances Campbell (whom she had grown to loathe), and returned to Scotland to live for a few years with the same Mylne family relations who had taken in her brother (killed several years before in a military skirmish). Inevitably, soon afterwards as a young woman 20 years of age, she set out for America, accompanied by her sister Camilla. Her book, *Views of Society and Manners in America*, published in 1821 upon her return to England, "was the first serious book about the United States written by an English woman" (Eckhardt, *Fanny Wright* 44). Her study of the United States was essentially so positive that "James Fenimore Cooper described her book as nauseous flattery" (Eckhardt, *Fanny Wright* 46). How was it, then, as Barbara Taylor records, that "by the end of the decade [the 1820s].... Fanny [had become] the most notorious feminist radical in America"? (Taylor 66). How is it possible that, in the space of less than ten years, she had not only stirred up the inevitable Tory reaction in Britain in response to her travel book's praise of American democracy, but also aroused the hatred of so many Americans in the very country she had so admired?

The answer lies largely in her many other American "firsts" and in the daring and conviction with which this energetic, young aristocratic woman battled injustice in a land she loved and considered the world's best hope. As Celia Eckhardt explains:

In 1825 she became the first woman in America to act publicly to oppose slavery. Twenty miles outside the little trading post so presumptuously named Memphis, in Tennessee, she established a commune whose purpose was to discover and then to demonstrate how slaves might be educated and responsibly freed. In 1828 she became the first woman in America to speak in public to a large secular audience of men and women, and the first to argue that women were men's equals and must be granted an equal role in all the business of public life. Along with Robert Owen's eldest son, Robert Dale Owen, she edited a liberal weekly newspaper, the *Free Enquirer*, and from 1828 to 1830 she used its pages, as she used lecture halls throughout the country, to fight for all the victims of the social and political hierarchies of her time. (*Fanny Wright* 1-2)

Frances Wright spoke with Thomas Jefferson, Andrew Jackson, General Lafayette and many other important public figures of the period, about the injustices of slavery in America and the best ways to bring about an end to this blight upon American freedom. With George Flower of Albion, Illinois, she founded the Nashoba colony to set America an example of a community where slaves were being taught skills and educated in order to be freed. When the colony failed, due to disease and scandal, both, she took the slaves to Haiti where they could eventually own their own land and live independent lives, believing that nowhere in America, north or south, could blacks, free or enslaved, escape abuse and prejudice.

Appearing on the lecture circuit, first in Robert Owen's utopian community of New Harmony, Indiana, then in Cincinnati, Ohio, and on throughout the Midwest and East, Frances Wright talked to large audiences, speaking out against other injustices she feared would harm the great experiment of American democracy. In her preface to her published lectures given in Cincinnati in 1828, she admitted that, upon her initial visit to the United States, "I studied her institutions, and mistook for the energy of enlightened liberty what was, perhaps, rather the restlessness of commercial enterprise.... It required a second visit, and more minute inspection, to enable me to see things under the sober light of truth, and to estimate both the excellences that are, and those that are yet wanting" ("Course of Popular Lectures" vi).

She argued for equal education for all, male and female, black and white, as essential for democratic life where all must have enlightened, well-trained minds: "Equality! where is it, if not in education? Equal rights! They cannot exist without equality of instruction" ("Free Inquiry" 25). She proposed a system of public education, boarding schools modelled on the schools of reformer Robert Owen in New Lanark, Scotland, and in New Harmony, Indiana, to be available to all children upon the age of two and to be paid for by property taxes and an additional tax upon the parents of school-age children. Under her system, older students would begin to repay the community for their free schooling through work appropriate to their age and to their newly acquired skills.

Increasingly, she became concerned with female education, lamenting "the neglected state of the female mind, and the consequent dependence of the female condition" (*Life, Letters, and Lectures* vii). For this reason, she opposed traditional marriages as not only ensuring female dependency on men but turning women into the legal property of their husbands while denying them the right to their own property. She spoke of her concern, as well, over religious revivals in which uneducated women, "half of the nation," were put "at the mercy of that worst species of quackery, practised under the name of religion" (*Life, Letters, and Lectures* vii). To Wright, a "crafty priesthood," busy filling its pockets with parishioners' money, stood out as a prime example of how the better educated, more prosperous few—lawyers, priests, and speculators—took advantage of the ill-educated, disadvantaged many in American democracy (just as they had in England) ("Address on the State of the Public Mind" 177, 176). Although she was to argue for religion as necessary in maintaining community in her most important book, *England, The Civilizer*, toward the end of her lifetime, religion for Frances Wright meant that which binds a people together in a common system of belief—rather than that which denounces, divides, degrades, or defiles human beings and their endeavors—the consequences of the "religious" zealotry she saw everywhere around her in American life.

In other activities, Frances Wright worked closely with Robert Dale Owen, of New Harmony, Indiana, the reformer Robert Owen's eldest son. Convinced that a free press was as essential as public education for "the American people—the only people free to choose between truth and error, good and evil" in her period, she co-edited the *Free Enquirer* (originally *The New Harmony Gazette*) with Robert Dale Owen, intending it to be "the first periodical established in the United States for the purpose of fearless and unbiassed enquiry on all subjects" (*Life, Letters, and Lectures* x). At the same time, she and Robert Dale Owen became instrumental in helping the New York Working Men's party organize their efforts toward the educational betterment of the working classes. She joined with workers in calling for reform legislation, such as the ten-hour law to reduce the long hours of their working day, and in demanding improvements in often deplorable working conditions. And, near the *Free Enquirer* office in New York, she opened a "Hall of Science"—as she had encouraged citizenry in other locales throughout her lecture tours to do—where the adult working public could attend debates and hear lectures on natural science, biological science, mathematics, reading, speaking, and other subjects of interest and value to them, developing the curiosity and agility of mind so necessary to a democratic society.

Steadily, Frances Wright worked to change the reality of America into its promise of freedom and equality for all—and, steadily, she made enemies. First, with Nashoba. As Paul Baker explains, "criticism was loud and heated concerning this 'one great brothel,' which seemingly had cast aside family ties, eliminated the bonds of religion and looked to the amalgamation of the two races." When the scandal arose, Frances Wright was in England recovering from a fever so severe that she almost died; James Richardson, whom she had left in charge of Nashoba, had begun to live with one of the slave women and to publicize their relationship in a log he had sent to a Baltimore editor (Baker xviii, xvii). However, Frances Wright continued to defend Nashoba and refused to alter her own anti-marriage, anti-religion, and pro-miscegenation stances—further exacerbating the scandal with her *Explanatory Notes, Respecting the Nature and Objects of the Institution of Nashoba and of the Principles Upon Which It Is Founded, Addressed to the Friends of Human Improvement in All Countries and All Nations*. Her views were unpopular in early nineteenth century America—especially taken out of context and separated as they were from her careful arguments for a non-partriarchal, non-sexist, non-racist, truly egalitarian society amidst the harsh legal realities of life in America for women, for blacks and for northern laborers in the early nineteenth century. Of course, after Frances Wright had assumed the co-editorship of the *Free Enquirer* and her lecture tour of the midwestern and eastern United States in the latter 1820s, the outcries against her increased. As she became even more active and more visible, the fireworks really began exploding.

On the lecture circuit, as she grew in stature and recognition as a public figure in nineteenth century America, Frances Wright increasingly began to be called names. She was known, Paul Baker reveals, as "the great Red Harlot of Infidelity" and "the whore of Babylon" (xix). Margaret Lane reports that another title, "Priestess of Beelzebub," dogged her steps, "follow[ing] her from town to town throughout her campaign for rational education and free enquiry" (32). According to Celia Eckhardt, "ministers took to calling Fanny the 'High Priestess of Infidelity,' and a Baltimore preacher said that she was neither man nor woman but someone sent from hell" (*Fanny Wright* 184). After Frances Wright spoke to packed houses in Boston, "The Reverend Lyman Beecher later wrote that regrettably she won over educated, refined women—'females of respectable standing in society'—and worst of all, women who had been friends to his own children" (Beecher 93). Another Beecher, Lyman's daughter Catherine Beecher, author of *A Treatise on Domestic Economy* (1841) and the elder sister of Harriet Beecher Stowe, no doubt won her father's approval by writing of Frances Wright:

who can look without disgust and abhorrence upon such an one as Fanny Wright, with her great masculine person, her loud voice, her untasteful attire, going about unprotected, and feeling no need of protection, mingling with men in stormy debate, and standing up with bare-faced impudence, to lecture to a public assembly....There she stands, with brazen front and brawny arms, attacking the safeguards of all that is venerable and sacred in religion, all that is safe and wise in law, all that is pure and lovely in domestic virtue. Her talents only make her the more conspicuous and offensive, her amiable disposition and sincerity, only make her folly and want of common sense the more pitiable, her freedom from private vices, if she is free, only indicates, that without delicacy, and without principles, she has so thrown off all feminine attractions, that freedom from temptation is her only, and shameful palladium. I cannot conceive any thing in the shape of a woman, more intolerably offensive and disgusting. (*Letters on the Difficulties of Religion* 23)

Pure or impure, amiable or irascible, brilliant or ignorant, in the case of Frances Wright, as Catherine Beecher here makes clear, it was all deemed the same. Frances Wright's strengths and virtues, themselves, became primary offenses. No matter what she did or which way she turned, Frances Wright was to find no escape from her attackers.

And soon the attacks became physical as well as verbal. In *Frances Wright and the "Great Experiment,"* Margaret Lane reports that, "at one lecture, a smoke-barrel was set alight, throwing the audience, but not Fanny, into a panic; at another, the gas-lighting was suddenly cut off, leaving the hall and an audience of 2,000 in darkness; after another, her carriage was

A DOWNRIGHT GABBLER,
or a goose that deserves to be hissed—

Frances Wright increasingly began to be called names (Lithograph caricature by J. Akin, 1830, courtesy of The New-York Historical Society, N.Y.C.)

overturned" (32). She resorted, finally, to a bodyguard of women and admirers for her public appearances (Baker xix). After one address in New York in 1838, a mob followed her to her home and violence continued in the streets for several hours (Eckhardt, *Fanny Wright*, 267-68; 273). Not long after, Frances Wright left the podium in America for good. Ironically, the young Frances Wright had said herself of America, "here there is no *mob*. An orator or a writer must make his way to the feelings of the American people through their reason" (*Views of Society* 211). This was the ideal America she had envisioned; the reality of America mocked her words and threatened her person for much of her adult life.

It was Frances Wright, and not the American people she idealized, who resorted to reason rather than emotion in responding to mob violence and brutal attacks. Her quiet and calm were not contagious, however, although they were often reported and commented on; perhaps they even fanned the flames higher. To her, "the senseless cry of 'infidel' " meant nothing. She believed that Washington, Jefferson, Adams, Franklin and others "who secured this country's independence, were all, according to the priestly acceptation of a meaningless word, *infidels*—that is, all disbelieved the compound Jewish and Christian system, and looked upon its mysteries and its miracles as upon nursery tales" (Wright, "Address, Containing a Review of the Times" 191). She knew that what she argued for and worked toward threatened those who were the most powerful individuals in American society and who had profited the most from the existing system and its inequities:

Who are...the foremost to cry out "heresy! and stop the mouth of knowledge? Who but those who live by the ignorance of the age, and the intolerance of the hour? Is any improvement suggested in our social arrangements, calculated to equalize property, labour, instruction, and enjoyment; to destroy crime by removing provocation; vice, by removing ignorance; and to build up virtue in the human breast by exchanging the spirit of self abasement for that of self respect—who are the foremost to treat the suggestions as visionary, the reform as impossible? Even they who live by the fears and the vices of their fellow creatures. ("Nature of Knowledge" 18)

Clearly, Frances Wright believed that her work was necessary and her causes just. She knew that, as a woman who dared to lecture in public, she appeared "presumptuous" but dared to argue further that "my sex and my situation tend rather to qualify than to incapacitate me for the undertaking" ("Nature of Knowledge" 16). She went on to explain that her circumstances had freed her from the debts of allegiance, money, service, or duty owed by most of those who occupied the public forum. However, she could speak openly and without fear, allied to, and subservient to, no one, as she was:

I am here to speak that for which some have not the courage and others not the independence. I am here, not to flatter the ear, but to probe the heart; not to minister to vanity, but to urge self-examination; assuredly, therefore, not to court applause, but to induce conviction. Must it be my misfortune to offend? Bear in mind only that I do it for conscience sake—for *your* sakes. I have wedded the cause of human improvement; staked it on my reputation, my fortune, and my life; and as, for it, I threw behind me in earliest youth the follies of my age, the luxuries of ease and European aristocracy, so do I, and so will I, persevere even as I began; and devote what remains to me of talent, strength, fortune, and existence, to the same sacred cause—the promotion of just knowledge, and the establishing of just practice, the increase of human happiness. ("Divisions of Knowledge" 44)

When she did give up the public platform, first in 1830, and again in 1839, she explained that she did so because she believed she could no longer be useful: "So long as I alone was concerned, the noise of priest and politician was alike indifferent to me, but I wish not my name to be made a scarecrow to the timid, or a stumbling-block to the innocently prejudiced" ("Parting Address" 220). She withdrew, then, from the lecture circuit, but never gave up her dedication to "the cause of human improvement" ("Divisions of Knowledge" 44).

Nor was she ever to overcome the image she had so early acquired as a senseless, yet dangerous, fanatic. Errors of fact as well as of interpretation have persisted into this century, as Michael Sadleir's commentary on Frances Wright makes clear:

She was one of the earliest of that long line of earnest, noisy women whose cacophonous reformism echoes down the nineteenth century.... She preached both free-love and contempt for men, with a fine disregard of consistency and a numbing eloquence.... She herself, at the end of a rousing series of lectures against the slavery of wedlock, married a French teacher of languages and died at Cincinnati in 1852, a respectable married woman, washed up on the banks of her own extremism and there stranded. (70-71)

Frances Wright did marry—that is true; but, as we shall see in the next section, she had divorced and become anything but a complacent, conventional matron by the time of her death. Sadleir errs in this—as well as in characterising her speeches as inconsistent and man-hating. The lectures were not to be allowed to speak for themselves; they were reprinted only in 1972. Instead, Frances Wright, willed to near-oblivion, has been allowed to fade from American history and literature with only an occasional outburst such as Sadleir's or a scanty reference to help carry on the stereotype.

Perhaps the most interesting story of all is the way in which Frances Wright has remained one of American history's "untouchables"—seldom seen, or when seen, viewed slightly askew. A remarkable instance of the latter—one of history's final injustices to Frances Wright—has been recorded by her biographer Celia Eckhardt (*Fanny Wright* 295). The historical marker recording her settlement in Tennessee not only misplaces Nashoba but misinforms the visitor about this nineteenth century colony. The marker errs in both the place and the date of Nashoba; however, its gravest error is an error of omission, suggesting, perhaps, that even now America is not ready to deal with Frances Wright and what she worked so hard to accomplish in the early 1800s. The marker mentions simply that Nashoba was an experimental community in cooperative living; it does not state that Frances Wright's experiment was designed and carried out in an effort to end slavery in America forever, to promote cooperative living between blacks and whites, and to encourage a lasting equality between the races through equal education. Could it be merely oversight that caused the entire significance of the experiment Frances Wright conducted to be "lost" even as it was being "memorialized"? In such ways we come to see how history can be both blotted and erased, simultaneously.

Chapter Two
Snobbish Conservative

Margaret Lane recalls a recent experience through which Trollope's reputation similarly is blotted even while she is being erased from the annals of history:

I recently had a letter from a professor in an American university, who wrote (since I had mentioned her) "Fanny Trollope was the"—and here he put some explosive asterisks—"of all time. Nobody asked her to go to Cincinnati, and certainly nobody asked her to stay," and he went on to advise me not to waste my time on her. (Lane 1)

How strange such vehemence as this appears more than a century after Frances Trollope's death. And yet we have seen it before in reference to both Frances Trollope and Frances Wright.[1] Again, as with Frances Wright, Frances Trollope's actions and writings often continue to arouse anger, in part because they were those of a forthright and independent woman who refused to conform to the female ideal of her own time—and of much of the twentieth century, as well. What is particularly interesting to note, however, is the way in which Mrs. Trollope has been stereotyped, and subsequently criticized, for being everything that Frances Wright was not.

Unlike the orphaned, sheltered, aristocratic Frances Wright, Frances Trollope grew up with a freedom unusual for middle and upper class girls of her period. The daughter of an English vicar in Heckfield, England, and of a mother who died when her youngest child, Frances, was still quite young, Frances Trollope became accustomed to roaming the countryside freely and to browsing at will in her father's library. There she developed what was to become a lifelong interest in literature and in the arts. In her twenties, she and her elder sister went to live in London with her older brother—and there she met Thomas Anthony Trollope, the young, aspiring lawyer who was to become her husband. Marrying in 1809, at the age of 30, Frances Trollope had seven children in eight years—losing one child at birth and one in infancy. Unfortunately, as Frances and Thomas Trollope's family commitments grew, Thomas' law practice began to decline, largely because of his volatile temper and his irritability with clients.

For some time after the family moved to a farmhouse in the village of Harrow, near London, Frances Trollope continued to experience the life of a conventional, nineteenth century, middle-class Englishwoman. She tended to servants, managed her household, mothered her children, and, especially,

13

enjoyed readings and dramas in her own drawing room and in those of others in Harrow society. Her circle of friends in Harrow was varied and sophisticated; in addition to her sons' Harrow school masters (some of them former teachers and friends of Harrow's local hero, Lord Byron), her circle came to include General Pepé, the Italian revolutionary, and Frances Wright, already grown famous for her travel book on America, who had met the Trollopes in Paris at the home of General Lafayette, French hero of the American War for Independence. In these times of revolution and unrest, Frances Trollope's Harrow-based friendships kept her abreast of radical thought and change. And although this was a period in her life of busy domesticity, Frances Trollope already showed signs of combining a somewhat conventional lifestyle with a questioning attitude. For one of her drawing room readings, for example, she wrote a poem satirizing the vicar of the local Harrow church for refusing to erect a memorial there for Lord Byron's little illegitimate daughter Allegra. Such unnecessary cruelty and rigid sanctimoniousness offended her sense of human decency.

Increasingly, however, her husband's financial and emotional problems came to affect the daily round of her social and domestic activities. First, the family was forced to rent out their beloved home of Julians Hill in Harrow—followed by their renovated farmhouse, Julian Cottage (which Anthony later made famous as Orley Farm). As Thomas Trollope planned to move the family to even more ramshackle quarters at Harrow Weald, Frances Trollope decided, instead, to heed her friend Frances Wright's call for interested persons to return with her to her anti-slavery settlement of Nashoba in Tennessee. Accompanied by her two young daughters, her 16-year old son Henry, and the children's French art instructor Auguste Hervieu (who planned to teach in the Nashoba school), Frances Trollope set sail for America and, at the age of 50, changed her life forever. From this period on, her life became much more a matter of public record and of public commentary than one largely of private concern and import.

In *Domestic Manners of the Americans* Frances Trollope suggests the extent to which her trip to the United States was to affect her: "I had a little leaning towards Sedition myself when I set out; but before I had half completed my tour, I was quite cured" (36). Arriving at Nashoba with Frances Wright, "one glance sufficed to convince me, that every idea I had formed of the place was as far as possible from the truth. Desolation was the only feeling—the only word that presented itself; but it was not spoken. I think, however, that Miss Wright was aware of the painful impression the sight of her forest-home produced on me" (23). Fearing for her children's health and thoroughly disillusioned by "the savage aspect of the scene," Frances Trollope prepared to leave Nashoba for the more civilized prospect of Cincinnati, Ohio (rumored to be the most promising city in the West) (*Domestic* 24). While she wondered how Frances Wright could ever have imagined that European friends such as herself might have been comfortable in Nashoba, she admitted, "even now, that I have seen the favourite fabric of her imagination fall to pieces beneath her feet, I cannot recall the self-devotion with which she gave herself to it without admiration" (*Domestic* 24). Frances Trollope could follow Frances Wright only so far; after that, she found it necessary to find her own way.

Arriving in Cincinnati, Frances Trollope discovered little more to her liking than she had in Frances Wright's Nashoba. Appalled by the lack of culture and refinement she found in this fast-growing city, she commented:

During nearly two years that I resided in Cincinnati, or its neighbourhood, I neither saw a beggar, nor a man of sufficient fortune to permit his ceasing his efforts to increase it: thus every bee in the hive is actively employed in search of that honey of Hybla, vulgarly called money; neither art, science, learning, nor pleasure, can seduce them from its pursuit. (*Domestic* 36)

Drawing on her own cultural background to help support herself and her family, and to help provide entertainment in a city that seemed to have little, Frances Trollope devised two popular shows for Cincinnati's Western Museum: "The Invisible Girl," where her son Henry answered questions cleverly and mysteriously from behind a curtain, impressing all with his learning and his skill in foreign languages; and "The Infernal Regions," for which she composed the script and persuaded the talented, young sculptor Hiram Powers to create a mechanized and electrified version of Dante's Hell.

Encouraged by her enormous (but, so far, largely unpaid) successes with the American public, Frances Trollope conceived of an immense project, a Bazaar, of which Henry would eventually become proprietor, across from the steamboat landings and near popular hotels on the Ohio riverfront. The Bazaar was to offer museum shops, art galleries, lecture halls, a ballroom, and commercial ventures, all under one roof—a project to be financed largely by Frances Trollope's inheritance. Almost immediately, however, the building became known as "Trollope's Folly," its design and its concept (based on Mr. William Bullock's Egyptian Hall of Piccadilly, London) seeming too pretentious and extravagant for the Western frontier. Disheartened and bankrupt, Frances Trollope was forced to leave "Trollope's Folly," its Egyptian styles, its rotunda, its balconies, galleries, and ballroom, behind her in Cincinnati, she and her children subsisting on Hervieu's occasional earnings for the remaining months of their American trip.

Returning to England, Frances Trollope immediately set about trying to reverse her family's desperate economic situation. Arising at four o'clock in the morning, and working from the hundreds of pages of notes she had taken on her trip to America, she wrote *Domestic Manners of the Americans* at the age of 53, within a few weeks of her return. Her intention clearly was to write a book that was very different from her friend Frances Wright's *Views of Society and Manners in America*, published 11 years earlier. Referring to herself in the third person in her Preface to the First Edition of *Domestic Manners of the Americans*, Frances Trollope declared:

Although much has already been written on the great experiment, as it has been called...she [the author] has endeavoured to show how greatly the advantage is on the side of those who are governed by the few, instead of the many. The chief object she has had in view is to encourage her countrymen to hold fast by a constitution that ensures all the blessings which flow from established habits and solid principles. If they forego these, they will incur the fearful risk of breaking up their repose by introducing the jarring tumult and universal degradation which invariably follow in the wild outcome of placing all the power of the State in the hands of the populace. (Mullen xxxiii)

Mob rule was very much associated with democratic processes in Frances Trollope's analysis of American society. Thus, Frances Trollope's first published work directly countered the views of that earlier, adulatory travel book on America by Frances Wright—and Frances Trollope immediately became the darling of the same Tories who had earlier attacked her young friend. While she met with instant success in Tory circles, Frances Trollope was not to remain in their good graces long.

Stereotyped ever after as the Tory conservative who wrote *Domestic Manners of the Americans*, Frances Trollope was, in fact, as Helen Heineman has suggested, "that strange anomaly, a Tory radical" (*The Triumphant* 185). Disheartened as she was by the materialism, crudity, violence and hypocrisy she had found in Jacksonian America, Frances Trollope was not the simple supporter of the status quo her Tory admirers at first thought her to be. A prolific author, writing from the age of 53 to 78 years of age, Frances Trollope completed 114 volumes—six travel books and 34 novels in all—many of which were works of social protest. Again Helen Heineman explains, "In using fiction to arouse public-consciousness about social abuses, Mrs. Trollope contributed an impressive list of 'firsts': the first antislavery novel, the first full-length exposure of evangelical excesses, the first novel on child labor in industrial areas, the first attack on the bastardy clauses of the New Poor Law" (*The Triumphant* 143-44). In no time at all, Frances Trollope had managed to arouse the anger of Tories as well as of Whigs—and through it all, despite her age and her many family obligations, she continued undaunted.

Beginning her public career late in life (at 53) with the publication of *Domestic Manners of the Americans*, Frances Trollope displayed a supple strength, a stubborn persistence and a very thick skin. Despite remarkable efforts on behalf of her family—she produced a three-volume novel, *Refugee in America*, the same year as *Domestic Manners of the Americans*—in 1834 the

Trollopes were forced to flee England and live in Bruges, Belgium, to escape their English creditors. That year, while Frances Trollope wrote three more books, she nursed three dying members of her family: her son, Henry, who died at the age of 23 (never well after their trip to America); her demoralized and defeated husband, Thomas; and, after returning again to England, her 18-year-old daughter Emily, another companion of her American trip.

Throughout her personal difficulties—which would eventually include the death of her one remaining daughter Cecilia—Frances Trollope continued to write. And, all the while, despite being under almost constant critical attack, she responded little at all, and then with gentle, good humor. Perhaps she had become inured to name-calling on her trip to America—for scandal, as Frances Trollope wrote to her friend Julia Pertz (26 Dec. 1827), followed her from the point of her departure from Harrow, "I have left the people in Harrow making great eyes at me but I care little for this. I expect to be very happy, and very free from care at Nashoba—and this will more than repay me for being the object of a few 'dear me's'!" (Heineman,*The Triumphant* 49). When her expectations of Nashoba were not fulfilled, and she had hastened on to Cincinnati, she created scandal there, as well. Frances Trollope wrote her son Tom that a letter of introduction from Lafayette contained "*in fact*, the first certain assurance [for Cincinnatians] that we are not a set of very accomplished swindlers!" (Heineman,*The Triumphant* 62). Despite Lafayette's letter, however, her problems in Cincinnati persisted. Frances Trollope's friendship with Auguste Hervieu, her conversations and business dealings with men, her insistence on taking walks unaccompanied on city streets and out-of-the-way paths, and her lack of interest in housekeeping all created talk. Helen Heineman comments that in Cincinnati Frances Trollope's "major flaw was a failure to fit into the pattern of American female domesticity" (*The Triumphant* 61). In addition, "Mrs. Trollope's unfamiliarity with the unspoken agreement to ignore the problem of the blacks in America was doubtless the basis of much later criticism of her social blunders and unpleasantly coarse frankness"(*The Triumphant* 61).

And if Frances Trollope found herself called "English old woman" (Trollope, *Domestic* 83) and frequently worse ("amazonian," "man-woman" and a "trollop" [Heineman, *Francis Trollope* 10]) while in America, the criticisms became more vicious after the publication of *Domestic Manners of the Americans*: "American reviewers were naturally furious with Mrs. Trollope. Interest in these reviews was so intense in England that a separate bound volume containing several of them was published" (Mullen xxii). While many of these reviews continued attacks on Frances Trollope's personal character, the criticisms which must have been most stinging were those of some of her former friends and acquaintances. Cincinnati's Timothy Flint, of whom she had spoken so highly in *Domestic Manners of the Americans*, commented in his

Contemporary caricature of Frances Trollope and family seated before Auguste Hervieu painting "The Landing of Lafayette in Cincinnati." (Reprinted by permission of Charles Scribner's Sons, an imprint of MacMillan Publishing Company, from Clara Longworth de Chambrun's *Cincinnati: The Queen City, 1939; 1967.*)

review of that same work that Frances Trollope was "as incapable as an infant of such a project [as the Bazaar] in her own country, [thus] in America her ruin was more complete than that of infantine folly." Further, Flint described her as " 'a short, plump figure, with a ruddy, round Saxon face of bright complexion... singularly unladylike'. Nevertheless, he did praise her for her wide knowledge of literature and her frequent kindness to the poor in Cincinnati. He said that there had been considerable gossip about Hervieu but he defended her from these unwarranted slurs" (Mullen xvi-xvii; xxii). Frances Trollope's former friend, General Lafayette, accused Frances Trollope of blatant self-interest in a letter to her lifelong friend, Harriet Garnett, commenting that "her abuse of the American character and American manners...has not a little contributed to make her very fashionable in the fine circles in England" (Heineman, *The Triumphant* 101). Of course, the Whig *Edinburgh Review* already had implied Frances Trollope's self-interest to the British public, revealing the deplorable state of the Trollope family finances in an effort to discredit both Frances Trollope's commentary and her character, at once (Stebbins 49).

Nevertheless, Frances Trollope published on and the "dear me's" (more than the few anticipated) persisted ("To Julia Garnett Pertz" [27 Dec. 1827] 49). As she pointed out injustices in England as well as in America, Tories joined Whigs in expressing their outrage:

Her contemporaries were shocked by the harsh bitterness of these novels [of social reform], and for her pioneering efforts Frances Trollope was much maligned by critics and reviewers....Unable to dispute her facts, critics directed their venomous attacks to her personality and sex and greeted her unusual subject matter by labelling these novels low, coarse, and vulgar, and her character hideous, revolting, and repulsive. (Heineman, *Francis Trollope* 58)

Her antislavery novel, *Jonathan Jefferson Whitlaw* (1836), won disapproval in England as well as in America:

The Athenaeum called *Whitlaw* an unpleasant and repulsive book; *The Spectator* criticized her unfavorable portrayal of southern planters who were, it insisted, "the gentlemen of the States." Fifty years later her sympathetic daughter-in-law thought the tale was "painful" and questioned the appropriateness of using such unhappy subject matter as the basis of fiction. In general, Trollope was accused of extravagance and misrepresentation. Yet today *Whitlaw* is a novel that demands respect for its serious treatment of an important subject. (Heineman, *Francis Trollope* 62)

British reviewers, also, were scandalized by Frances Trollope's portrait of a seductive, evangelical minister in *The Vicar of Wrexhill* (1837), by her attack on English manufacturers in *The Life and Adventures of Michael Armstrong, The Factory Boy* (1840), and by her depiction of workinghouse conditions and the effects of England's New Poor Laws on the lives of the impoverished, particularly women, in *The Fallen Woman: Jessie Phillips, A Tale of the Present Day* (1843).[2] As Helen Heineman notes, "repeatedly, the word vulgar was used to describe her, yet there is no note in her personal life or professional writings that would today draw such an appellation. In the 1830s the word was synonymous with free, frank, and uncoventional attitudes, particularly in women" (*Francis Trollope* 136).

William Makepeace Thackeray was one of those who was offended by Mrs. Trollope's unladylike, indeed, in his view, unliterary, subject matter, objecting as he did to fiction that was "heavy and pretentious" because it abandoned fantasy to treat the subject of social issues (Review of "St. Patrick Eve," Heineman, *The Triumphant* 144). More importantly, her fellow author and son, Anthony Trollope, chastised his mother in his *Autobiography* for having chosen, as a woman, to write fiction of social protest:

With her, politics were always an affair of the heart—as indeed were all her convictions. Of reasoning from causes I think that she knew nothing. Her heart was in every way so perfect, her desire to do good to all around her so thorough, and her power of self-sacrifice so complete, that she generally got herself right in spite of her want of logic; but it must be acknowledged that she was emotional. (22)

Further, Anthony Trollope said of his mother, "She was neither clear-sighted nor accurate and in her attempts to describe morals, mannners, and even facts, was unable to avoid the pitfalls of exaggeration" (*An Autobiography* 33). Upon Frances Trollope's death, as Lucy Poate Stebbins and Richard Poate Stebbins reveal, "neither of her sons made much of her extraordinary talents; in their opinion, the epitaph which could be carved on the monument of many a lesser woman suited her life and works: She was cheerful, industrious, and affectionate" (222). In their study *The Trollopes: The Chronicle of a Writing Family*, Lucy Poate Stebbins and Richard Poate Stebbins theorize about Anthony's unconscious rivalry with his prolific, popular, writing mother:

[Anthony] would not admit that his mother possessed extraordinary talent, because he wanted to keep her inferior to his father and incidentally to himself; he said she was healthy and industrious; her exhuberance overflowed in effortless creation. Having thus set limits to her ability he began to believe that talent was never essential to success; the chief requisite was work; he could scarcely think of himself as a creative genius and deny his mother's claims, when, alas! they two were so much alike. (222, 293)

The weight of Anthony's opinion helped to crush his mother's reputation and keep her out of sight, while he continued to remain in view, for over a century.

While *Domestic Manners of the Americans* alone of all Frances Trollope's works has stayed in print and continued to generate comment from her own time on to the present day, Frances Trollope's other writings quickly disappeared. Richard Mullen writes in the introduction to the recent Oxford edition of *Domestic Manners of the Americans* (1984) of the timeliness of Frances Trollope's concerns with

the prevalence of violence, the dangers of fundamentalist religion, and the emptiness of American cities at night. Whereas so many other travellers wrote about long-dead debates or vanished institutions, Mrs. Trollope, like Tocqueville, had the perception to see enduring aspects of American democracy. She had, after all, been in America at a crucial period, when the America of the Founding Fathers was about to be made into the rougher and more democratic America of Andrew Jackson. It is more than symbolic that Jackson himself makes an appearance in *Domestic Manners*. The American Republic— as old as Mrs. Trollope herself—was changing into a popular democracy, a change she witnessed and described. (xxiv)

Frances Trollope's study of America, however, managed to endure in spite of a steady diminishment of her insights and her abilities—carried out at times through her son Anthony's own commentary and by comparison to his own accomplishments. In their study of the Trollope family, Lucy Poate Stebbins and Richard Poate Stebbins examine *Domestic Manners of the Americans* in the light of Anthony Trollope's *North America*, concluding:

When she [Frances Trollope] had been in America she had been little and almost old, shabby and ill-attended, and people had dared to be rude to her; they had not been intentionally insolent to the important-looking, well-dressed English author, Anthony Trollope; thus, his ire had less excuse. Yet it must be admitted that he was the better able to differentiate between what annoyed him personally and what was in itself an evil. (209)

Anthony's autobiographical comment that his mother was over-emotional, illogical and subjective was to take firm root even though disputed by his elder brother Tom (Sadleir 59).

Unfortunately, most of the attention Frances Trollope has received from literary critics (until the work of Helen Heineman in the 1980s) has come from those who have been interested in Anthony Trollope's fiction. C. P. Snow in *Trollope: His Life and Art* (1975) dismisses Frances Trollope in this way:

She loved [her eldest son] Tom, whom even before Mr. Trollope died she made into a surrogate husband. She loved her other children when they were within sight, and otherwise forgot them almost entirely.... Often, despite her ebullience and outpouringness, her emotions switched off...she might have thought twice about money. She never did except, almost literally, until the bailiffs were at the door. She liked living in the state which she thought suitable.... There are good arguments for thinking that she was responsible for the scale of Julians, their grand house on the Harrow farm. She went on to be responsible for more and graver follies. More likely than not, there was a resonance between her bouncing euphoria and her husband's self-justifying hopes. (17-18)

Snow must place blame for the unhappy state of the Trollope family affairs somewhere and uses Anthony's few comments on his mother in his *Autobiography* to center his criticism on Frances Trollope. In so doing, Snow ignores or downplays a depression in rural England in the late 1820s and 1830s which affected the Trollopes' Harrow property adversely; the role of Thomas Anthony Trollope's declining law practice and his growing irritability and ill-health in the family's misfortunes; as well as Frances Trollope's own enterprising, resilient inventiveness and productivity on behalf of her family's welfare (63).

Michael Sadleir in *Trollope: A Commentary* (1975) also quotes often from Anthony's *Autobiography* in making points about Frances Trollope's capabilities, writing that Frances Trollope "was the ordinary Englishwoman, with certain elements carried to a higher power.... She was prone to unreflecting generalized dislikes; stubborn alike toward ideas and in adversity, and lacking in that pride of individuality which throws persons of a different type into automatic opposition to herd-bias" (58). And Eileen Bigland, writing in 1954, relies on Anthony Trollope in stereotyping Frances Trollope as an ambitious, selfish, and thoughtless woman: "underneath the gaiety, the wit, the restless dartings after new friends and interests lay a grimly ambitious mind that did not hesitate to sacrifice anybody or anything in order to gain a certain end" (46). Bigland, too, reiterates that Anthony was the child Frances Trollope had "loved least," speculating that Frances Trollope "perhaps even then...recognized the latent power within and instinctively resented it" (58).

With several decades of feminist criticism behind us, the misogyny of such critical assessments as those we have just looked at seems apparent; and yet these are all recent judgments of Frances Trollope which devalue her accomplishments and criticize her at once for being female (for being emotional, illogical, flighty and extravagant) and for not being female enough (for being non-nurturing, selfish, ambitious and hard). The strongest influence upon those critical judgments has been, as we have seen, her youngest son Anthony's brief autobiographical reflections—rather than a close examination of Frances Trollope's own life and works. And, as Lucy Poate Stebbins and Richard Poate Stebbins suggest (even as they concur with Anthony's judgments), Anthony was caught in a dilemma; he wanted to love his father and to grow up as a successful man in British society, yet his father was irritable, defeated, and difficult—a failure. Anthony would choose to model himself on his mother and rely on her help initially in getting published but would denigrate her, at the same time, thereby making Frances Trollope seem more different from himself than she really was and of less value in his life than she really had been (293). To achieve stature as a man in his society, Anthony continued to insist on the inferior place of women in the scheme of things, while at the same time sympathizing with strong, rebellious females in his novels. In response to questions of women's rights and women's suffrage, he would argue that:

They [women] are the nursing mothers of mankind, and in that law their fate is written with all its joys and all its privileges. That women should have their rights no man will deny. To my thinking neither increase of work nor increase of political influence are among them. The best right a woman has is the right to a husband, and that is the right to which I would recommend every young woman here in the States to turn her best attention. (*North America* 1: 266)[5]

That his own mother had not been the "nursing mother of mankind" that he had desired, that she had had the "right" that he would grant her, the right to a husband, but very little protection and advantage on that account, that she had found it necessary to support herself and her family for the latter part of her adulthood, and that she had worked every morning for 25 of the last 30 years of her life, arising at four in the morning to write for several hours before her day began (as would be his habit, as well), Anthony could not afford to examine too closely. Nor did he wish to call attention to the novels she wrote in which she had espoused powerful views and depicted sympathetic, clever men and women as forerunners to his own work.

One of the most popular and controversial authors of early nineteenth century England had been reduced to a stereotype that would endure from the time of her death into the present. As Michael Sadleir remarks, "Who would believe, reading these pallid courtesies [newspaper notices of her death], that Frances Trollope in her day provoked more anger and applause than almost any writer of her time? Who would guess that books of hers once lashed critics and public into furies of resentment, into rhapsodies of praise" (112). With that said, Sadleir laments "the eviction of her books even from the hall of recollection" and passes on the stereotype of Frances Trollope that has prevailed, to discourage further interest in her life and in her works in our own time, calling her "an emotional rather than an imaginative person"—a sorry judgment upon any author (115).

Early in her writing career, Frances Trollope understood and satirized the process by which a writer becomes "known" and definitive judgments are made after just one work has been published or one influential opinion has prevailed. In *Charles Chesterfield: or, The Adventures of a Youth of Genius* (1841), Mr. Marchmont, the editor of *The Regenerator*, tells a young, bewildered Charles how to go about reviewing an author: "all we require to know is the name of the author in the cases where the name is known, or the precepts in which he writes where it is not" (8). The review, then, Marchmont explains, writes itself without any unnecessary contact with the new work in question or any chance for the "fallibility of the judgment of man" to interfere with and complicate ready assessment (9). A shocked Charles calls this the "steam-engine principle" of reviewing, protesting the need for "a patient and attentive reading" in order to form an "honest" opinion (10). By 1841, however, Mrs. Trollope understood full well what had happened to her works in the first decade following the publication of *Domestic Manners of the Americans*. Whatever a dismayed, but young and naive, Charles Chesterfield might think, Frances Trollope herself realized that as many as one hundred and fourteen volumes, a lifetime of work, could be neatly reduced and dismissed with a quick word or two—just enough to last an eternity.

The "conservative" Frances Trollope and the "radical" Frances Wright thus shared in common the experience of being stereotyped within their own lifetimes. While these stereotypes were diametrically opposed—one being placed on the extreme right and the other on the extreme left of the political spectrum—they were, at the same time, as we have seen, tagged with similar epithets. One was judged a "trollop" (in more than just name) for her daring behavior, the other a "harlot." Both were branded as thoughtless, illogical, over-emotional, impulsive, as well as immoral. But, most importantly, they were seen as female, an unfortunate enough condition, it would seem, in and of itself, but, even worse, as "deviant women" who did not know where they belonged and who defiantly overstepped the required boundaries of humility and subordination. The punishment for each was, again, to be the same: immediate categorization, swift rejection and virtual extinction from the selective annals of history and literature as women who did not belong. In an effort to help repair some of the damage done to these two remarkable women, we need to re-examine their works, to reassess their reputations, to acknowledge their influence, and to move beyond the stereotypes of their lives.

Part

❖2❖

Differences

Differences

Without doubt, important differences existed between Frances Trollope and Frances Wright. While initially these differences may have sparked their interest in each other, eventually they assured that each woman would go her separate way. After Frances Trollope's brief—and disillusioning—experience at Nashoba, the two women never again planned another joint venture (despite a shared enthusiasm for travel, for adventure, for writing, for reading, for good conversation, and for a busy, active lifestyle). While Camilla Wright once visited briefly with Frances Trollope in Cincinnati, Frances Wright never did (even while lecturing there). And, although Frances Trollope attended two of Frances Wright's lectures and followed Wright's public career, the older woman never sought out the younger woman's company again. The friendship between the two had come to a quick, but definite, end—only a few years after its beginning.

Most likely, the Nashoba experience which severed their friendship hurt both women. Outwardly, despite the distance they maintained, there was only civility. Frances Wright graciously loaned Frances Trollope $300 from Nashoba's treasury to establish herself and her family in Cincinnati. Several years later, Frances Wright refused "to respond to General Lafayette's urgent plea that she would write something to defend her beloved America from the mischievous conclusions of Mrs. Trollope's newly published book, *Domestic Manners of the Americans*. Fanny's word, he was sure, would carry weight, and he begged her to redress the wrong to the Americans by her one-time friend, but Fanny was silent" (Lane 39). Frances Trollope, in a foreign country, her life in disarray with three children in tow who required food, shelter and clothing, also tried to be careful in regard to her former friend. In her published account of her Nashoba experience in *Domestic Manners of the Americans*, Frances Trollope expressed admiration for the way her "philosophical friend" could do without the "necessaries of life," commenting "nor was there any mixture of affectation in this indifference—it was a circumstance really and truly beneath her notice" (24). Privately, in the rough draft of her travel book, however, Trollope expressed concern over her young friend's eccentricities:

The Frances Wright of Nashoba, in dress, looks, and manner, bore no more resemblance to the Miss Wright I had known and admired in London and Paris than did her log cabin to the Tuileries or Buckingham Palace....I never saw, I never heard or read, of any enthusiasm approaching hers, except in some few instances, in ages past, of religious fanaticism. ("The Rough Draft" 27-28n)

She worried that Frances Wright's growing zealotry—as revealed in Wright's *Explanatory Notes* about Nashoba—was a sign that Wright was losing touch with reality. Trollope wrote privately to common friends such as Charles Wilkes in New York, "Poor Fanny Wright! I own to you that my firm conviction is, that the brain fever which attacked her last year, has affected her intellect. There is no other mode of accounting for her words or her actions."

Reluctant as they were to disclaim each other publicly, the two women clearly parted company privately. Neither had understood the other. Had they done so, Frances Wright would never have encouraged Frances Trollope to come to America nor would the latter have agreed to undertake such an adventure in the first place. What they had misunderstood about each other, however, was not so much a matter of philosophy or of ideology (as history has assumed) as a matter of human character. In actuality, the most important differences between Frances Trollope and Frances Wright seem to have been ones of personality rather than of public policy—or, to put it another way, the differences which existed in their writings and in their lifestyles were often the consequences of two contrasting natures. These separate natures, and the way they came to influence the public careers and works of Frances Trollope and Frances Wright, need to be more fully understood and explored.

Chapter Three
The Lonely Idealist

Frances Wright's bitter childhood experiences left lifelong scars. For someone who lived a large part of her adult life in full, public view, lecturing on stage before thousands of people, meeting with important, international figures of her time, giving her views on topics ranging from family relationships to religion, economics, slavery, labor and education in the *Free Enquirer* as well as in her speeches and other writings, Frances Wright remained a rather lonely figure. Orphaned before she was three, raised separately from her brother and sister by guardians she barely knew (and later despised), she came to feel very much alone and very much alienated from those who were closest to her. As Celia Eckhardt has concluded, the loss of her parents "proved to be the most terrible thing that ever happened to Fanny Wright," teaching her "the hard lessons of childhood solitude" ("Of Fanny and Camilla Wright" 41).

When, at the age of 11, she was reunited with her younger sister Camilla, Frances still continued to feel solitary and apart. In fact, her burden seemed to have been increased. Writing in her autobiography, Frances recalled "the heart solitude of orphanship...the absence of all sympathy with the views and characters of those among whom her childhood was thrown, [and]...the presence of a sister who looked to her for guidance, and leaned upon her for support" (*Biography* 9). Another child might have rejoiced in the opportunity for a renewed, sisterly companionship. Frances's soul already had become too weighed down by the inequities she had witnessed in the world and the injustices she herself had endured as an orphan at the hands of her young aunt:

Fanny hated their aunt. Her reasons for this corroding hatred remain obscure. Everything about Frances Campbell suggests a woman of the utmost propriety.... But whether Fanny's hatred derived from real child abuse, as she implied, or was the fruit of her projected anger at her parents' loss, it was no ordinary passion. It directed the course of her future.... She saw that the wealthy landowners of Dawlish, who were Miss Campbell's friends, drove the poor contemptuously from their land, and she resolved to be a champion of the humble. (Eckhardt, "Of Fanny and Camilla Wright" 42)

In her autobiography, Frances Wright recorded this early commitment to the struggle for human justice. Her world became the world of ideals, of ideas, and of books—the self-contained world of the mind—early on in her youth.

Solitary and self-reliant, without great need for the stimulation or succor offered by ordinary, day-to-day, human relationships, Frances Wright often miscalculated the effect of her actions upon others around her. An extraordinary mind—that of a Jeremy Bentham or a General Lafayette, for instance—could excite her own intellect and captivate her attention for weeks and months at a time. The more routine, daily proprieties and concerns of men and women, however, did not concern her. This, of course, led to problems for Frances Wright—problems that became public matters as she, while still a young woman in her early twenties, attained visibility and social prominence after the publication of *Views of Society and Manners in America* in 1821. First, when General Lafayette admired her book, she reciprocated his attention with enthusiasm for the famous general's ideas,

Contemptuous of gossip,...Fanny saw Lafayette on occasion alone. Old enough to be her grandfather but notorious for his interest in pretty young women, Lafayette accepted her devotion with the grand seigneur's appetite for worship. It should have come as no surprise that scandalous rumors began in the spring of 1824, suggesting that Fanny was his mistress and exercised undue influence over him. Lafayette's family, who had gradually chilled to them [Camilla and Frances], now turned decidedly against the Wrights, insisting, among other things, that when he accepted President James Monroe's invitation to come to America in the fall as the Nation's guest, Fanny and Camilla, if they went at all, should not accompany him on the same ship. Fanny tried to persuade Lafayette to still the gossip by either marrying her or adopting her and Camilla, but Lafayette demurred and the family got their way. (Eckhardt, "Of Fanny and Camilla Wright" 44)

Oil on canvas of Frances Wright, by Henry Inman, about 1824. (Courtesy of The New York Historical Society, N.Y.C.)

On the heels of creating one family upheaval, Frances next created yet another. Following General Lafayette and his disgruntled family on her second visit to America, Frances Wright became absorbed in finding a solution to America's problem of slavery. After visiting Robert Owen's New Harmony, Indiana, settlement, she entered into a partnership with a man she had met in nearby Albion, Illinois—George Flower—to form a model community to educate and free slaves at Nashoba in Tennessee. Celia Eckhardt speculates that, during their involvement, Frances Wright may have had an affair with Flower. Whatever the exact nature of their relationship, it was so close and so intense that Eliza Flower became upset and jealous, finally insisting on her husband's departure with his family from Nashoba (Eckhardt, "Of Fanny and Camilla Wright" 46).

Clearly the orphaned Frances Wright did not understand the power of traditional family ties nor the demands of nuclear family relationships. Her unhappy experiences with the families of Lafayette and Flower, however, made her even more vehemently negative about "families" than her grandfather and her aunt Campbell had made her already. And, of course, as Frances Wright grew more committed to resisting the traditional family and changing its nature, she grew more and more out of step with public opinion. Fixating on "how intolerably crippling marriage was" after the loss of Flower as her Nashoba partner (Eckhardt, "Of Fanny and Camilla Wright" 46), Frances grew adamant in her *Explanatory Notes* in defense of the settlement's experiment in communal living. In the face of the enormous scandal created by the publication (in her absence) of Scotsman James Richardson's liaison with one of the black women at Nashoba, Frances Wright wrote to Richardson privately that he should have been more circumspect: "All principles are liable to misinterpretation but none so much as ours," noting that he would cause "unnecessary hostility, and misconception" (Eckhardt, *Fanny Wright* 149). Yet in her *Explanatory Notes*, written immediately afterwards, Frances Wright insisted on making a point of Nashoba's nontraditional concept of family and community: "No woman can forfeit her individual rights or independent existence, and no man assert over her any right or power whatsoever, beyond what he may exercise on her free and voluntary affections."

Nashoba represented Frances Wright's ideal community. In her correspondence with Mary Shelley, Frances Wright had pictured Nashoba as "an establishment where affection shall form the only marriage, kind feeling and kind action the only religion, respect for the feelings and liberties of others the only restraint, and union of interest the bond of peace and security" (Eckhardt, *Fanny Wright* 151). In part, Wright was following the Owenite principles of Robert Owen's New Lanark, Scotland, and New Harmony, Indiana. As Barbara Taylor explains, "the Owenite commitment to collectivized family life and female equality set them apart not only from their conservative opponents but also from most other radical movements of the period (including

Chartism)" (xiii). However, Taylor goes on to point out, "Of all the leading Owenite feminists, only Fanny Wright ever advocated the total abolition of marriage in favour of liberated liaisons, and even she gave way at the prospect of bearing an illegitimate child" (69).

But Frances Wright never gave way in her attempt to redefine the role of women. In her last, and most important, work, *England, The Civilizer*, she decried the way in which the female had been confined historically within "the narrowest precinct of the family circle...forcibly closing her eyes upon the claims of the great human family without that circle...estranging her soul from the conception of all the glorious powers as yet dormant within her;... becoming the stringent conservative sustainer of the established order of society, whatever that may be..." (13). Society could only be improved, Wright felt, if, "The school, and the loving community that surrounded it, would provide an alternative to the home itself and to what was often 'the forcible union of unsuitable and unsuited parents [which] can little promote the happiness of the offspring' " (*Explanatory Notes*). Thus, she advocated boarding schools for children beginning at the age of two, with older school children repaying their debt to the community for the free public education provided them through the use of their newly acquired skills on society's behalf.

Her ideal was one of loving couples and of a community of dedicated individuals who together cared for and educated all the children for the common good. She was dismayed by the restrictive, crippling powers of the traditional family—yet it was Frances Wright's attempt to practice traditional family living herself which finally defeated her. First, she had felt responsible for her sister Camilla, taking the younger, more frail, woman with her from Dawlish to Scotland, then again on her voyages to America, and on into the American frontier as a settler in the experimental Nashoba community. While attempting to act responsibly toward Camilla, Frances clearly never understood fully her own power and influence over her sister, nor could she effectively decrease her younger sister's dependency upon her or help Camilla to realize her own potential. Thus, Frances's relationship with Camilla proved increasingly burdensome and strained, to their mutual frustration and pain. When an ailing Frances left Camilla behind in Nashoba while setting forth herself to recuperate in Europe, their uncle James Mylne was outraged; how could Frances have left the delicate Camilla "dispirited and broken-hearted by her [sister's absence]...to encounter all the horrors of a forest solitude"? (Eckhardt, *Fanny Wright* 149). Their friends, the Garnett sisters and Frances Trollope, expressed concern, as well, over Frances's seemingly callous treatment of her devoted sister (Heineman, *Restless Angels* 76, 87). If Frances felt that her abrupt departure might strengthen Camilla and foster within her younger sister an independence of spirit and a new strength of character, Frances proved sadly mistaken. Perhaps Frances was too ill herself (she needed to be lifted on board ship, she was so weak) to think clearly about Camilla's situation; or Camilla herself may have prevailed, dreading as she did the thought of another long sea voyage (Owen, *Owen's Travel Journal* 23-25). Whatever Frances's reasons, by the time of her return to Nashoba, Richardson's log had been published revealing Camilla Wright's knowledge of his relationship with Mamselle Josephine and her consent to disciplining the slaves according to their former slave treatment (with floggings) if they continued to violate the new rules that were to govern their conduct at Nashoba. In addition, Frances discovered that the lonely, dependent Camilla only a few weeks before had married Richesson Whitby, an Owenite from New Harmony who had taken George Flower's place at Nashoba.

And yet Camilla soon made clear that her choice of Whitby was not one that was intended to replace Frances in her life. After all, Camilla once had said of her older sister, "her equal never can and never will be found" (Eckhardt ,"Of Fanny and Camilla Wright" 45). Although pregnant with Whitby's child, Camilla followed still in her sister's steps, leaving Whitby behind to have her baby by herself in Memphis. Meanwhile, Frances had left Camilla alone to endure a difficult childbirth while continuing her own lecture commitments and writing projects. Before her departure, Frances most certainly must have expressed her unhappiness over the decisions Camilla had made during her absence—over her younger sister's seeming lack of good judgment and her ineffectuality in exerting a sensible influence over Richardson's behavior at Nashoba. Whatever their differences, Camilla again followed Frances as soon as her strength had returned, arriving at the Riker Estate in New York to serve as housekeeper for the *Free Enquirer* community house her elder sister had established there. Suddenly, Camilla suffered the death of her infant son— followed by yet another separation from her older sister as Frances Wright departed to carry out her plans to free the Nashoba slaves in Haiti. Writing Harriet Garnett of her sense of hurt and her growing alienation from the sister she had worshipped, Camilla confessed, "the sister—the friend with whom from my earliest childhood I have felt my being identified—for whom I have suffered much and with whom I have sympathized still more is no longer the sharer of my thoughts and feelings and only ceased to be so from my discovery that *I shared not hers*" (Eckhardt, "Of Fanny and Camilla Wright" 48). In her loneliness and hurt upon the death of her son, bewildered and alienated by Frances's hectic, public life, exposed publicly (and, perhaps, criticized privately by her sister) for her acts of judgment and her moral philosophy, Camilla had begun to experience the painful birth of her own identity. Even though Camilla once more was to accompany her sister to France, where Frances was to have her *Free Enquirer* co-worker Phiquepal D'Arusmont's child (conceived on the journey to Haiti), she remained sadly estranged from her older sister. This time Camilla chose to live apart from Frances. And this time, too, it was she who stayed away while Frances suffered through the agonies of childbirth without a sister's care.

And then, abruptly, only a month after Frances's child was born, Camilla died. As Celia Eckhardt writes:

The circumstances of their last year and a half together made Fanny's loss [of her sister] all the more irreparable. Whatever had happened between them—whatever harsh words were said, whatever the wounds given and received—Fanny had failed Camilla, and she knew that. Camilla's death left her with a formidable psychic struggle for survival.

For the next few years, everyone who wrote about Fanny wrote of a woman who carried bravely on, but who was at the same time remote and demoralized. She withdrew into a thorny isolation: within five years she lost or repudiated every important friendship [with Lafayette, the Garnett sisters, Robert Dale Owen, the Mylne family] she had known when Camilla was alive. (*Fanny Wright* 232)

The loss of her sister's love, Camilla's death before their relationship could be healed, the birth of her illegitimate child, her marriage to Phiquepal D'Arusmont, the birth and death of a second infant—all caused Frances Wright to turn away from public life, from old friends and acquaintances, and to retreat, for a short period of her life, into the traditional family she had despised in a futile attempt to atone for the wrongs she had caused both her younger sister and her illegitimate child. She decided to marry Phiquepal, protect her daughter's reputation, and create a conventional family of her own.

Once more, however, family defeated the solitary and independent Frances Wright—this time permanently and devastatingly. When Harriet Garnett visited the newly married Frances Wright D'Arusmont in Paris in November of 1831, she found a dedicated mother, isolated from the outside world, absorbed in tending by herself to the daily tasks of caring for and feeding her infant daughter. Afterwards Harriet Garnett wrote her sister, Julia Garnett Pertz, "it was her—and yet not her.... I thought of the past—of you and poor Cam,—and I own I felt very unhappy. I have not had the courage to return, and shall probably seldom see her I have loved so well—too well alas!" (Heineman, *Restless Angels* 87-88). During this period of her life, Frances Wright tried to make the conventional role of mother and wife fit her stately, worldly character. The result was the dispirited, forlorn, abject creature Harriet Garnett had found in Paris—"her—and yet not her," not Frances Wright herself, the woman who had moved audiences of thousands in America with her eloquence and her vision, who had moved Frances Trollope to come with her to the New World, and who had moved Harriet Garnett and Julia Garnett Pertz, as she had her younger sister, Jeremy Bentham, Lafayette, and Robert Dale Owen, among others, to worship their dear friend.

The role, an act of will and not of nature, could not sustain. Frances's family life did not endure. In the spring of 1834 Frances Wright gave a series of lectures in London and then in America. By 1836, Phiquepal and Frances most often lived apart, traveling separately—their daughter Sylva sometimes with one, sometimes with the other, and finally situated in a boarding school in France. The D'Arusmont family structure had begun to unravel. When Frances Wright inherited property in Dundee, Scotland, from a second cousin in 1844, Celia Eckhardt reveals that Frances was made "wealthy once again, and the greed that her wealth inspired finally destroyed her family" (*Fanny Wright* 284). A battle began which was to destroy Frances Wright's mental, and finally her physical, health—a battle that would last the rest of her lifetime. That there should ever have been the need for such a struggle brings us, once more, to the complexity of Frances Wright's character.

Before her marriage to D'Arusmont, Frances Wright had spoken and written often on the issue of legal equality for married women. In the *Free Enquirer*, just two years before her own marriage, she had decried the way in which the law "allowed robbery and all but murder against the unhappy female who swears away, at one and the same moment, her person and her property, as it but too often is, her peace, her honor, and her life" (*29 April 1829*). The words were to be prophetic in describing her own subsequent married life to Phiquepal D'Arusmont. Knowing that the law was unjust to married women, knowing further that D'Arusmont was a man whom many of her own associates disliked and distrusted (a man Walt Whitman later would call "a damned scoundrel" [Traubel 2: 204]), and knowing that D'Arusmont had no property to bring into their marriage to balance her own, in marrying Phiquepal D'Arusmont "she made no legal provision to keep her property in her own hands" (Eckhardt, *Fanny Wright* 232). It may be that, in refusing to act in what she knew was her own best interest, Frances Wright was attempting in some way to punish herself, first for having failed her sister Camilla and then for having brought an illegitimate child into the world. More than that, as we have seen, Frances Wright had tried to remake herself into a "family" person, perhaps out of this same guilt and need for self-punishment. Casting aside her own long-standing hostility to the traditional family, she had begun to follow the path society deemed correct for women to take, the path of sacrificing herself (and her fortune) for others in the role of wife and mother.

It is doubtful, however, that her motives were merely self-destructive. It was one thing to tell others to protect their property; Frances Wright herself, however, had never been much concerned with holding onto her wealth or providing for her own physical comfort. The words that are carved on her tombstone, words written first in 1829, two years before her marriage, voice her pledge of self-sacrifice for a cause more important than her own life: "I have wedded the cause of human improvement; staked on it my reputation, my fortune, and my life" ("Divisions of Knowledge" 44). Self-abnegation was basic to Frances Wright's character. It is with amazement that Frances Trollope recorded the way in which her young, wealthy, aristocratic friend at Nashoba contentedly made "her meals on a bit of Indian corn bread, and a cup of very indifferent cold water, and while doing so, smiled with a sort of complacency that we may conceive Peter the Hermit felt when eating his acorns in the wilderness" ("The Rough Draft" 28n). Joel Brown, a Cincinnati carpenter who knew Frances Wright 20 years later in the period immediately preceding her death, similarly admits to being startled by the simplicity of Frances Wright's life. He reported that her furnishings were basic and few when she moved into the house he was building for her in downtown Cincinnati and that she was oblivious to the mess and confusion of the construction still in progress around her; nor could he help noting, once more, her meager meals consisting mainly of a little boiled beef or an egg, a potato, crackers, tea or coffee ("Unpublished memoir" 6). Julia Garnett Pertz, writing after the scandal surrounding Nashoba, may have been prescient in analyzing Frances Wright's final demise in saying, "her very virtues—her sensibility—her humanity, her generous forgetfulness of self, have been her ruin" ("To Sismondi" 53).

So absorbed was Frances Wright in the world of ideas, in her concern for the public good, and for the future of humanity, that she remained almost suicidally forgetful of herself—just as she seemed often forgetful of others close to her, as well. And, again, Frances Wright underestimated the effect of her powerful personality and of her independent, activist commitment on those closest to her. Although Phiquepal D'Arusmont's relationship with Frances Wright had begun when she was editor of the *Free Enquirer*, a founding figure of the New York Working Men's Party, a public lecturer known throughout the Midwest and East, and a Nashoba reformer freeing her slaves in Haiti, he clearly became outraged when Frances Wright continued to remain devoted to these same causes for reform after their marriage. Celia Eckhardt comments that, in their bitter fight over Frances Wright's inherited property,

all the rage of a man so long dwarfed by a powerful woman poured onto his page: "Your life was essentially an external life. You loved virtue deeply, but you loved also, and, perhaps even more, grandeur and glory; and in your estimation, unknown, I am sure, to your utmost soul, your husband and child ranked only as mere appendages to your personal existence." (*Fanny Wright* 286)

That Frances Wright remained more dedicated to the world outside than to that inside her own home, that she believed she had something to say that needed to be heard beyond her own dinner table, cannot be doubted; but that she pursued her public career out of a need for applause, as Phiquepal had suggested, does not seem consistent with the denial of self for humanity's cause which so many individuals, from Lafayette to Robert Dale Owen, Amos Gilbert to Mary

Shelley, Walt Whitman to Frances Trollope herself, had attested to in confirming Frances Wright's own sense of the motivating force in her life. In Walt Whitman's words, "She was a brilliant woman, of beauty and estate, who was never satisfied unless she was busy doing good—public good, private good" (Traubel 1: 80).

It now seems probable that, as the sole provider throughout her marriage, Frances Wright only too late came to feel concern for her own economic welfare. As Margaret Lane explains, in 1844 Frances Wright took the advice of her Scottish lawyers and took "a dead of trust, which would make her daughter a considerable heiress and give D'Arusmont a comfortable income for life, but entirely exclude him from control of the capital"; it was at this time that D'Arusmont angrily began to file "suit after suit to gain control of her property" (Lane 43). Shortly afterwards, "reduced to writing from London for a pittance of her own inheritance to live on," Frances Wright signed over trust deeds for her properties, to her daughter Sylva and to her husband—

deeds she soon repudiated on the grounds she had been coerced. According to Fanny, after she signed the final document, Phiquepal threw off the mask, "saying that he had got what he wanted: that he and Sylva were independent of her and could do without her." She went to Nashoba to live, and by the end of 1849, Phiquepal and Alexis [Phiquepal's adopted son who had started a brewery business in Cincinnati, apparently with Frances's money] were again talking about cutting her allowance. She claimed that because she refused to register and thereby validate the Nashoba Trust Deed in Shelby County, they stopped her support altogether. ("D'Arusmont v.s. D'Arusmont and Others" 548-62)

Frances then filed two suits of her own, one for divorce in Shelby County, Tennessee, and a chancery suit in Cincinnati, "no doubt hop[ing] that her case would set the precedent in Ohio for giving married women control over their own property" ("D'Arusmont V.S. D'Arusmont and Others," Eckhardt, *Fanny Wright* 286). Although Frances Wright was to win both cases, (that for divorce in 1851), the case concerning her inheritance was not settled until after her death.

Enduring never-ending legal battles which rapidly depleted her mental and physical strength, Frances Wright admitted,

Nothing but the conviction that this [legal] course is calculated to open her [Sylva's] eyes to the real character of the tortuous path of intrigue and vain ambition in which she has been involved, by a mad and a bad man [Phiquepal D'Arusmont], would have moved me to engage in it, or sustained me in pursuing it. (Amos Gilbert 39-40)

Yet nothing Frances Wright was to say or do could ever bring her daughter

Sylva back to her. The independent and self-sufficient Frances Wright was to be unexpectedly and devastatingly shaken by the loss of her daughter's love, just as she had been years before by her sister Camilla's emotional withdrawal and sudden death. In writing to her Cincinnati lawyer, W. Y. Gholson, Frances Wright despaired when she concluded that she must now "resign myself to the loss of my child" (Nov. 13, 1851).

Two months later, slipping and breaking her thigh on ice in Cincinnati, Frances Wright endured a painful and futile period of convalescence during which her daughter refused to visit her (even while staying in Cincinnati). Pleadingly Wright wrote to Gholson, telling him of mental anguish so great that she could not afford to hear or think about her family affairs any longer:

the sight of the old friend who called on me last night simply to talk to me of things I must never think of—law suits, my daughter, land and money—Oh My Dear Sir never let me hear those names again. You will do all that has to be done and do all for the best. (June 6, 1852)

As she lay dying on the thirteenth of December, 1852, Frances Wright drew up a will in which, despite all the hurt and pain Sylva's acts of cruelty and hostility had caused her in the years preceding, she left the majority of her estate to her daughter, "who has been alienated from me but to whom with said property I give my blessing and forgiveness for the sorrow she has caused her mother," giving a kiss to a Cincinnati acquaintance to pass on to Sylva (Sept. 13, 1852). If throughout her life her fortune had been staked on causes she believed in—on Nashoba and the *Free Enquirer*, for instance—upon her death it reverted to the family (where Phiquepal had wished it to remain). Ironically, however, her heiress, Sylva, remained unforgiving. Persuading W. Y. Gholson to give her her mother's unpublished papers, Sylva allowed these works to disappear (Eckhardt, *Fanny Wright* 295). Further, in 1874, testifying before Congress against woman's suffrage, Sylva argued:

As the daughter of Frances Wright, whom the Female Suffragists are pleased to consider as having *opened* the door to their pretensions,....*shut* it forever, from the strongest convictions that they can only bring misery and degradation upon the whole sex, and thereby wreck human happiness in America! (Eckhardt, *Fanny Wright 290*)

Defiant of conventions as Frances Wright had been—a woman who first had raised the issues of female rights and female suffrage publicly in America, who had founded the first experimental colony to bring an end to slavery in the South, who had edited a paper openly attacking religious bigotry and chicanery in the New World—she had not been able to withstand the force of the traditional family and its demands on her own life. Always there was family around her—a grandfather, an aunt, an uncle, cousins, her younger sister, a husband, a daughter—in the midst of whom she remained, somehow, always aloof, the solitary, independent, remote and reflective visionary. Alone as she remained, Frances Wright still could not forgive herself nor forget her failures in the eyes of family members who, while unable to give her what she needed, expected Frances to give unstintingly to them of her time, her devotion, her wealth (when needed), and, above all else, her constant companionship. To have acceded wholly to the demands of family would have been to forego her public career (unlike the famous men, revered by their public and families alike, who surrounded her). To give up her work, however, was to give up on the ideas she believed in—for Frances Wright was an activist who believed that ideas needed to be put into practice and reforms needed to be acted out.

Frances Wright took her role seriously, writing in the Preface to her lectures, that she felt it was her "duty to present [her views] to the American people" (x). In fact, Frances Wright may have seen herself as something of a "messiah" (Eckhardt, *Fanny Wright* 172), a quality the older Frances Trollope gently mocks in commenting in a letter to Lafayette on Wright's Cincinnati lecture in 1829, "Fanny appears in good spirits, and anticipates confidently the regeneration of the whole human race from her present exertions" (60). Nevertheless, Trollope herself attests to Frances Wright's eloquence and her extraordinary talents as an orator:

I shared the surprise, but not the wonder; I knew her extraordinary gift of eloquence, her almost unequalled command of words, and the wonderful power of her rich and thrilling voice; and I doubted not that if it was her will to do it, she had the power of commanding the attention, and enchanting the ear of any audience before whom it was her pleasure to appear. (*Domestic* 57)

Trollope further comments that Wright's "tall and majestic figure, the deep and almost solemn expression of her eyes, the simple contour of her finely formed head,...all contributed to produce an effect unlike anything I had ever seen before, or ever expect to see again" (*Domestic* 57). Robert Dale Owen described her as a "Mercury," an admirable figure whose "principles and opinions accorded more completely with my own than those of almost any other person" (Eckhardt, "Of Fanny and Camilla Wright" 41; *Owen's Travel Journal* 43). Remembering his attendance at Frances Wright's Sunday speeches in New York when he was still a boy, Walt Whitman declared: "She has always been to me one of the sweetest of sweet memories: we all loved her, fell down before her: her very appearance seemed to enthrall us" (Traubel 2: 205). Again, Whitman eulogizes Frances Wright: "She was one of the few characters to excite in me a wholesale respect and love: she was beautiful in bodily shape and gifts of soul.... There was a majesty about her" (Traubel 2: 499).

When Whitman recalled Frances Wright's powerful, oratorical skills, he talked of her speaking "informally, colloquially" to the crowds who gathered on Sunday to listen to her in the old Tammany Hall. Yet today her speeches often appear ponderous and wooden on the printed page without the aid of her meaningful pauses and the rich emphasis of her powerful speaking voice to underline her meanings. Here, for instance, is a sentence from one of her speeches, mind-numbing in its length and breadth of scope, alike:

until every son and daughter in this galaxy of commonwealths shall be equally provided with the means of instruction—shall be raised in the habits of healthy industry—be protected equally from the sufferings and vice attendant on poverty and on riches—be trained as equals to understand and to exercise the rights set forth in this charter—all your laws and your provisions, your preaching and your punishments, your churches, your prisons, your partial colleges and inefficient schools, your asylums and your hospitals, your restricted commerce and protected manufactures, your canals and your railroads, your taxes and your bounties, your inventions and your improvements, multiplied without object and without end, will work no real benefit to man—will do nothing towards the alleviation of one of the weighty evils which now press on the population—will and can, tend to no other consequences than further to vitiate the feelings, confound the understandings, deprave the habits, and render yet more disproportionate the condition of humankind. ("Address II" 138)

Her speeches must be read aloud, read majestically, to sustain.

Her other prose, too, is difficult. Whitman loved Frances Wright's *A Few Days in Athens*, written when she was only 18, a book he called formative for himself and one he frequently recommended to others as "sparkling with life," even if somewhat "immature, perhaps, crude, but strong" (Traubel 2: 209). In fact, Whitman admitted to admiring the style of *A Few Days in Athens* despite its faults, a style he concluded was "the style of all the greatest sages—Epicurus, Epictetus, Emerson, Darwin: the modesty—the readiness to yield, to see what they might have excuses for not seeing. All modern science is saturated with the same spirit, and in this exists its excuse for being" (Traubel 2: 517).

Wright's greatest work, written in her mature years, *England, The Civilizer*, still displays a similar cumbersome and rough, yet brilliant, quality. From its typical essay-length title, *England, The Civilizer: Her History Developed In Its Principles; With Reference To The Civilizational History of Modern Europe (American Inclusive,) And With A View To The Denouement Of The Difficulties Of The Hour*, to sentences such as the following, it combines startling, sweeping insights with a histrionic, rhetorical, at times almost unreadable, prose manner:

Up to the time present, society—as ever submitted to male government under one another of its forms, variously styled the patriarchal, monarchal, oligarchal, aristocratic, democratic, despotic military, or—the last variety of which it is susceptible—the money jobbing, scheming, all intriguing, all defrauding, all confounding, the hired and hireling, bank-ruled and by corruption ruling, legislative—up to the time present, society submitted, under government, to the master-action of the selfish principle, stifles, tramples under foot, or even perverts the very nature of the generous. (11)

History is here condensed, categorized, defined and revealed in just one sentence, while Wright, at the same time, contrasts what she calls the selfish, male, governing principle with its generous, female, subservient counterpart—impulses which must be combined, she argues later, for the future good of the human race. If her prose is difficult, her ideas are visionary, as Celia Eckhardt reveals:

it would be ninety years before another woman rediscovered those important ideas that gained credence only as the twentieth century neared its end. In *Three Guineas*, Virginia Woolf found, as Fanny had, that the world men had made was inclined to war and she understood that the instinct to battle was sex-related. (*Fanny Wright* 281)

While other women—Ernestine Rose, Elizabeth Cady Stanton and Susan B. Anthony—would also follow Wright in making such a connection, Frances Wright's ideas remained ahead of her times.

Her writing was as grand, majestic and sweeping as her person—and as highly serious, as well. As Celia Eckhardt explains, from childhood on, Frances Wright had felt "disgust for frivolous reading, conversation, and occupation"—the experiences of the drawing room she had shunned at an early age (*Fanny Wright* 9). Without ever developing "the psychic protection of a sense of humor," she confronted life head-on (*Fanny Wright* 9). In Robert Dale Owen's view, she had been " 'a little soured perhaps by an unhappy infancy and childhood.' He thought her less light-hearted than he and said she took a gloomier view of the world: not habitually sad, she was nevertheless restless and occasionally despondent. He saw much to admire in her, he later wrote, but nothing to love" (Owen, *Owen's Travel Journal* 42 and "An Earnest Sewing of Wild Oats," 74-75; Owen, *Threading My Way* 299). For Frances Wright, however, life had to be dealt with in a straightforward, if solemn way. She believed in a practical education for everyone, women and men, blacks and whites, and regretted her own less useful education in her aunt's drawing room and library. In the words of Joel Brown,

My wife says she was the most ignorant housekeeper She ever Saw, could not sweep a room and do it correctly, could not pack a Trunk properly—This she regretted very much—She often remarked, Her Gardeen had done her injustice, by not giving her a practable education.... How much better it would have been for me if I had learnt general housework [she said], than learning aristocratical noncense [sic]. (6)

Frances Wright considered herself a realist. As her character Mitrodorus tells Theon in *A Few Days in Athens*, "In studying the existences which surround us, it is clearly our business to use our eyes, and not our imaginations. To see things as they are, is all we should attempt, and is all that is possible to be done" (188).

Clearly, Frances Wright believed that she saw with her eyes and not with her imagination, and yet her own highly serious, courageous and confrontive stances were often unconsciously idealistic, as well. She admitted that, when she had written *Views of Society and Manners of the Americans* in 1821, she had mistaken "for the energy of enlightened liberty what was, perhaps, rather the restlessness of commercial enterprise" (Preface, *Life, Letters, and Lectures* vi). Nevertheless, afterwards, despite evidence to the contrary, "she refused to believe that Americans would deliberately choose the pursuit of material goods and social distinction over the pleasures of egalitarian society. She believed that the impulse to lord it over one's fellows represented a failure of understanding rather than a permanent human characteristic" (Eckhardt, *Fanny Wright* 172). She devoted many of her speeches to the cause of "universal free public education [which she thought] could develop the republican spirit that would allow America's republican institutions to work.... [She had] a nineteenth century belief in the saving grace of education" (Eckhardt, *Fanny Wright* 173). Even as her anti-slavery experiment of Nashoba was failing, she wrote of the day when "the white man and the black, and their children, approached in feeling and education, [would] gradually blend into one their blood and hue" (Wright, *Explanatory Notes*).

Frances Wright took on the forces of religion head-on, as she had in *A Few Days in Athens*, where Epicurus announces that he had "found the first link in the chain of evil; I have found it—in all countries—among all tribes and tongues and nations; I have found it, Fellow-men, I have found it in—RELIGION!.... It is Religion—that poisoner of human felicity! It is Religion—that blind guide of human reason!" (199). Frances Wright, in speaking out in this way, confronted societal values in America, a country so preoccupied with religion that Frances Trollope (the daughter herself of a clergyman) commented that "religion was tea-table talk and its strict observance a fashionable mark of distinction" (Eckhardt, *Fanny Wright* 171). Wright outraged the religious community even further when she and Robert Dale Owen "wrote respectfully of Richard Carlile's pioneering British birth-control book, *Every Woman's Book*. They argued that legislation could not regulate the affections of men and women and that evil was the consequence not of man's fallen state but rather of ignorance and bad institutions" (Eckhardt, *Fanny Wright* 194).

Admitting the failure of the American democratic society to fulfill its promises of equality for all, Frances Wright "formulated a philosophical interpretation of history, envisioning a final change, sometime in the future, to a social organization having communal ownership of all real property" (Baker, Introduction to *Views of Society* xxii). At the conclusion of *England, The Civilizer*, although she could no longer speak in public in America without fearing for her safety, and her marriage to Phiquepal D'Arusmont had made her private life insufferable, Frances Wright envisioned a time when "the dove of peace descends upon earth, and love becomes the universal bond of the species, by our recognizing happiness for the unique end of our being, and by uniting as one family to fertilize one common earth; each secure in the aid and protection of all, without care for the day or anxiety for the future" (470).

Most of all, however, Frances Wright revealed her idealism in the way she had ignored the most profound reality of American life, what Frances Trollope was to call the "seven-fold shield of habitual insignificance" which "guarded" women in the United States (*Domestic* 57). As Celia Eckhardt comments, "She saw how thoroughly women were excluded from public life, but failed to see how profoundly that exclusion crippled them and affected her" (*Fanny Wright* 46). Frances Wright believed she would be listened to, that she could effect change in American society, and that the "defect" of her sex could be overcome by her own belief in herself, by the soundness of her reason, and by the sincerity of her commitment to the good of humanity. Both in her public life and in her private life, however, she would be held up to the prevailing standard of female domesticity—and found wanting.

Frances Wright was not realistic enough to know, finally, that she had attempted the impossible nor to understand the greed, the envy and the need for power which motivated many of the Americans she had sought to help. Unhappily, as well, she had failed to sense these same base motives in the man she had married. Innocently, she had written of a common concern for the working classes and for the uneducated which "has occupied my mind as that of my husband for years. The similarity of our researches, which induced our union, has aided our [work towards reform]..." ("To John M. Morgan"). In this hope, perhaps, most of all, Frances Wright was to prove herself tragically mistaken and fatally idealistic—dying a lonely, broken woman unable to find solace herself, much less heal the sicknesses of society as she had worked so hard to do.

Chapter Four
Witty Realist

While Frances Wright's independent spirit was being broken by the greed and cruelty of her own family and the American people she had tried to help, Frances Trollope's will was growing stronger in the face of her own overwhelming problems. In going to Nashoba, Frances Trollope admitted to her friend Harriet Garnett (7 Dec. 1828) that she had hoped to find tranquillity "in the absence of Mr. Trollope. He is a good honourable man—but his temper is dreadful—every year increases his irritability—and also, its lamentable effect upon the children" (Heineman, *The Triumphant* 63). Later, in Cincinnati, where she found tranquillity even more distant than her temperamental husband in Harrow, Frances Trollope began, out of necessity, to invent ways to provide for herself and for her children—creating the "Invisible Girl" and "The Infernal Regions" attractions for the Western Museum, then venturing upon her ambitious Bazaar project. After the failure of the latter, when Frances Trollope was already 51 years of age, she suffered the indignity, terror, and confusion of bankruptcy—bankruptcy in a foreign land. Then again at 55, following yet another bankruptcy one year after her return to Harrow, she planned both her husband's narrow escape and her family's safe refuge from their English creditors.

And yet, with each of these difficulties—and more to come as her husband and three of her children, one after another, grew sick and died, with Frances Trollope tending their illnesses, arranging their burials, moving the family, and organizing one household after another from Bruges, to London, Paris, Vienna, Penrith, and Florence—Frances Trollope became more determined to persevere and more resourceful in her plans than ever before. Her zest for life remained intact, amazingly undamaged by her many wearying and sorrowful experiences. Critical of his mother in other ways, Anthony Trollope had only praise for her resiliency and her sense of humor:

Of the mixture of joviality and industry which formed her character, it is almost impossible to speak with exaggeration..... But the joviality was all for others. She could dance with other people's legs, eat and drink with other people's palates, be proud with the lustre of other people's finery.... of all people I have known she was the most joyous, or, at any rate, the most capable of joy. (*An Autobiography* 24-25)

Anthony spoke with amazement, too, of his mother's ability to write under the most dire of situations: "I have written many novels under many conditions; but I doubt much whether I could write one when my whole heart was by the bedside of a dying son" (*An Autobiography* 24-25).

In happier days, Frances Trollope had organized her family and neighbors in writing *The Magpie*, a homespun journal "dedicated to 'Literature, Politics, Science, and Art,' " signing herself with characteristic self-mockery as "Grub Street" (Stebbins 53). In America, with her Nashoba and Cincinnati Bazaar plans in shambles around her, Frances Trollope would put her writing talent, her sense of humor, and her inexhaustible energy to earnest use, planning one more way to save her family from desperate circumstances, this time by writing a travel book on America.

And so *Domestic Manners of the Americans* was born—and Frances Trollope became an internationally known, discussed, and reviewed author (heretofore known only to a small circle of family and friends as "Grub Street"). Humor, an essential element of her nature, would be central, as well, both to the popularity and to the controversy surrounding her travel book—remaining key to the readability of *Domestic Manners of the Americans* today. And humor was, as well, one of the book's main subjects—or, rather, the lack thereof which Frances Trollope had perceived in the American character and in American culture as a whole. As Frances Trollope's spokesperson, Caroline Gordon, comments frankly in *Refugee in America* (to the annoyance of her American acquaintances), "one of my most particular complaints about you is, that your people never do look gay and happy together; I have never heard a hearty laugh since I entered the country" (1: 159). Frances Trollope herself had found Americans too obsessed with the business of life (seemingly, the business of making money) and far too solemn in their demeanor for her more cheerful nature. In *Domestic Manners of the Americans*, she makes frequent observations on the seeming wretchedness of the Americans, even those at their leisure in the midst of social gatherings, engaged in consuming "massive" quantities of food apparently to reward themselves "for whatever they may have suffered in keeping awake...it always appeared to me that they [Americans] remained together as long as they could bear it, and then they rise *en masse*, cloak, bonnet, shawl, and exit" (50). Noting that billiards were against the law, that a $50 penalty existed for selling a pack of cards, that public balls and concerts, even private dinner-parties, seemed depressingly infrequent in puritanical America, Frances Trollope commented, "I never saw any people who appeared to live so much without amusement as the Cincinnatians" (59).

Not so Frances Trollope, whose ready wit and propensity for enjoying life sustained her in her private life, as they sustained her readers in page after page, volume after volume, from the first to the last of her works, whether written by the author in the grip of economic necessity, personal anguish, or bodily pain. She faced her critics unperturbed and unrepentant, maintaining the social

PORTRAIT OF

FRANCES TROLLOPE

Portrait of Frances Trollope, from Auguste Hervieu's frontispiece for the Fifth Edition of *Domestic Manners of the Americans* (1839).

realism and social commentary of her fiction, while teasing: "Of course, I draw from life.... But I always pulp my acquaintances before serving them up. You would never recognize a pig in a sausage" (Stebbins 142). When her critics attacked her style as well as her content, she remained steadfastly sanguine through this unpleasantness, as well. According to Richard Mullen's recent introduction to *Domestic Manners of the Americans,*

She was then attacked for a "want of delicacy in style and sentiment." Actually, this was to be a frequent criticism of all of Mrs. Trollope's writings as she often used words that the growing puritanism of the nineteenth century found "vulgar." This, is, of course, precisely one reason why she remains so readable today, unlike many more "genteel" writers. (xxi)

In fact, Frances Trollope delighted in the colloquial and everyday, while relishing innovations, too, as they crept into the English language. She had entertained all of Europe with her "Americanisms" in both *Domestic Manners of the Americans* and *Refugee in America*. Amused by the frequency with which certain names recurred in American families, she created scenes in her "Yankee" works such as this one: "'Put on the kettle, Benjamin Franklin; fetch down the maple sugar from the shelf, Sally; bring over all the mugs, Monroe, my man' " (1: 56). Her American girls talk about being "jam" (dressed up) [*Refugee*, 1: 70]; her American women call each other "honey" [*Domestic* 83] and speak of their "helps" (servants) [*Refugee* 2: 108]; her American men admire "fight[ing] it out ...like Christians" [*Refugee* 2: 179] as well as "getting along" [*Domestic* 17] (as they term suffering through the hardships of the frontier). After the publication of *Domestic Manners of the Americans*, Frances Trollope was informed by the Countess of Morley in London, "that I had quite put English out of fashion and that every one was talking Yankee talk" ("To Thomas Adolphus Trollope" 102). Frances Trollope's delight in Americanisms would continue into her last novel, *Fashionable Life; or, Paris and London* (1856), where she explains: "It is not a gay task, even for such an idle story-teller as myself, to turn from such a scene as I have described above [to a much more painful one]...but, to use again a very expressive transatlantic phrase, 'I have got to do it' " (3: 14). Nor could Frances Trollope resist the peculiarities of language at home, as when she comments in *Uncle Walter*, "his Lordship did not 'polk' (the last May Fair supplement to 'Johnson's Dictionary,' if we be correctly informed, contains this verb)" (1: 222).

If language itself amused Frances Trollope, more especially did the manners and actions of the people using it. In the same novel, *Uncle Walter*, Frances Trollope savages the marriage game as practiced in nineteenth century England. She ridicules the "sundry thoughtful mothers and pretty daughters, none of whom were inclined to neglect this fortunate opportunity of entering themselves for the 'great Goldstable stakes' " as they strove to capture the wealthy, innocent Lord Goldstable (1: 237). When Kate Harrington's mother prepares a clever trap to ensnare this rich, young man for her daughter, Frances Trollope jests: "Experienced mamas will readily understand me, when I say that such a spot [for a téte á téte] is of as much important use to their operations, as a landing-net to an angler" (1: 195). Painstakingly, Trollope describes the lavish preparations Lady Augusta makes (and the miseries, immediate and future, cloaked by their promise):

The first floor was as brilliant as a profusion of wax-lights, and a profusion of flowers could make it; the supper, which was to be served at two, A.M., had been prepared in Gunter's very best style; the music was excellent; and any one unaccustomed to such things might really have supposed that they were going to enjoy themselves exceedingly, if they had taken a review of the preparations before the arrival of the actors who were destined to fill the scene.

Our readers, however, are, of course, not so rustically ignorant, and so wholly unaccustomed to fashionable parties, as to suppose anything so preposterously ridiculous, and so utterly unlike the truth. *They* know, unless indeed they are absolutely, and altogether nobodies, how much, and how little, of real enjoyment is to be hoped for, when space enough for one hundred is to be occupied by three. (*Uncle Walter* 1: 193)

Human greed, selfishness, hypocrisy and ignorance in their many forms become the real sources of entertainment for Frances Trollope and her readers.

The outrageous Widow Barnaby especially served to entertain her creator, Frances Trollope, and the nineteenth century reading public. The author's relationship to her favorite creation is a complex and interesting one. On the one hand, the Widow Barnaby represents everything that Mrs. Trollope loved to ridicule and expose in her fiction: human selfishness, materialism, pretense and vanity. On the other, as an energetic, older woman who lived by her wits and no longer depended on the benevolence of a man to take care of her, the Widow Barnaby was a woman not unlike Frances Trollope herself. As Mrs. Trollope admitted to her readers at the outset of *The Barnabys in America* (1843), "I scruple not to confess that with all her [the Widow Barnaby's] faults, and she has some, I love her dearly; I owe her many mirthful moments, and the deeper pleasure still of believing that she has brought mirthful moments to others also" (1:3). Through the Widow Barnaby, Frances Trollope is able, paradoxically, both to poke fun at and to defend herself, at the same time.

In *The Barnabys in America*, Frances Trollope sends her favorite character to America, "a land which all the world knows I cherish in my memory with peculiar delight" (1: 3). When the Widow Barnaby parallels her creator's life, further, by announcing her intention to write a travel book on

America, she is warned by Mrs. Judge Johnson of others preceding her who have set an unwholesome precedent for English travel books on America (foremost among them, of course, Frances Trollope herself): "There has been a great deal of ill blood brewed, and evil seed sown between our two countries by the vile abominable lies and slanders that some of our travelling authors have propagated against us; and to such a lady as you are, I expect this must be as hateful as it is to us" (*The Barnabys in America* 1: 280). Frances Trollope, I am sure, laughed heartily as she turned the Widow Barnaby into the oft-reviled and caricatured version of herself stereotyped in numerous reviews after the publication of *Domestic Manners of the Americans*. For the Widow Barnaby was as determined to make money from her travel book as the penniless Frances Trollope must have been—and as ready to win her fortune by any means, fair or foul, as Frances Trollope had been accused of having set out most callously to do.

In theorizing about the best way to accomplish her ends, however, the greedy Widow Barnaby parts company with her author, Frances Trollope, revealing the innocence and honesty of the latter:

It would be just as easy for me to write all truth as all lies, about this queer place, and all these monstrous odd people, but wouldn't I be a fool if I did any such thing?—and is it but one bit more trouble to write all these monstrous fine words, just like what I have read over, and over again, in novels,—is it one bit more trouble, I should like to know, writing them all in one sense instead of the other? (*The Barnabys in America* 2: 26)

And so, the Widow Barnaby creates a "fine," if fictional, picture of America, completely unlike that painted by Frances Trollope herself, one guaranteed to gain the Widow ready financial backing, lavish accommodations, continuous entertainment, and constant applause on her travels throughout America, as when she reads this passage to one of her Yankee audiences:

Nobody properly qualified to write upon this wonderful country could behold a single town, a single street, a single house, a single individual of it, for just one single half-hour, without feeling all over to his very heart, convinced, that not all the countries of the old world put together are worthy to compare, in any one respect, from the very greatest to the very least, with the free-born, the free-bred, the immortal, and ten thousand times more glorious country, generally called that of the "Stars and the Stripes!" (*The Barnabys in America* 2: 44)

Thus, the Widow Barnaby triumphs on American soil, allowing Frances Trollope to savor another victory in her string of novels satirizing America following the publication of *Domestic Manners of the Americans*. Having been scorned and humiliated at every level of society throughout her tour of the

United States, charged unfair prices and cheated into bankruptcy when she attempted to build her Bazaar, Frances Trollope, a decade later, sent America this extremely clever, resourceful, energetic, and, above all else, unscrupulous, version of herself to settle a few old scores—the Widow Barnaby outmaneuvering, outwitting and outraging the equally enterprising, if smugly complacent, Americans at their own game.

Although she is clearly defending herself from her critics in *The Barnabys in America*, Frances Trollope does so characteristically, laughing at herself all the while. She maintained her cheerfulness, at least in part, by refusing to take her own life and work too seriously. In her first, unpublished preface to *Domestic Manners of the Americans*, she confesses: "I greatly doubt if my book contains much valuable instruction; nay I should not be much surprised if it were called trifling; for to tell the honest truth I suspect that it is...gossiping" ("The Rough Draft" 431). (On the contrary, as Richard Mullen suggests in his recent introduction to the Oxford edition of *Domestic Manners of the Americans*, her book and its criticisms have withstood the test of time remarkably well through her detailed analysis of some of the most significant and lasting elements of American society.) In *Domestic Manners of the Americans*, itself, Frances Trollope remarks, in her self-effacing way:

I am in no way competent to judge of the political institutions of America; and if I should occasionally make an observation on their effects, as they meet my superficial glance, they will be made in the spirit and with the feeling of a woman, who is apt to tell what her first impressions may be, but unapt to reason back from effects to their causes. . . . but there are points of national peculiarity of which women may judge as ably as men—all that constitutes the external of society may be fairly trusted to us. (39)

That said—the misfortune of her sex apologized for and the ominscience of her work discounted—Frances Trollope proceeds, under her own name (unlike Frances Wright, who published anonymously as an "English woman"), to comment freely and wittily on whatever engaged her fancy—politics, of course, foremost on the list of subjects covered. Pleasant and self-effacing as she remained, Frances Trollope quietly insisted on penetrating the social facade and exposing the underlying truths beneath, whatever the unpleasant consequences might be.

In this insistence and in other ways, Frances Trollope's character, as with that of Frances Wright, reveals a complex mixture of the conventional and the unconventional, the adventurous and the traditional, the conservative and the liberal. A woman who enjoyed her family, living out her days in the company of one or more of her children, Frances Trollope, nevertheless, had set out on a journey to America leaving behind her husband, as well as two of her sons (Anthony and Tom—an act for which Anthony seemed never fully to have forgiven her). Furthermore, her restless spirit caused her to abandon family at other times, as well, as she moved away from Hadley (and her son Anthony), then away from Penrith (and her daughter Cecilia), in her search for a place which would satisfy her basic needs and her basic nature. At last she found that place in Florence, Italy, where she was accompanied by her son Tom—making a final home there, far away from the graves of many of her family members and away from the established homes of surviving children she loved (and those children's—Cecilia and Anthony's—children, her grandchildren), as well.

In making this choice, Frances Trollope recognized her own needs as important, showing a remarkable insistence, once more, on living where she could feel culturally at home, as well as physically and materially comfortable. She had literally "earned" the right—in providing for all of her family's creature comforts for so long—to satisfy her own special wants, and she did not scruple in her later years to provide for these. In defining for herself the essence of the "good life" (as in her inclination to be jovial and to meet life with a ready sense of humor), Frances Trollope differed greatly from her younger, more serious and ascetic friend, Frances Wright. As Celia Eckhardt comments, on the voyage from England to America Frances Trollope "had begun to suspect that she and Fanny Wright might have very different ideas about the basic requirements of civilized life" (*Fanny Wright* 160). The subsequent months of Frances Trollope's American sojourn filled out whatever remained sketchy in her notion of the "essential life" (as she came to portray it in her writing).

Unlike Frances Wright, described by Frances Trollope as eating cornbread and drinking water while standing under a leaky roof in her Nashoba cabin, looking about her "with the air of a conqueror...[who] had triumphed over all human weakness" (*smalley* 28n), Frances Trollope found "the 'simple' manner of living in Western America...distasteful" (*Domestic* 37). For this judgment and for other acts, Frances Trollope has often been criticized as "snobbish." Richard Mullen repeats the story of the aspiring Trollopes in Harrow who "boasted a liveried footman, even if it meant economizing on candles" (*Domestic* x). Anthony Trollope recalls that his mother "loved society" (*An Autobiography* 21), that "she was extravagant and liked to have money to spend" (25). C. P. Snow, as we have seen earlier, blamed Frances Trollope's extravagances in furnishing their Harrow homes for the decline in the family's resources (18). And countless American and British reviewers of *Domestic Manners of the Americans* scorned Frances Trollope's descriptions of the American frontier as those of a pretentious social climber trying to impress the British aristocracy (xxi-xxiii).

Certainly, it is true that Frances Trollope valued the comforts of life. Unlike Frances Wright, who had never wanted for money and had rejected the drawing room manners and "aristocratic noncense [sic]" of her youth for a more simple and practical life, Frances Trollope came more and more, through the hardships that she had witnessed and those she had experienced, to appreciate a refined and graceful lifestyle (Brown 6). What Frances Trollope abhorred most about the "simple life" she saw in America, however, was "its levelling effects on the manners of the people [rather than]...the personal privations that it rendered necessary" (*Domestic* 37). She elaborated on the inter-relationship she found between manners and society in America:

It requires an abler pen than mine to trace the connection which I am persuaded exists between these deficiencies [in refinement] and the minds and manners of the people. All animal wants are supplied profusely at Cincinnati, and at a very easy rate; but, alas! these go but a little way in the history of a day's enjoyment. The total and universal want of good, or even pleasing, manners, both in males and females, is so remarkable, that I was constantly endeavouring to account for it. (*Domestic* 37-38)

People ate, drank, slept, and, of course, worked in America, "that land of universal money-getting" (*Refugee* 3: 40) where Trollope believed she had discovered "a race...selling their lives for gold" (*Domestic* 27-28). Meanwhile, at all levels of American society, Frances Trollope saw people neglecting what seemed central to her and central, she felt, to civilized people in any country: literature, art, architecture, conversation and theatre, all necessary, she believed, to stimulate and engage the minds of the people, grace their environment, elevate their character, and ennoble the resulting social interaction among them. Without these, freedom and material well-being were not worth having, Frances Trollope felt, in America or anywhere else:

All the freedom enjoyed in America beyond what is enjoyed in England, is enjoyed solely by the disorderly at the expense of the orderly; and were I a stouter knight, either of the sword or of the pen, I would fearlessly throw down my gauntlet, and challenge the whole republic to prove the contrary: but being, as I am, a feeble looker-on, with a needle, for my spear, and "I talk" for my device, I must be contented with the power of stating the fact, perfectly certain that I shall be contradicted by one loud shout from Maine to Georgia. (*Domestic* 88-89)

To state such a "fact" (that America was a crude and violent country) was, of course, to throw down a gauntlet—an act of courage not soon forgiven or forgotten by the United States and its supporters throughout the world.

For Frances Wright, the elevation of human character would begin with a free, practical education for all in a democratic society. She was, as Frances Trollope called her, a "philosophical" woman who theorized about improving humanity as a whole, writing and speaking in universal and abstract terms (*Domestic* 24). Not so Frances Trollope. As Helen Heineman suggests about the Nashoba experience they shared together, "Frances Trollope saw the somber reality" (*The Triumphant* 49). While Frances Wright felt that she had gained nothing of value in her many years of drawing room experiences, the more gregarious Frances Trollope had not only enjoyed her share of light-hearted moments in such social gatherings as Frances Wright had rejected, but had learned there most of what she felt she would need to know about life. The lessons she learned in the drawing room, in fact, served her well throughout her writing career. For there Frances Trollope had become a sharp, critical observer of the particular both in human character and in human interaction; she carried her interest and her understanding of men and women out into the world on her many travels and on her research trips for her reform novels.

Frances Trollope's writings are characterized by vivid detail and realistic descriptions, as in this memorable account of dinnertime on a Mississippi steamboat from *Domestic Manners of the Americans*:

The total want of all the usual courtesies of the table, the voracious rapidity with which the viands were seized and devoured; the strange uncouth phrases and pronunciation; the loathesome spitting, from the contamination of which it was absolutely impossible to protect our dresses; the frightful manner of feeding with their knives, till the whole blade seemed to enter into the mouth; and the still more frightful mannner of cleaning the teeth afterwards with a pocket-knife, soon forced us to feel that we were not surrounded by the generals, colonels, and majors of the old world; and that the dinner-hour was to be anything rather that an hour of enjoyment. (15)

Later on her American journey, Frances Trollope encountered "freeholders" who, "often possessing several slaves," had "as few of the comforts of life as the very poorest English peasant" (*Domestic* 203). Rather than glance away from these sorry scenes, Frances Trollope looked closely at the frontier families she saw on her trip up the Mississippi into Ohio and beyond, reflecting especially on the condition of the women she studied. The situation, she comments, of the American farmer's

wife and daughters is incomparably worse [than his]. It is they who are indeed the slaves of the soil. One has but to look at the wife of an American cottager, and ask her age, to be convinced that the life she leads is one of hardship, privation, and labour. It is rare to see a woman in this station who has reached the age of thirty without losing every trace of youth and beauty. (*Domestic* 97)

More particularly, she immortalizes one farmer's wife through this portrayal of her situation:

She did not look in health, and said they had all had ague in "the fall," but she seemed contented and proud of her independence; though it was in somewhat a mournful accent that she said: "Tis strange to us to see company. I expect the sun may rise and set a hundred times, before I shall see another *human* being that does not belong to the family." (*Domestic* 42)

For the social Frances Trollope, "there was something awful and almost unnatural in [the woman's] loneliness"—and Frances Trollope's empathy is clear in this portrait of a frail, solitary figure upright against the stark background of the American frontier (*Domestic* 43).

In her fiction, as well, Frances Trollope insisted on dispelling illusions and revealing the truths she had seen in the human behavior and human society around her. A European who had herself been lured by the promise of America only to be driven to despair on sight by the utopian community of Nashoba; a woman who had been deceived about the quality of education and the lifestyle her son Henry would experience in New Harmony, Indiana, another cooperative, utopian community; and a visitor who felt she had not only been mistreated but also cheated into bankruptcy in Cincinnati, Ohio, in the land of equal opportunity and justice for all, Frances Trollope created a "fiction" which would startle the idealistic reader into a recognition of the reality of the America she had discovered. In *Refugee in America* she describes the community of "Perfect Bliss," visited by the hopeful Madame de Clairville (another Trollope surrogate),

a French woman who, though forty, was still handsome, and though poor, was still elegant. As her story is very similar to what has occurred to more than one foreigner in America, a slight sketch of it must be given.... (1: 210)

Madame de Clairville's husband, in search of the ideal community, had accepted the life of hard work he had found in "Perfect Bliss," even though his "visions had been of scientific lectures, amateur concerts, private theatricals and universal philanthropy [Frances Trollope's own dream, as well?]" (*Refugee* 1: 212). What he could not accept was that his wife, too, must spend her time laboring hard amidst health-threatening conditions while "all the little comforts which he had spent his last thousand francs to purchase at New York, were seized upon, as general stock, and a scanty pittance of necessaries doled out to them at each meal" (*Refugee* 1: 213).

After her husband's death, within a year of this brave venture, Madame de Clairville found herself alone, yet "able to manage for herself, better than he had done for her. There was still an active principle of hope alive within her; she determined to return to her country and her child, and felt but little alarmed, and not at all discouraged, by the difficulties in her way" (*Refugee* 1: 215). So, too, the pragmatic, realistic Frances Trollope must have felt, though battered by so many unfamiliar and unfortunate experiences in America, as a woman for the first time on her own in the absence of her husband, drawing on her own imaginative and physical resources, keeping the "active principle of hope alive within her," using the strength within her while, at the same time, making its discovery. As with Madame de Clairville, Frances Trollope, too, had learned to be distrustful of abstract ideas: "she had learnt to comprehend thoroughly the theory and the practice of a community founded on the principles of general equality and universal benevolence" (*Refugee* 1: 215). Frances Trollope (and the most sensitive and intelligent of her heroines) would pay less attention to what people said and watch, even more closely than before, what they did and how they lived in determining the quality of life they had established.

A traditional woman in many ways, Frances Trollope was not, as she has been accused of being, a simple defender of the status quo, eager to please the aristocracy and make a fortune and name for herself. Even when opposing the English Reform Act of 1832 by writing *Domestic Manners of the Americans*, Frances Trollope expressed her concern about elevating the quality of life for a majority of the people. The American democratic ideals, most assuredly, she felt, had failed to accomplish this end. The quality of the lives of the majority of people she had seen in America was sorry, indeed. The American system seemed to her not only to encourage the greed, crudity and violence of a few (rather than equality for all), but actually to elevate those who succeeded in bullying others, placing them in positions of prominence and authority. Jonathan Jefferson Whitlaw, the villain of her anti-slavery novel by the same name, had learned from his riverman father that "all men...whose lives are spent in turning everything to profit,...[must] judge quickly and promptly" if they are to succeed on their own (1: 104). Whitlaw, Jr., an able son, had put these frontier virtues to good use in Jacksonian America, seizing opportunity after opportunity to further himself at the expense of others, until he became the all-powerful slave overseer of a vast plantation in Louisiana. When Whitlaw explains his ethic to the Englishman Mr. Croft, advising the latter that he is "sure to be cheated in selling his American property" by businessmen looking out for their own best interests, Mr. Croft is astounded by the "every man for himself," "live by your wits," American philosophy: "Indeed, sir! [he exclaims to Whitlaw]—that's giving no good character to your men of business" (2: 281). Profit and power seem to Trollope to outweigh all considerations of human decency, character, and cooperation in America; her observations of America in the 1820s-1830s suggested that there wealth was admired—and decency, generally discredited and despised.

Thus it does not surprise Frances Trollope to find "less alms-giving in America than in any other Christian country on the face of the globe. It is not in the temper of the people either to give or to receive" (*Domestic* 99). Cincinnati minister Timothy Flint, critical of his former friend Frances Trollope and her portrait of his city in his review of *Domestic Manners of the Americans*, nevertheless comments on "her frequent kindness to the poor of Cincinnati," despite her own pennilessness while in residence there (*Domestic* xxii). Warm, compassionate and generous by nature, Frances Trollope became outraged when confronted by the "horrible atrocity" of slavery, as well as by the bleak prospects of the white underclass in a country where "the sufferings of the destitute...are not liberally relieved by individual charity" (*Domestic* 98-99).

For Frances Trollope, as a writer and a woman, life's goal was not to amass profit at any cost; it was, instead, to unite virtue and economic well-being for as many people as possible. She opposed slavery as morally unjustifiable— punishing those in her fiction who had profited from the slave trade and from slave labor (such as Jonathan Jefferson Whitlaw, Colonel Dart, Colonel Beauchamp, and Judge Johnson) and allowing the aged slave woman Juno to continue her life undisturbed and unpunished after plotting and executing the murder of the evil overseer Whitlaw at the end of *Jonathan Jefferson Whitlaw*. By permitting the latter, Frances Trollope challenged Victorian morality, as she did, as well, in the conclusion of her novel *The Life and Adventures of Michael Armstrong: The Factory Boy*. After rescuing child laborers Michael and Edward Armstrong from the cruelties of the factory system, Trollope's heroine, Mary Brotherton, not only provides for their education and their economic well-being but marries the working-class Edward, as well. Frances Trollope insists in her fiction that gentlemanly and gentlewomanly behavior are matters of moral character, not class distinction. Thus, Jonathan Jefferson Whitlaw's impoverished, uneducated Aunt Clio, "estimable and even admirable in no common degree," while related to an unscrupulous, unprincipled nephew, must be rewarded for her compassion and generosity in the later novel, *The Barnabys in America* (*Whitlaw* 1: 96). So, too, Frances Trollope brings about the "long-waited-for happiness" (3: 288) of Clara Holmwood, heroine of *Fashionable Life; or, Paris and London*, a wealthy woman rejected by Henry Hamilton that "it [might] never be said that the penniless son of the Earl of Springwood sold himself to a corn-factor's daughter for hard cash!" (1: 123). Henry's honor clearly comes before his feelings or those of the woman he loves. Later, the author admits to her "readers, if I am lucky enough to have any," that she has created "a vision. A mere blunder and delusion" in the intricacies of her plot— taking Clara's money away through a misunderstanding, then giving it back to her on the instant the older, but still passionate, Henry Hamilton has proposed and obligated himself to the stately, if nouveau riche, heroine of her last novel (3: 288).

Through such endings, Frances Trollope joined other English novelists of her period in "construct[ing] plots by which love and property could be celebrated simultaneously or even synonymously" (Welsh, *The City of Dickens* 67).Yet it must be remembered that her happy, and fortuitously, prosperous, couples are not always of the same class. Trollope joins the radical ranks of

"middle-class idealogues [who] had attacked the cynical property marriages of
the upper classes and posed in their place 'unions of the affections,' freely-
contracted 'companionate marriages' held together by heart-strings rather than
purse-strings" (Taylor 33). For Frances Trollope, as for Clara Holmwood, so
much concern for blood lines, to the exclusion of minds and hearts, merely
perplexes:

"Perhaps," thought Clara, "the mysterious problem explanatory of the flow of
aristocratic blood, may be in some degree analogous to the doctrines of electricity, only
somewhat more difficult of comprehension." (*Fashionable Life* 3: 254)

Once more, however, we see Frances Trollope's romanticism tempered by
no-nonsense realism. For Frances Trollope does not trust her heroines to love
and to lifelong dependence on a husband. In the words of Uncle Walter to his
beloved niece Kate Harrington:

"But, alas! my love, the long and sad experience, learned by the study of mankind,
teaches us but too plainly that it is not safe to trust to such pure and beautiful enthusiasm.
Or why should we see so many lamentable instances of miserable marriages?" (*Uncle
Walter* 3: 13-14)

Thus, Frances Trollope counsels her heroines to take radical stances towards
their financial affairs in marriage. Unlike Frances Wright, Frances Trollope
herself had kept her own property upon her marriage (only to lose it in America
when she gambled on the success of her Cincinnati Bazaar). With warnings to
her readers about ill-tempered husbands (*One Fault*, 1840) and the prevalence
of the unhappily married (*The Young Countess: or, Love and Jealousy*, 1848),
Frances Trollope advises her heroines to protect themselves as much as
possible. In *Mrs. Mathews* (1851) Mary arranges a separate allowance for
herself upon marriage, as well as her own space in the house and the right to
dispose of her property as she chooses. In *The Widow Married* (1840), the wily
Mr. O'Donagough is portrayed as having met his match in his new bride, Mrs.
Allen (the Widow Barnaby):

...nay, his notions of a well-regulated family economy, might have led him to prefer
taking his lady's income under his own immediate and separate control; but here, after a
somewhat spirited threat on occasion of the first two quarterly payments, he gave in;
Mrs. Allen not being a woman to give way easily, where she felt herself to be right. (36-
37)

Trollope's female characters need ready wits to protect themselves from the
exploitation of the unscrupulous men in their lives and from the cruelties of the

world they live in.

Frances Trollope, then, endows her heroines with a physical, moral and intellectual strength similar to that she had discovered in herself on her American journey and used from that time forward, into the last decade of her life, to meet the world head-on. Insistent on the need for virtue and justice in human affairs, Frances Trollope was also insistent on looking at human society realistically in her fiction of social protest and reform. Unlike Lady Augusta in *Uncle Walter*, she did not believe that "Utopian fancies will not do in civilized life" (2: 24). On the contrary, a "civilized life" ought to be the very fulfillment of those utopian dreams, in Trollope's view. Manners should not exist without kindness, wealth without generosity, culture without wisdom. For this reason, she satirized the hypocrisy, greed, ignorance, and vanity which passed for civilized behavior in the Old World—as well as their cruder variants in the New. It was her very belief in the possibility of a more refined and humane world that caused her to criticize cleverly what she saw taking place around her.

While she found everywhere, in societies she visited throughout the Western world, much to expose, she did not despair. For Frances Trollope's basic nature was cheerful. Through all her economic trials and personal sorrows, she found in daily living much to enjoy, please, and delight her. Never ceasing in her search for a better society, she came, at last, to Florence, Italy, where her restless spirit (sustained always by "the active principle of hope alive within her") (*Refugee* 1: 215) found a final contentment.

Beset by many of the same difficulties as Frances Wright—the loss of a parent (Frances Wright had lost both) at an early age; a difficult marriage; a complex relationship with a child (Anthony for Frances Trollope, Sylva for Frances Wright) who would later come to devalue her; as well as widespread criticism and stereotyping of her character and her writing—Frances Trollope's personal response remained the antithesis of Frances Wright's. Whether present at birth or nurtured into being by a more tranquil childhood (if one less materially advantaged than that experienced by the uprooted orphan Frances Wright—Frances Trollope having enjoyed familiar, pastoral surroundings near her father's vicarage into her twenties when her father remarried), Frances Trollope's nature remained playful, good-humored and composed until her death. A witty realist, always at home in the company of others (even when "pulping" them for her fiction), Frances Trollope presents us, seemingly, with the reverse image of the lonely, idealistic Frances Wright.

Part
❖3❖
Common Causes

Common Causes

So distinct were the personalities of Frances Trollope and Frances Wright that even their most recent biographers have found it difficult not to take sides. Helen Heineman, in *Frances Trollope: The Triumphant Feminine*, defends Frances Trollope's departure from Nashoba by stating:

If Mrs. Trollope had been a foolish enthusiast flinching at the first sight of unpleasant reality, how much more reprehensible was Miss Wright, who had tired of the day-to-day living out of her high ideals and had abandoned ship, as described by her adoring sister in a passage of confession and rationalization. "She thought it would be a poor appropriation of her talents to sit down and devote herself to the emancipation of a few slaves, besides its being an employment for which she was altogether and in every respect incompetent." (Camilla Wright [Whitby], "To Harriet Garnett" in *The Triumphant* 60).

In other words, if Frances Trollope could be accused of being a foolish woman, Frances Wright could be accused of being a heartless one. On the other hand, Frances Wright's biographer Celia Eckhardt portrays Frances Trollope as seemingly a flighty, shallow woman next to the ministerial reformer whom she has studied so closely: "At the same time Fanny's temptation to woo Mrs. Trollope to America must have been nearly irresistable. For all her occasional foolishness, Frances Trollope was a delightful woman" (*Fanny Wright* 154). A flighty, foolish Frances Trollope, an egotistical, reckless Frances Wright—their stereotypes survive, even in the most important scholarship to date on these two women. It seems difficult, despite the distance of more than a century, for scholars and critics to find compatability with both Frances Trollope and Frances Wright, at the same time.

Truly, they were different, as we have seen, clashing both in their distinctive personalities and in their divergent lifestyles. Yet these two women were to argue for many of the same causes in their works and to reach remarkably similar conclusions about nineteenth century American and British societies—and similar conclusions, as well, concerning necessary courses of action for humanity's future. Both women were to call for social reform, both stressed the need for a more humane civilization, and both believed that female leadership would be necessary for the advancement of culture. In the particulars of their criticisms, reforms and ideals, as well, as we shall see, they were most often in agreement. For two women whose friendship was so brief, whose personalities were so opposite, whose lives developed so differently, and whose paths were never again to cross after 1830, the ideas they espoused and the causes they fought for were to remain remarkably similar until their deaths in the mid-nineteenth century.

Chapter Five
Frances Wright's Civilizers

As soon as Frances Wright began to lecture in America, she began to urge social reform. America had not lived up to her high ideals—nor to its own promise. By 1830, less than ten years after the publication of her adulatory *A View of Society and Manners in America*, Frances Wright was asking her American audiences:

...who that looks to your jails, to your penitentiaries, to your houses of refuge, to your hospitals, to your asylums, to your hovels of wretchedness, to your haunts of intemperance, to your victims lost in vice and hardened in profligacy, to childhood without protection, to youth without guidance, to the widow without sustenance, to the female destitute and female outcast, sentenced to shame and sold to degradation—who that looks to these shall say, that inquiry hath not a world to explore, and improvement yet a world to reform! ("Free Inquiry" 36)

Everywhere around her in America, Frances Wright saw poverty, inhumanity, degradation and disease either ignored entirely, dealt with inadequately, or institutionalized through systems such as slavery in the South and wage slavery in the North. Even before Frances Trollope wrote *Domestic Manners of the Americans*, commenting upon the immense distance between American rhetoric and American practice, Frances Wright would tell her Philadelphia listeners in 1829, "Go! mark all the wrongs and the wretchedness with which the eye and the ear and the heart are familiar, and then echo in triumph and celebrate in jubilee the insulting declaration—*all men are free and equal!*" ("Of Existing Evils" 107). Frances Wright had had a dream of America—and she spoke and wrote passionately to move others to share her vision.

Justifying or ignoring its own violence and injustice, the American system of government came to seem to Frances Wright as unfortunate as the European systems she had scorned:

A majority! Of what! The experienced? The intelligent? The virtuous? The industrious? No: a majority as of brute force counted by numbers, and of the male sex. A worse rule, at the present point of time, could scarcely be devised or followed; unless indeed it should be that which submits, as in Europe, the control of all things and all interests to a *minority* of landed and moneyed monopolists—upheld by the brute force of armies, coercive law, and all the machinery and corrupting influence of government. ("Letter V" 27)

Male government by the violent, greedy few—or by the violent, greedy many—offered humanity, in Frances Wright's view, very little choice. By 1848, in her last work, *England, The Civilizer*, Frances Wright would say of America that, "its virtue is gone and its vice becomes apparent. Its critics [Frances Trollope, of course, significant among them] may hold it as cheap as they please; and they will scarcely hold it cheaper than I do" (*England, The Civilizer* 18). Yet she still harbored hope that America would change its course, calling on her adopted homeland one more time: "Oh, last and fairest born among the nations; but now so deeply tainted with the worst pollutions of the age! Pause, pause in time! Throw down the sword, and seize the wand of science! Hold forth to Mexico the hand of generous aid!" (*England, The Civilizer* 412). Frances Wright's cries were to be of little avail against the doctrine of manifest destiny and the development of American imperialism in the nineteenth century; nevertheless, she maintained her idealism, calling for cooperative policies both at home and abroad.

The true advancement of American society, and of civilization as a whole, Frances Wright believed, would result only from the linking together of the head and the heart, the rational and the emotional, the scientific and the generous, the male and the female in human affairs. America's achievements thus far had never reflected such a life-giving, life-sustaining, union of forces—and, in truth, were not, in Frances Wright's eyes, "achievements" at all:

Civilization is not made up—as some suppose—of wealth and want, luxury and misery, excess and starvation. Nor yet of railroads, steam power, electric telegraphs, fine houses, household furniture, large cities, gaols, judges, gibbets, churches, law, physic, trade, traders, trinkets, and trumpery, tax gatherers and taxation. Oh! civilization, true civilization, is made up of all that is beautiful and all that is glorious. Beaming faces, joyous hearts, intelligent minds, polished manners, affection, confidence, well developed, well directed energies, industry, skill, art, taste, genius, and—the guide, the stay, the light, the soul of all—science! (*England, The Civilizer* 383-84)

For Frances Wright, the general well-being, the general industry, the general intelligence, and the general culture of a people must be the measure of its civilization. America's technological advances in and of themselves, the extreme profits of its few, and the proliferation of its material goods could neither counter-balance nor excuse the starvation, misery, want, and poverty still as much in evidence in the New World as in the Old. For "true civilization" to exist world-wide, a "fair exchange of positive surplus, value for value, must hold the world in confraternity of feeling, and solidarity of interests" (*England, The Civilizer* 425). Capitalism and industrialism had not brought about the "true civilization" Frances Wright envisioned—one where wealth was shared, at home and abroad, and the well-being of all was adjoined to (in fact, guaranteed by) the well-being of the individual. The proof of "true civilization" would be an energetic, purposeful, well-informed, well-mannered and virtuous citizenry. Until the "majority" in American society were educated enough to make thoughtful choices, as well as both comfortable and secure enough themselves to be caring about their fellow citizens, rule by the "majority" seemed to be doomed to failure.

What could be done and who could accomplish the difficult—if not impossible—task of ushering "in a right spirit a new era"? (*England, The Civilizer* 468). As Frances Wright concluded in *England, The Civilizer,*

> Society has been so long driven by the selfish principle singly, that it may be hard for her to receive inspiration from the generous…the outstanding generation has grown up, and lived, in the service of *self* only; and felt nothing for, and known nothing of, the collective species…. Woman must give the tone in this; and place herself everywhere on the side of humanity, union, order, right reason, and right feeling. (468)

Frances Wright believed that the generous instinct which had been cultivated in the female held the key to the advance of civilization. In her wide-ranging review of human history and society in *England, The Civilizer*, Frances Wright located the evil endangering the future of humanity (evident in the modern industrial and capitalist continuation of a competitive, greedy, and violent past), in the on-going imbalance between the sexes:

> But now the master error in the whole male conception of things is readily distinguished. It sees no motive power but brute force direct; force indirect, which is corruption or fraud; or a rivalry of forces, of corruptions, or of frauds. It sets nations and society by the ears, and—in its theory at least—all nature too…the effective power in the moral world must be the result of the two human instincts acting conjointly and in unison. This can only be when the two persons in human kind—man and woman—shall exert equal influence in a state of equal independence. The result of this will be justice. (22)

War, corruption, rivalry, competition—all had resulted from the human selfishness perpetuated by male dominance over the female; the life-giving, nurturing functions carried out by women in society had, thereby, been rendered unimportant and ineffective.

Frances Wright believed that all human action could be traced to two sources: "love of self and love in the female. Both, in united action, are indispensable to collective existence. In isolated action, destructive" (*England,*

The Civilizer 21). The male instinct, the selfish principle, had dominated throughout history: "man...feels, calculates, aspires, dares, grasps, conquers, constructs, destroys, for self alone, and keeps all things in a state of standing warfare, litigation, and confusion" (*England, The Civilizer* 13). Only a new exertion of the female, or generous, principle, she felt, could restore the balance and redirect the course of history:

In human kind, the female instinct assumes a character commensurate with the wider range of the human faculties, and originates, sustains, and promotes the whole scheme of progressive civilization. Through and by woman alone, the male barbarism is tamed, and the fierce savage drawn to acknowledge sympathy with his fellow. But, moreover, through and by woman alone, is society at any time held together, or progress made toward the ultimate confraternity of the species. (*England, The Civilizer* 11)

The historic powerlessness of women, in Wright's eyes, had allowed the male force, unchecked, to grow into barbarism and savagery—to bring nation against nation, enterprise against enterprise, male against female. If the two human instincts (cultivated separately in the two sexes) could come together in a state of equality, independence and harmony, the result would be, at last, "true civilization."

Even in Frances Wright's earliest writings, we can find her bewilderment at the existing relationship between the sexes. In *A Few Days in Athens*, she describes the house of Pythagoras, "with the men all peace, method, virtue, learning and absurdity; with the women all silence, order, ignorance, modesty, and stupidity" (145). The separation of human qualities by sex to further "male" learning and method, on the one hand, "female" modesty and ignorance, on the other, had led only, she suggests, to the ungrounded, specious "absurdity" of men, the untutored, ahistorical "stupidity" of women. Frances Wright was well aware of the "vulgar persuasion, that the ignorance of women, by favouring their subordination, ensures their utility" ("Free Inquiry" 32). In denying women an education, the vote, a legal right to their children, their earnings, their property, or the right to make binding contracts (other than the marriage contract), the "new" American civilization was continuing to follow centuries-old patterns of restricting the lives of women (while "freeing" the most privileged men towards the dizzying heights of ambitious, unrealistic absurdity), ensuring dull and docile female laborers, obtuse and selfish male leaders, and an entire female population denied influence upon the public practices of society as a whole.

Yet, as Frances Wright pointed out in speech after speech on her journeys throughout America, as the daily care-givers of the family and the nurturers of the nation's children, American women, in reality, had enormous power—power to do ultimate damage to society and to America's future. She warned,

"Think it no longer indifferent whether those who are to form the opinions, sway the habits, decide the destinies of the species—and that not through their children only, but through their lovers and husbands—are enlightened friends or capricious servants, reasoning beings or blind followers of superstition" ("Free Inquiry" 32). The situation of women, in fact, Frances Wright believed, could only reflect the state of human civilization as a whole:

Let women stand where they may in the scale of improvement, their position decides that of the race. Are they cultivated?—so is society polished and enlightened. Are they ignorant?—so is it gross and insipid. Are they wise?—so is the human condition prosperous. Are they foolish?—so is it unstable and unpromising. Are they free?—so is the human character elevated. Are they enslaved?—so is the whole race degraded...every departure from principle, how speciously soever it may appear to administer to our selfish interests, invariably saps their very foundation! ("Free Inquiry" 24)

The future of America must inevitably continue the misery and injustice of the human past, she warns in one of her earliest lectures, if husbands never come to know "the delight which intercourse with the other sex can give,...the sympathy of mind with mind, and heart with heart," or fathers always say to their daughters, "They can never *be any thing*; in fact, they *are nothing*. We had best give them up to their mothers, who may take them to Sunday's preaching: and with the aid of a little music, a little dancing, and a few fine gowns, [can] fit them for the market of marriage" ("Free Inquiry" 31-32; 30).

As long as the two sexes continue unequal, Frances Wright said, "human improvement must advance but feebly. It is in vain that we would circumscribe the power of one half of our race, and that half by far the most important and influential. If they exert it not for good, they will for evil; if they advance not knowledge, they will perpetuate ignorance" ("Free Inquiry" 24). Following the philosophy of Mary Wollstonecraft (whom she admired), of the long-standing tradition of English women writers who had voiced their concerns about society's neglect of, and injustices towards, women (a tradition Dale Spender outlines in *Mothers of the Novel*), and the Owenite commitment to the equality of women traced by Barbara Taylor in *Eve and the New Jerusalem*, Frances Wright became America's most prominent (and most unpopular) critic of female subjugation and its most outspoken advocate for the education of women in the early nineteenth century.

Obliterating female ignorance would be the first step in the advancement of society. That accomplished, women for so long the "conservators of the species," would command new respect and offer a newly enlightened, more "generous," guidance towards society's healing ("Letter III" 16). Balance would be restored between the sexes, "until power is annihilated on one side, fear and obedience on the other, and both restored to their birthright—equality" ("Free Inquiry" 32). Such an equality between the sexes would, Frances Wright believed, lead to equality between the races, between social classes, and between warring nation states. As she told her former countrymen at the site of an English university under construction (several decades before Emily Davies had succeeded in founding Girton College, Cambridge, for women in 1869), "Raise such an edifice for your young women, and ye have enlightened the nation" ("Free Inquiry" 31). As women would rise, they would enlighten the young, instill their spirit of cooperation into the community beyond their firesides, and elevate the quality of civilization as a whole, "O! what would it be if her virtuous instincts were enlightened by knowledge; if her all-quickening— as all-enduring energies, were at once strengthened, steadied, rightly aimed and justly balanced by wisdom and experience!" ("Letter VII" 46).

With knowledge, women—Frances Wright believed—would become the "civilizers" of human kind; without it, they would, in fact, both perpetrate evil and be, themselves, its victims: "Knowledge is power, and in the present warring and wicked state of society, a nation, a people, or a class without knowledge is always trampled on" ("Letter VI" 33). With its women and other large segments of its population still uneducated, America could never succeed in fulfilling its promise of freedom and justice for the many:

Is this such a republic, while we see endowed colleges for the rich, and barely *common schools* for the poor; while but one drop of coloured blood shall stamp a fellow creature for a slave, or, at the least, degrade him below sympathy; and while one half of the whole population [the female half] is left in civil bondage, and, as it were sentenced to mental imbecility? ("Free Inquiry" 25)

At Nashoba Frances Wright had sought to educate male and female, black and white, children together; in the Halls of Science and Schools of Industry, for which she lectured to raise funds throughout the United States, she had hoped to encourage a "national, rational, and equal education" for laboring men and women, and their children, whatever their ages or circumstances ("Free Inquiry" 36). For Frances Wright, a system of free, public education remained "the only safeguard of youth and the only bulwark of a free constitution," as well as "the only possible cure for every vice in our existing practice, error in our opinions, and evil in our condition...." ("Address on the State of the Public Mind" 139).

One of the ideas Walt Whitman would gain from Frances Wright (and later perpetuate in his own works—having heard her lectures in the New York Hall of Science and read her *Free Enquiry* columns as a boy) was the idea that American democracy depended for its very survival on a well-educated citizenry.[1]

Auguste Hervieu's illustration of Frances Wright's anti-slavery community Nashoba for *Domestic Manners of the Americans* (1832).

The right to vote would be meaningless unless those who voted could also think for themselves and reason through complex social and moral issues. To do such independent thinking, citizens would need access to equal instruction. Yet it would not be sufficient, she warned, simply to have the existing "inefficient schools...multiplied without object and without end" ("Address II" 138-39). Citizens must not merely be educated, but educated in such a way as to inspire "a fearless spirit of inquiry" in every heart ("Nature of Knowledge" 19). If education continued to be:

left solely in the hands of hired servants of the public—let them be teachers of religion, professors of colleges, authors of books, or editors of journals or periodical publications, dependent upon their literary labours for their daily bread, so long shall we hear but half the truth; and well if we hear so much. Our teachers, political, scientific, moral, or religious, or writers, grave or gay, are *compelled* to administer to our prejudices and to perpetuate our ignorance. They dare not speak that which, by endangering their popularity, would endanger their fortunes. ("Nature of Knowledge" 16)

Thus, an enlightened citizenry, able to judge freely and capably on its own the value of numerous civic proposals, public persons and moral issues must be schooled in a new system of public education: one dedicated to the promotion of open inquiry into all subjects, without fear of punishment, and one dedicated to ensuring the safety and well-being of daring, unconventional thinkers, teachers, and writers. Until such a system of education should be inaugurated in America, Frances Wright felt that the "many" (with or without the vote) would constitute merely a "flock of sheep" preyed upon by the "flock of wolves" (whether politicians, entrepreneurs, clergy, or lawyers), and, she warned, "the larger the flock of wolves, the worse for the flock of sheep" (*England, The Civilizer* 329).

Education dedicated to "free inquiry," alone, could empower the ignorant and helpless. With the end of the ignorance of women would come, Frances Wright believed, the end of the pernicious influence of one group of wolves, the American evangelicial clergy, over females (witnessed at revivals such as those held near Cincinnati in the late 1820s and commented upon both in Wright's Preface to *Life, Letters, and Lectures* and Trollope's *Domestic Manners of the Americans*): "Let priestcraft devise his nets, multiply his emissaries, pour his wily lesson into female ears" ("Address III" 177); priests as the *"fishers of women"* creating "meshes...to entangle the female of every age" would be confounded, at last, by educated women able to think and speak for themselves ("Nature of Knowledge" 20). Wright believed: "truth shall baffle his [the priest's] wits; and break his sword of flesh with the sword of the mind" ("Address III" 178).

The laboring classes would also gain power through knowledge. In "An

Address To Young Mechanics," Frances Wright decried "the aristocratical distinctions" perpetuated through the existing, unequal system of education, whereby "some [are] raised unwisely to submit, and others unwisely to govern" (200). As long as the wealthy few continued to receive an "erroneous and imperfect education" in the history and methodologies of power and privilege, the laboring classes, Frances Wright warned, would always experience civilization's "progress" in the form of "robbery": "...their canals, railroads, and all the scheme of internal improvement, *is now conducted* to the advantage of speculators and capitalists, real or pretended, and to the ruin of the honest labourers, and farther depression of the wages of industry" ("An Address to Young Mechanics" 200; "Address on the State of the Public Mind" 76). Frances Wright believed that society, in its existing, topsy-turvy state, rewarded "the least useful, nay, frequently the most decidedly mischievous" of occupations: "the soldier who lives by our crimes, the lawyer by our quarrels and our rapacity, and the priest by our credulity or our hypocrisy...." The farmer, the craftsman and the laborer who serve legitimate human needs through honest work, on the other hand, continue to endure in poverty and ignorance (*Explanatory Notes*).

In the hands of the privileged, educated few, knowledge had been used to perpetuate the imbalance of power, Wright suggested, with

art and science...applied, not to relieve the labour of industry, but to depreciate its value—while human beings count but as an appendage to the machinery they keep in motion, and the tender strength and dawning intellect of infancy are crippled by forced labour, improper diet, neglect, ill usage, and bad example, think not that canals and railroads are to advance the nation, nor that steamboats and spinning-jennies are to save the world. ("Address II" 139)

An unequal and basically aristocratic education seemed to Frances Wright to perpetuate civilization's most barbarous evils: the continuation of male dominance, the empowerment of the wealthy few, and the triumph of human greed and selfishness over cooperative action and the survival of the species.

In her criticism of capitalism's exploitation of child and adult labor and her efforts to create a less competitive, more cooperative future, Frances Wright was not alone. Nor was she alone in her defeat. As Barbara Taylor concludes in her discussion of the nineteenth century English Owenite movement,

By the 1860's, capitalism had shown itself to be not only more resilient than any of its early critics could have anticipated, but also capable of internal reconstruction and rehabilitation—processes which the Owenites themselves could not have foreseen and for which their own theories provided no explanation. The hope of simply moving beyond the boundaries of the competitive system into a new mode of cooperative, communal existence faded as it gradually became evident that there was no longer any "outside" left to go to. (Taylor 262)

And with the end of the dream of cooperation between management and labor died another to which Frances Wright had dedicated her entire life: "The utopian dream which foresaw women's liberation as part of a general process of 'social regeneration' had dimmed and died—and with it went the ideological tie between feminism and working-class radicalism" (Taylor 263-64).

Ironically, Frances Wright—who had taken so much criticism for her "masculinity," for having "unsexed" herself through her ambition, her public role, her daring, her very tall, erect, and seemingly powerful person (including from Frances Trollope who commented to Julia Pertz on "that dry, cold, masculine, dictatorial manner that had been growing...since Frances Wright commenced her public lectures") had not only been concerned with issues of human exploitation and female liberation all along; she had dedicated her entire life to the spirit of what she called the "female principle," to "that which looks to the conservation and happiness of the species" (Eckhardt, *Fanny Wright* 210; Wright, "Letter III" 16). As Owenite Anna Wheeler told a London audience in 1829: "grateful posterity will no doubt associate her name with...the name of COOPERATION" (*The British Co-operator* 67). Calling first for cooperation between the sexes, Frances Wright envisioned an end to the world she despised, a world of

brute force quelling the inspiration of mind; noise drowning reason; disputation knowledge; fraud subtracting from weakness what violence may have failed to rob; law usurping the place of justice; selfish interest that of generous friendship; prostitution, contraband or legal [i.e., marriage], that of love; theology of religion; and rapacious government that of benign administration. ("Letter III" 16)

She called on the males of the species to recognize the interdependence of the sexes, which: "Mutually dependent...must ever be giving and receiving, or they must be losing:—receiving or losing in knowledge, in virtue, in enjoyment" ("Free Inquiry" 31). She advised "that happiness to be experienced by *any*, must be shared by *all*; that the real interests of the whole human family are one, even as their nature is itself the same" ("Lecture V" 82). Framing another idea Walt Whitman would learn from her and carry forward after her death in his own writing, she emphasized the obligations of the citizen as "both an individual, and...one of a collective sum. In these two characters, he claims advantages and he owes duties...."[2] Advocating the breakdown of the nation state into smaller, more cooperative units, Frances Wright in *England, The Civilizer* outlined the specific duties and services the individual would owe in a cooperative society, concluding: "receiving all from the public, he owes all to the public" (456). The individual's relationship to such a society, however, would be a reciprocal one, with society, in turn, giving the individual, among other things: "employment at all times"; "all succour in event of sickness"; "support in old age"; and "education [for his or her] children in the public establishments" (455-56). Having come, she said, "past the age of iron" in the progress of human history, "We ought also to be past the age of paper. We ought to be approaching the age of science" (293-94). In such an age, Wright envisioned at the conclusion of *England, The Civilizer*, we would

develop with greater power all the resources of our globe. Elevate ever higher and higher the standard of human excellence, and invigorate the graspings of human ambition after the great, the good, the beautiful, and the true.... Liberty becomes the portion of our race, by *the union of all for the independence of each*. The dove of peace descends upon earth, and love becomes the universal bond of the species, by our recognizing happiness for the unique end of our being, and by uniting as one family to fertilize one common earth; each secure in the aid and protection of all, without care for the day or anxiety for the future. (470)

In all of her ideas, her writing, and her practice throughout her lifetime, Frances Wright exemplified—indeed, became the very embodiment of—the generous and cooperative principle, the "female principle," she had called upon to save the world.

Her life, from its beginning, had been one long search for a truly cooperative society. On her first trip to America in 1818, she thought she had found a new land of possibility. Having called for the end of slavery and admonished the United States for its devaluation of women in *Views of Society and Manners in America*, she, nevertheless, believed Americans were "singularly enlightened in the art of government: they have learned that there is no strength without union, and no union without good fellowship, and no good fellowship without fair dealing" (171). When she later understood that her first impression of a cooperative union of states dedicated to fair play and fair exchange had been an erroneous one, and when her communal experiment of Nashoba itself had failed, she lectured throughout America, calling upon its youth to work for the improvement and reform she had always sought and still dreamed possible:

Youth is accounted hasty, and is so, for it is inexperienced. Yet do I believe it far more capable of self-correction and self-government, at the present time, than maturer age. To the young, then, do I look for most zeal in the cause of reform, and most tenderness of its honour...on the side of honesty, but also on that of good manners, forbearance, and moderation. ("An Address to Young Mechanics" 205)

In demanding a free system of education for all the young, she further declared: "Were it only in our power to enlighten part of the rising generation, and should the interests of the world decide our choice of the portion, it were the females, and not the males we should select" ("Free Inquiry" 31). To the future mothers of the race, those who had been given the role of "nurturers" and "conservers" of the species, and to all youth of every race, would fall the task of reform: "Time is it to check the ambition of an organized clergy, the demoralizing effects of a false system of law, to heal the strife fomented by sectarian religion and legal disputes; to bring down the pride of ideal wealth, and to raise honest industry to honour" ("Lecture VII" 102). While she called for "a change in the *very soul* of society—in its thoughts, in its feelings, in its habits, in its motives, in its social economy, in its moral character" ("Address Containing A Review of the Times" 196), she insisted that this change must be accomplished peacefully by a "gradual, but radical reform...*through* ...*legislatures*" ("Address III" 178).

Frances Wright had never given up the dream of a cooperative, just society, and a responsible, caring citizenry, which had been hers since youth. Although she had been forced, finally, to move from the public sphere of lecturing to the private sphere of writing, she worked constantly, until her death, in the cause of a higher form of civilization. Human decency was possible, she insisted; good manners, a sense of justice, compassion for the aged, the ill, the infant, all were facets of the human character that could be, and must be, brought forth for the survival of the species. When critics attacked her from every side, she pointed out their often blatant motives of self-interest:

Is any improvement suggested in our social arrangements, calculated to equalize prosperity, labour, instruction, and enjoyment; to destroy crime by removing provocation; vice, by removing ignorance; and to build up virtue in the human breast by exchanging the spirit of self-abasement for that of self-respect—who are the foremost to treat the suggestions as visionary, the reforms as impossible? Even they who live by the fears and the vices of their fellow creatures... ("Nature of Knowledge" 18)

Frances Wright did not doubt the nobility, the resiliency, and the regenerative powers of the human spirit when encouraged towards improvement. How could she, a woman who had, herself, accomplished so much and worked so hard, one individual dedicated to the cause of reform? To her alone, as Paul Baker reveals in his litany of Frances Wright's achievements through her experiments, lectures and writings, can be credited all the following:

...her pioneering work with the Negro, attempting to solve the slavery problem through gradual emancipation;...her experiment in communitarianism, in establishing a pilot project for general social reform;...her continued advocacy of unversal, free, practical education for children of both sexes;...her efforts to help the American workingman better his condition;...her work in women's rights, including her ideas on legal equality for women, protection of their property rights, more liberal marriage laws, and birth control;...the example of a "liberated woman" that she herself set;...[and] her attacks on imprisonment for debt and capital punishment.... (Introduction, *Views on Society and Manners* xxii)

For proof of the elevated spirit of which she believed humanity capable, we need look no further than Frances Wright herself.

Chapter Six
Frances Trollope's Heroines

Although her satirist's voice was experienced in pointing out human selfishness, weakness and vanity, Frances Trollope also wrote in the hope of effecting eventual change. As with her resilient heroine Mrs. Barnaby, who suffered comeuppance after comeuppance, Frances Trollope met life "with renewed hope and renewed ambition, and felt as fresh in spirit, and as ready to set off again in pursuit of new plots, and new projects, as if she had never met with a disappointment in her life" (*The Widow Married* 1: 44). In the face both of her many critics and the continuing follies of her fellow creatures, Mrs. Trollope persisted in her calls for social reform. In the words of the Reverend Mr. Bell in *Michael Armstrong*, "Some individual voices have been most gloriously raised [in the cause of labor reform]...and if they will be steadfast and enduring, they must and will prevail—for human nature, with all its vices, is not framed to look coldly on such horrors, and permit them."[1] For Trollope, human nature is flawed—but redeemable.

Certainly, "civilized man" (in the form of a Jonathan Jefferson Whitlaw, for instance) could be a dismaying sight, one that "terrified...even more than the painted and scarred features of the Indians" who comfort and protect Lucy Bligh in *Jonathan Jefferson Whitlaw* (3: 132). Mrs. Trollope had been well aware, from the outset of her writing career at 53 until its conclusion at 77, that much of what passed for civilized behavior in the Western World she had traveled so extensively was nothing more than fashionable whim, full-blown insanity, or blatant self-interest. She realized, further, that the self-interests and concerns of the upper classes prevailed and that social class often decided the "right" or the "wrong" of an issue. When the Reverend Henry Harrington ranted against "irreligious apple-women and rebellious news-vendors" who dared to break the sabbath in *Uncle Walter*, the narrator pointed to the parks where throngs of "lordly sabbath-breakers [made it]...abundantly clear to the great unwashed that their rulers were only humbugging them when they enacted Sabbath Observance Bills, and harangued against the wickedness of all popular Sunday recreations" (1: 3; 2). Why should the Reverend Harrington be so outraged about the Sunday vendors and the throngs of poor fleeing "their close, crowded homes, and dim alleys, to solace their toilsome lives" (1: 3), yet utter not a syllable about fashionable carriages or leisurely gentlemen to be found wandering those same public parks? In the same novel, in a similar vein, Uncle Walter will expose the double standard of a society " 'which thinks no language strong enough to upbraid the degraded creature who sells herself, when the price paid is to save her from starvation,...[then] smile[s] upon and approve[s] the very same act, when not the necessaries, but the luxuries of life are the legalized payment' " (1: 309).

Speaking out against these social class inequities, exposing the hypocrisy of the virtuous and complacent rich, Frances Trollope called for new laws to protect the poor, the invisible and the voiceless in nineteenth century society. At the same time she was insistent that she would not contribute to the chaos of the modern world in the name of progress. Refusing to write the promised sequel to *Michael Armstrong* after "those in whose behalf she hoped to move the sympathy of their country [were] found busy in scenes of outrage and lawless violence," Frances Trollope insisted as fully as she had in *Domestic Manners of the Americans* on orderly, thoughtful, decorous process as the only means to true civilization (*Michael Armstrong* iv). As with Mary Brotherton in *Michael Armstrong*—and Trollope's former friend Frances Wright, as well—Frances Trollope held that reform must be brought about as the abolition of the slave trade had been achieved in Britain: " 'It was brought about, nurse Tremlett, by the voices of the people of England, which were for years raised quietly, and with no break of law or order, but with patient and unstinting perserverence against this great sin, till the lengthened cry could be no longer resisted, and the law they perserveringly asked for, was granted to them' " (*Michael Armstrong* 221). If, indeed, the elevation of humanity was to be achieved, it must be accomplished, Frances Trollope believed, through the honorable and decent actions of indignant men and women.

Frances Trollope's novels of social reform were intended to move the people of America and England about issues of injustice. In work after work, Frances Trollope revealed social problems and stirred her complacent readers to demand social change, through: *The Life and Adventures of Jonathan Jefferson Whitlaw: or Scenes on the Mississippi* (1836) with its exposé of American slavery; *The Vicar of Wrexhill* (1837) with its portrayal of the hypocrisy of British evangelical clergy; *The Life and Adventures of Michael Armstrong, the Factory Boy* (1839) with its revelations about the apprentice system and the abuses of child labor in England; *Jessie Phillips: a Tale of the New Poor Law* (1843) with its depiction of the harsh conditions of the poor houses and the plight of "fallen" women (who no longer could bring charges against the fathers of their illegitimate children) under the New Poor Law of 1834; and her many works challenging traditional marriage arrangements for their injustices toward women, from *One Fault: a Novel* (1840), to *Mrs. Mathews, or Family Mysteries* (1851) and *Fashionable Life: or Paris and London* (1856). While arguing for gradual, legal processes of reform, Frances Trollope wrote courageously with the satirist's "moral imperative" (Welsh 10), insistently demanding that surfaces be examined, injustices be revealed, and society's "hidden moral disorder"

(Welsh 15) be addressed. It was Frances Trollope who—before Dickens—not only exhibited an intense satiric concern with society's problems but also suggested, as would Dickens, that the cure for society's ills "reside[d] in some relation with the female sex" (Welsh 150). In an age where the public world was dominated by the male, and the spiritual world, through Puritanism, had taken on "the most masculine form that Christianity has yet assumed" (Lecky 368),[2] Frances Trollope was to posit possible relief and redemption through the feminization of society. Her fiction's structural paradigm reveals a belief that the future of civilization rests on the shoulders of bright, *young* women, her worldly heroines. Over and over she repeats a pattern which insists on the saving power and moral influence of the youthful heroine in a corrupt world. In doing so, Frances Trollope displayed an acute interest in the future of humanity, significant insight into the causes and effects of human injustice, and psychological understanding foreshadowing a number of contemporary theorists.

While parents, according to society, were to be honored and respected, Frances Trollope's elders often prove perilous guides and poor examples for her young heroines to follow. Frances Trollope's mothers, like those of Jane Austen, often fail to nurture and prepare their daughters wisely for adulthood.[3] Lady Dowling in *The Life and Adventures of Michael Armstrong, The Factory Boy* (1840), although "a faithful and exceedingly fond wife [who] doted upon all her children" (63), cannot provide her daughter Martha with moral guidance and thoughtful advice concerning Martha's obligation to the factory children in Lord Dowling's factory. She is, it seems, far too busy overseeing workers of her own:

There was hardly an individual within ten miles who was not aware that Lady Dowling kept two carriages, six horses, one coachman, one postilion, five gardeners, two grooms, three footmen, one butler, and a page—not to mention two nurses, four nursery maids, and more ladies'-maids, housemaids, cookmaids, kitchen-maids, laundry-maids, still-room maids, dairy-maids, and the like than any other lady in the county. (3)

Lady Augusta Harrington, in *Uncle Walter: a Novel* (1852), is another "good" mother who devotes most of her time to fulfilling her "duty to her daughter" (1: 43). As concerned with appearances as *Michael Armstrong's* Lady Dowling, Lady Augusta shows Kate off in carriage-rides in the park and gives her a "coming-out" party which, the narrator explains,

owed its origins in no respect and in no degree to any feelings of kindness, hospitality or friendship whatever, but wholly and solely for vanity and ostentation, stimulated, however, by the hope that every penny expended would be repaid by a *quid pro quo* of some sort or other. (1: 168)

Lady Augusta, it seems, is incapable of considering her daughter Kate's welfare in any other than in economic terms. Frances Trollope quickly reveals that Kate has already surpassed her mother in the development of both mind and spirit: "As for Lady Augusta, she exercised a most conscientious, scrupulous, and vigilant control over her daughter's wardrobe and toilette, but it never occurred to her to open a volume in Kate's room, any more than in her own" (1: 37). The narrator admits that,

[it] must be confessed that Lady Augusta added that deep-seated vulgarity of mind which is the inevitable product of a life spent in looking up to that on which we ought to look down, reverencing that which deserves no reverence, mistaking small things, and small people, for great things, and great people, and in contracting all thoughts and all feelings within the narrow circle of a paltry, yet arbitrary conventionalism. (1: 70)

While other older women outside the family could provide role models for Trollope's young heroines, they seldom do. Lady de Paddington in *Uncle Walter* aids Lady Augusta in the latter's plan to thrust the naive, vacuous, but wealthy, Lord Goldstable upon a poor, unsuspecting Kate. Mrs. Gabbley in *Michael Armstrong* is the neighborhood gossip described by Lady Augusta as "crawl[ing] in [your] donkey-cart, like a snail in [your] shell, leaving your slime as you go" (354). Mrs. Gabbley is too busy meddling in others' affairs, exploiting their human misery, to offer kind-hearted advice: to Martha Dowling during her family's eviction for bankruptcy; to the orphaned, wealthy Mary Brotherton whose friendship Mrs. Gabbley only cultivates with an eye to the latter's own advantage; or to either Martha or Mary as they seek moral guidance concerning their responsibility to the impoverished, mistreated children employed in their fathers' factories. Adult women are capable of admirable behavior—but only when they leave the traditional female pastimes of visiting, gossiping and social climbing behind, as do Clara Holmwood, Clara's Aunt Sarah, Lady Amelia Wharton, and her daughter Annie, who set up their own household together in Paris, for the mutual benefit of all. As the narrator in *Fashionable Life* comments, "If all people set about carrying out their own arrangements, and their own intentions, in as business-like and rational a manner as did the female co-partnership I am describing, there would be much fewer disappointments in life" (1: 242).

The greed, vanity, selfishness and ignorance of Trollope's conventional female "mentors" can, at times, erupt into acts of overt, outrageous cruelty to others. In *The Life and Adventures of Jonathan Jefferson Whitlaw* (1836), young Lucy Bligh watches helplessly as Mrs. Shepherd, "in a perfect ecstasy of rage," beats the slave girl Dido for doing nothing more than giving Lucy a message from the black man Caesar:

The little trembling Dido was immediately brought before this dread tribunal [of Mrs. Shephard and the other seamstresses] and the scene that followed cannot be dwelt upon. The strength of more than one active practiced female arm was exhausted in lacerating the back and limbs of the unfortunate child whose ill-timed good nature had produced such terrible results...poor Lucy, in the agony of her soul at this spectacle, not only attempted to interpose an ineffectual effort to prevent it, but uttered words of such indignant reprobation at the executions, as certainly convinced all present that she was in truth an enemy in that camp where slavery was held to be the sovereign good and sovereign safety. (3: 115-16)

Occasionally, adults in Trollope's fiction do act as examples for her heroines. Elizabeth Hubert's parents in *The Widow Married*, for instance, or Mary Steinmark's family in *Jonathan Jefferson Whitlaw*, guide their daughters carefully to enable them someday to exert an intelligent, humane, and civilizing force upon society. Interestingly enough, it is most often the father's guidance which Trollope stresses, her sensible mothers often remaining shadowy background figures (as is Mrs. Steinmark in *Jonathan Jefferson Whitlaw*) or being deceased (as is Mrs. Gordon in *The Refugee in America*). In the case of the latter work, the young Caroline Gordon's upbringing by her father mirrors that of Eleanor Oglander, her father's youthful flame:

The cultivation of the fine mind of Eleanor had been the study, the occupation, and the happiness of her accomplished father, almost from the hour of her birth: —the decoration of the fine person of Caroline [Armitage, Caroline Gordon's mother] had been the study, the occupation, and the happiness of her accomplished mother. (1: 5-6)

The novel concludes with the widower Mr. Gordon's marriage to his old love Eleanor Oglander (the Lady Darcy), and with his tribute not only to her intelligence, but also to the heroism and "even-mindedness" of his courageous, adventurous, daughter and protegé, Caroline: " 'on this occasion, the male part of the dramatic personae must, one and all, hide their diminished heads before the females' " (3: 298). Yet it is the male part, the father, who has nurtured so carefully the minds and abilities of Eleanor Oglander and Caroline Gordon, alike.

Frances Trollope certainly reflects here her own life experiences—having received from her widowed father encouragement to cultivate her mind in his library and support to pursue her literary and artistic interests freely beyond the customary, domestic, female sphere. If girls are to be shaped and guided by their elders, Frances Trollope suggests in her fiction, it must be effected through a broadened education and an enlarged experience, as traditionally practiced with young men of the period, and actively encouraged by fathers or other male mentors. Here Trollope anticipates contemporary scholars' studies of women of achievement, such as Carolyn Heilbrun's *Reinventing Womanhood*, in suggesting the traditional importance of the father-daughter relationship and of male guidance for women who would move beyond the conventional female role.[4]

Trollope also suggests that even when a strong father figure is not a positive role model for his daughter, he can still have a positive influence upon her life. Her works suggest that when fathers are men of achievement in the world—men of importance and wealth in their communities—their daughters can learn from them the power one individual can come to exert in the world in influencing the course of human affairs for good or for ill. Frances Trollope's heroines gain power through the advantages of the education, prestige and money bestowed upon them by their fathers, but they desire to use that power and privilege as do Frances Wright's "civilizers," achieving good and redressing the wrongs committed by their fathers upon society. Over and over we find this fictional pattern in Trollope's novels. In *The Barnabys in America*, for instance, Annie Beauchamp, whose father Colonel Beauchamp owns "Big-Gang Bank" with its hundreds of slaves, enjoys the advantages of great wealth and opportunity. Nevertheless, she has been made wretched by witnessing her father's inhumane participation in the deplorable system of slavery. Her friend Clio Whitlaw predicts, " 'pretty Annie will free every nigger upon the estate, and then sell every acre of it, and be off to some right-down free country, as soon as it comes into her hands' " (2: 209-10). When the slaves revolt, killing Colonel Beauchamp before Annie has an opportunity to make Miss Whitlaw's prediction come true, Annie Beauchamp rescues her mother, then leaves slave-holding America, her ill-gained wealth, and her false position behind her for good. (Of course, she does so in the company of the doting Frederic Egerton, with every expectation of becoming his wife and having a comfortable future; yet it is implied that her pinciples outweigh all thoughts for her personal security and that those same principles, in fact, are what attracted such a noble suitor in the first place.)

Other Trollope heroines risk financial ruin and disinheritance through their rebellious acts against greedy, unscrupulous, conniving fathers. In *Uncle Walter*, when Kate Harrington refuses to marry Lord Goldstable, her mother Lady Augusta reminds Kate of a daughter's powerlessness to withstand the will of her parents:

"You will marry Lord Goldstable....You are a minor, an infant in the eye of the law, and therefore, most fortunately! you have no power, either to reject or to accept any such proposal [as her suitor Mr. Caldwell's], without the consent of your parents....You are *not* to become the wife of a man, who has got to work for the means of existence. But you *are* to become the wife of a highly descended young nobleman, with an income of eighty thousand a-year." (1: 289; 291)

Kate is fortunate to have the sympathies of both her Uncle Walter and her brother Henry on her side. They discuss the marriage game, in this case, "the great Goldstable stakes," with shared disgust and horror:

"Am I to understand then, Henry, that you too are of opinion that it is the wish of your father and mother to coerce the affection of their daughter, in order to give them an opportunity of selling her?"…

"I can assure you, uncle, that our practice in that respect puts the method of the Constantinople dealers to shame. There the fair ones, we are told, do shrink pitifully from the exhibition made of them, and evidently dislike the *trotting out*. But with the superior methods of our market, the pretty creatures are fully as anxious for the sale, as the seller." (1: 303; 305)

When the well-read, thoughtful Kate proves uncooperative in the business of this market trade, her father proves a formidable opponent, no less greedy than his parishioners, despite being "Doctor of Divinity, Warden of All Saints' College in the University of Oxford, Prefendary of the Cathedral Church of Glastonbury, and Rector of a large and wealthy parish at the west end of the metropolis" (2: 4).

Another vicar's daughter, Henrietta Cartwright, is compelled to break her silence and to confess that her father, respected as he is as the Vicar of Wrexhill (in the 1837 novel by the same name), revered as a moral leader and inspiring teacher in the community, is really manipulative and evil in his actions:

"Watch Mr. Cartwright a little while, Rosalind Torrington, as I have done for the six last years of my hateful life, and you may obtain perhaps some faint ideas of the crooked, complex machinery—the movements and counter-movements, the shiftings and the balancings, by which his zig-zag course is regulated. Human passions are in him for ever struggling with, and combating, what may be called, in their strength, *superhuman* avarice and ambition.

To touch, to influence, to lead, to rule, to tyrannize over the hearts and souls of all he approaches, is the great object of his life. He would willingly do this in the hearts of men—but for the most part he has found them tough; and he now, I think, seems to rest all his hopes of fame, wealth, and station on the power he can obtain over women. (127)

Indeed, Henrietta reveals that her father has not only married Mrs. Mowbray, fathered her child, and forced her to change her will to one excluding her grown children in favor of himself, but has, at the same time, fathered another child— that of the suddenly departed Mrs. Simpson.

In *Charles Chesterfield: or the Adventures of a Youth of Genius* (1841),

Auguste Hervieu's sketch of Mary Brotherton showing compassion for the poor Drake sisters in *Michael Armstrong* (1840).

another Trollope heroine, Clara Meddows, is also compelled to take direct action to counter her father's wickedness. Clara's father, Sir George, is another of Trollope's powerful father figures who reveals a "love of being unprincipled upon principle" (3: 46). At first Clara is described in this way: "Clearly as she saw, and deeply as she deplored the contemptible character of her father, she had never breathed a thought on the subject, save to her own aching heart" (3: 46). Depth of understanding and silent suffering are not enough, however. Frances Trollope demands action from her heroines, even at the expense of their family feeling and loyalty. When Clara learns that Sir George has swindled Charles Chesterfield's legacy of 4,000 pounds, she goes to her agent, Mr. Stephen Barton, and transfers her inheritance to Charles Chesterfield in order to restore the innocent young man's inheritance. In consequence, Clara faces the loss of everything she values in the world,

knowing herself to be utterly destitute; certain of having her race and name disgraced for ever, and for ever, in the eyes of Arthur Dalrymple [her suitor]; and anticipating with no very agreeable feelings the interview which awaited her with her father on the morrow. Still she was satisfied, and felt no shadow of regret for the sacrifice she had made. (3: 137)

Trollope's heroines take strength from their fathers, ironically using that strength, when necessary, against those same fathers over issues of human decency, dignity and justice.

Again, in *The Life and Adventures of Michael Armstrong, the Factory Boy* (1840), obedient, loving daughters slowly awaken to the horrors of the factory system through which their fathers have amassed exceptional wealth. Martha Dowling, described as "the only spark of refinement of which the Dowling family could boast," nevertheless,

adored her hard-hearted, vicious, unprincipled, illiterate, vulgar father, as heartily as if he had been the mode of everything she most admired and approved. Nay, it may be that she loved him better, or, at any rate, more strongly still...like the pitying fondness with which a mother dotes on a deformed child, who sees only that [as] it is less lovable it has more need of love than the rest. (53; 53-54)

Martha prefers not to think about how her factory-owning father has gained his wealth. So, too, with Mary Brotherton whose father, had he been alive, would only have scolded her if she had "indicat[ed] her belief, that she was formed of the same sort of materials as the wretches who toiled for him" (84). As Mary Brotherton talks to the factory workers and learns of their mistreatment and impoverishment, however, she comes to understand the hypocrisy of her abolitionist father whose "own mills daily sent millions of groans to be registered in heaven from joyless young hearts and aching infant limbs" (150). Exploiting child workers in his own community, he yet had subscribed to abolitionist societies abroad and cried "benevolent lamentations over the sable sons of Africa, all uttered comfortably from a safe arm-chair, while digestion was gently going on, and his well-fed person in a state of the most perfect enjoyment" (150-51).

And so Mary Brotherton begins to "employ [her] preposterous wealth in assisting the miserable race from whose labours it has been extracted" (221). Martha Dowling, too, having learned of the plight of laborers from Mary, follows in acts of individual charity to child workers, as well. Yet individual charity, these heroines find, is not enough. They must work to support political reform in the form of the Ten Hour Law, limiting childrens' labor to ten hours a day, rather than the sixteen they often worked—a position not to be adopted as law in England until seven years after *Michael Armstrong*'s publication in 1840. Trollope suggests here another radical idea: that care for the well-being of others must be made societal, not relational—not relegated to the custodial nurturing of individual women. While women must assume leadership roles in bringing about social reform, it is political change that is advocated—not the occasional act of female charity and kindness—in redressing large scale social ills and inequities.

Frances Trollope shows that her heroines have cultivated their minds as well as their hearts in becoming concerned with issues of human injustice. In doing so, they develop sufficient strength in the integrity of their convictions to withstand the force of social conventions, as when the wealthy Mary Brotherton marries the laborer Edward Armstrong, after rescuing him from the factory and educating him with her money. Throughout *Michael Armstrong*, Mary Brotherton reveals an independent spirit, moving herself and others beyond popular belief and practice in the course of the novel's action. Reason has led Mary Brotherton to reject the commonplace philosophy of her period:

"How comes it that ALL the people—the only phrases I have heard upon the subject were very comprehensive—how comes it, Martha Dowling, that ALL the people, young and old, who work in the factories are classed as ignorant and depraved?...if thousands of human beings in a Christian country are stigmatized as wicked, because their destiny has placed them in a peculiar employment, that employment ought to be swept for ever and for ever from the land, though the wealth that flowed from it outweighed the treasures of Mexico." (107-08)

If human injustice (in an exploitive factory system) causes human depravity (ignorance, alcoholism, apathy, corruption), as was so widely believed, then, Mary Brotherton argues, the unjust system must be abandoned, despite the profit it engenders. Questioning such a profitable system of production, as

Trollope does here, was no more popular in nineteenth century England than the abolitionist cause in the American South or Ten Hour Law advocacy in the North in America during the same decades. One British reviewer expressed his outrage over Frances Trollope's brashness (behind her heroine Mary Brotherton's rebellious voice and acts) in this way:

the author of *Michael Armstrong* deserves as richly to have eighteen months in Chester Gaol as any that are there now for using violent language against the "monster cotton mills."...Mill owners cannot refuse the smallest economy that offers in working the mills, on pain of ruin; and without forfeiting a claim to common humanity, they may be brought to look on the suffering of their operatives, as a general looks on the carnage and mutilation of his soldiers. ("Review," Heineman, *Frances Trollope* 75)

The price for defying social convention, for author or heroine, could be very high, indeed.

Frances Trollope's heroines are young—"seventeen was really the age of rational womanhood"—but they are not naive (*Charles Chesterfield* 3: 249). They are not as easily victimized by flattery or deceived by platitudes as their elders can be (Mrs. Simpson and Mrs. Mowbray by the Vicar of Wrexhill, for instance). Trollope's heroines read books; in Kate Harrington's library, we are told, are volumes, "it may be feared, some few which the Doctor [her father] would have been more surprised than pleased to find there, had it ever entered his head to visit his daughter's book-shelves, and to examine their contents" (*Uncle Walter* 1: 37). The Reverend Mr. Harrington believed, "the solid rock of classical learning [to be] the foundation of a truly liberal education"—for men, of course. On the other hand, Kate Harrington, her friend Mr. Caldwell, her Uncle Walter, and the spinster Wigginsville sisters all read and discuss modern literature and contemporary scientific thought as they grapple with the problems of the modern age (*Uncle Walter* 1: 10). It is, as Uncle Walter says, an "age [when the] treatise on universal knowledge is past. We have no admirable Crichtons now, who know everything; but we have specialities who, each in their own way [advance the cause of knowledge]" (*Uncle Walter* 3: 40). It is, as well, an age which exposes the pretensions of teachers such as the traditional James Harrington "who have far more indulgence for ignorance linked with submission, than for information if allied to independence" (*Uncle Walter* 2: 171). Kate Harrington is a modern, independent woman in the cultivation of her mind and in the course of her actions.

Another Trollope heroine and avid reader, Mrs. Barnaby's niece Agnes, finds herself at odds with her guardian over both her reading and her distaste for the female "system of visiting and gossiping" in which Mrs. Barnaby engages (as did her mother before her, leaving her mother "no time...to do more for [her daughters'] advantage than take care that they had enough to eat") (*The Widow*

Barnaby 1: 9). Uneducated and neglected by her own provincial mother, Mrs. Barnaby scolds Agnes for "wasting" her time to no purpose:

"Now, here's a leaf done already, and wait a minute and you'll see a whole bunch of grapes done in spotting. There is some sense in that: but poring over a lot of rubbishy words is an absolute sin, for it is wasting the time that Heaven gives us, and doing no good to our fellow creatures."

"And the grapes! Thought Agnes, but she said nothing." (*The Widow Barnaby* 1: 320)

How similar is this scene to those the upperclass Florence Nightingale reports suffering in the company of her conventional mother and sister during the mid-nineteenth century: "[Florence Nightingale] found that her own 'duties' left her with no time at all to herself and yet what did these inescapable duties amount to? Sorting out the china cupboard, picking and arranging flowers, sewing useless ornamental articles, going on visits and worst of all talking, talking, talking but never *saying* anything" (Forster 99). Frances Trollope's heroines would have agreed with nineteenth century educational reformer Emily Davies that, "Girls could do so little in life because they were educated to do so little. Change their education and their prospects were immediately changed, their horizons automatically widened" (Forster 136). Unlike Emily Davies, however, Frances Trollope allows her heroines a modern, although informal, education rather than the traditional education Davies would insist on inaugurating (at Girton College, Cambridge) in imitation of the male system (Forster 135).

Encouraged by their reading, Frances Trollope's heroines venture out into the world to learn what they can of life by asking questions and by exploring new pathways, at times unpleasant ones in the slum areas of an industrial city (Mary Brotherton) or the crude frontier of a strange, new land (Caroline Gordon). Mr. Gordon in *The Refugee in America* (1832), realizing the fulfillment of his daughter's full potential, "looked at her with evident delight. 'It would have been a pity, dear Caroline, should I have died without finding out what a heroine you are, and this would probably have happened if we had never crossed the Atlantic' " (1: 199). Frances Trollope suggests in her fiction that what we become is a product both of our education and of our experience; as Mr. Bell tells Mary Brotherton in *Michael Armstrong* (before she has had a chance to find this out for herself and put it into effect by educating the laboring Fanny Fletcher or Michael and Edward Armstrong), " 'You are as yet too young a lady for me to expect that you should have very deeply studied the nature of the human mind, or made yourself fully aware how greatly the habits and character of all human beings depend upon education, and the circumstances in which they are placed' " (203). Knowledge from books and knowledge from experience work together to move humanity beyond the narrowness of environmental circumstances and social conformity in Frances Trollope's fiction.

Much less preoccupied with dress, with fashion, with public appearance and social convention than the women who would guide them, Frances Trollope's heroines look for truth in a world of deceit and corruption, attempting to act with intelligence, honesty and fairness towards others. Through education and experience, Trollope insists, women can develop the knowledge of themselves and of the world that has made men too "tough" for deceitful, professional manipulators such as the evangelist Mr. Cartwright in *The Vicar of Wrexhill*. But Trollope's heroines are androgynous figures in whom a feminine feeling for others, human connectedness, love and care remain combined with a sharp, flinty intellect and a strong, tenacious will. For Frances Trollope, "that mixed expression of feeling and intelligence...makes the perfection of woman" (*Refugee* 1: 271). For as with Frances Wright, Frances Trollope portrayed the counterbalancing influence of the female in society as the cure for the maladies of the nineteenth century. Frances Trollope's protagonists are mature, adult women (despite their youth)—unlike Charles Dickens's "most distinctive heroines, Nell, Florence, Agnes, and Dorritt—the little mothers—and a good many others [who] are in one degree or another children" (Welsh 195). Dickens's child mothers, constant, nurturing, selfless angels of the home, offer succor and warmth to battered males who seek shelter there. Trollope's heroines, on the other hand, are shown to be worldly-wise and venturesome; they are the daughters, companions, or adversaries of men who can engage with them idea for idea. Without such self-development, Frances Trollope suggests, her heroines would be virtually useless to themselves or to others. Without knowledge of the human evils and human possibilities at work in the world, Trollope implies, her heroines would become helpless victims or ignorant perpetrators of evil themselves—women who would very much resemble so many of their female elders in her fiction. In her young heroines Frances Trollope celebrates women as achieving adults—not symbols of child-like innocence or home-bound naivete whose only role is to provide themselves and others escape from a troubled world.

Of course, no one Frances Trollope knew resembled this kind of "new" woman better than had her friend Frances Wright, 15 years her junior. Before setting forth to America, Frances Trollope was to tell her friend Julia Garnett Pertz: "Never was there I am persuaded such a being as Fanny Wright—no never—and I am not the only one who thinks so. Some of my friends declare that if worship may be offered, it must be to her—that she is at once all that woman should be—and something more than woman ever was—and I know not what beside" (Heineman, *Restless Angels* 56). If three years later, Frances Trollope would write to Julia Pertz, "'God knows what will become of us all,'" Trollope could never deny Frances Wright's influence on her life (Heineman,

Restless Angels 184). Yet Frances Trollope feared that her young friend's influence, in cooperation with her own adventurous spirit, had brought her to ruin.

Rather than destroying her life, her trip to America with Frances Wright had, in fact, enabled Frances Trollope to find her political voice and enabled her to use her education and her intelligence to significant purpose in the world. Through Wright's example, Frances Trollope had found her own vocation (writing) and many common causes to share with Wright. She would follow Frances Wright in speaking out in opposition to slavery, to child labor, to legal restrictions on married women, and in advocating the ten-hour day for workers and the role of women in effecting a better world.

By the close of their lives, their views had become remarkably similar. Frances Wright had come to agree with Frances Trollope that frontier America was lawless and crude. She came to feel about the Nashoba Trollope had rejected, "In principle we were right, but [in]...practice in the existing operation, we were wrong" ("To Harriet Garnett and Julia Garnett Pertz," Heineman, *Restless Angels* 88). The "conservative" Frances Trollope, on the other hand, had come to rejoice in the changes that had followed the revolution in Italy (where she lived her last years in Florence). She wrote her friend Harriet Garnett that, " 'the rapid improvement of the people is inconceivable' "; Harriet pointed out to her sister Julia Pertz, "She [Frances Trollope] writes with as much ardour on the subject as our warmest liberals do,—and is in reality a good liberal herself. When I congratulated her on the change, she said, 'I should be sorry to live and not be able to improve with the times. My eyes are now thank Heaven open' " (Heineman, *Triumphant Feminine* 251). And, as would Frances Wright, Frances Trollope, too, would choose to live in exile from England. Refusing to travel to Great Britain for the Great Exhibition of 1851, Frances Trollope revealed a reluctance Harriet Garnett understood, a reluctance to return to " 'this dear, aristocratical selfish land' " (Heineman, *Triumphant Feminine* 251). Frances Wright and Frances Trollope both insisted on pointing out in their writing the cruelty and indifference to human suffering underlying the mask of a genteel and gracious civilization in nineteenth century Britain.

Continuing to hope for the future, Frances Trollope followed Frances Wright in working for reform until her death. Frances Trollope's young fictional heroines, as we have seen, offer the promise of change in a selfish world. Her fictional paradigm contradicts the long-established pattern Patricia Spacks explores in *The Female Imagination*:

it is difficult to think of any serious literary work by a woman that celebrates female adolescence....Female aspiration is a joke. Female rebellion may be perfectly justified but there's no good universe next door, no way out, young potential revolutionaries can't find their revolution. So they marry in defeat or go mad in a complicated form of triumph...they express women's anger and self-hatred and the feeling that there's no way out. (200)[5]

Frances Trollope's heroines, on the contrary, have causes they believe in, values they uphold, and the self-respect and self-development necessary to fight for them. They differ from other nineteenth century heroines discussed by Sandra Gilbert and Susan Gubar in *The Madwoman in the Attic*, "who have to fight their internalization of patriarchal strictures for even a faint trace memory of what they might have become" (59). Frances Trollope's heroines offer the world the same hope as Frances Wright's "civilizers"—the hope that educated, enlightened, young women, working alongside men, can help balance masculine intellect and will with feminine concern for the "conservation, care, and happiness of the species" (*England, The Civilizer* 12-13). While Dickens's solution to human selfishness and cruelty, the child-mother nursing the wounds of her returning male combatants, has been the one history has continued to cling to as ideal,[6] it is one that Dickens's contemporaries, Frances Trollope and Frances Wright, rejected both in their own rebellious lives and in their innovative works, as well. Dickens's stance, while disillusioned, reflects the traditionalism Christopher Lasch outlines in *Haven in a Heartless World* (1979):

From the beginning, the glorification of domestic life simultaneously condemned the social order of which the family allegedly served as the foundation. In urging a retreat to private satisfactions, the custodians of domestic virtue implicitly acknowledged capitalism's devastation of all forms of collective life, while at the same time they discouraged attempts to repair the damage by depicting it as the price that had to be paid for material and moral improvement. (169)

Frances Trollope, stereotyped for more than a century as a "conservative," in reality advocated deep-seated social reform. Long after her relationship with her young, spiritual guide, Frances Wright, had faltered and come to an end, Frances Trollope continued to imagine fictional heroines who could confront corrupt male authority figures, set out into the world to redress wrongs, and alter the future of civilization, becoming what Frances Wright once had been for her, "all that women should be—and something more than woman ever was—and I know not what beside" ("To Julia Garnett Pertz" [7 Oct. 1827], Heineman, *Restless Angels* 56).

Part

❖4❖

Literary and Political Influences

Literary and Political Influences

Despite their many common views, Frances Wright and Frances Trollope found themselves dismissed as political extremists of the left and of the right by intelligent contemporaries as well as by popular critics. Robert Browning argued heatedly with Elizabeth Barrett Browning over socializing with Frances Trollope, considering the author of *Domestic Manners of the Americans* too conservative for their company—seemingly unaware that Frances Trollope had written on behalf of the same liberal antislavery and women's rights causes as his own wife (Browning, "To Mrs. Martin," *The Letters of Elizabeth Barrett Browning* 476). Margaret Fuller would attempt, too, to disassociate herself from Frances Wright, leaving her

out of *Woman [in the Nineteenth Century]* by design, probably for reasons of conviction or of discretion. She could afford to be more charitable toward Mary Wollstonecraft because she was dead and George Sand because she was French, but Fanny Wright (now Madame D'Arusmont, but separated from her husband) was alive and living in the United States. Her inflammatory lectures were too recent in the public mind. (Urbanski 63)

Marie Urbanski concludes that Margaret Fuller left Wright's influence on her thought "unacknowledged" rather than be attacked as too radical herself (65). Nevertheless, Wright's influence remains obvious in Fuller's work.

However controversial their views, and however much popular critics and, at times, prominent nineteenth century figures sought to deny their importance, Frances Wright and Frances Trollope had affected the social ideas, political movements, and influential literature of their times in ways that have never been fully appreciated. In part this neglect has been due to the difficulty of tracing an influence that remained unacknowledged or denied in the immediate (as with Margaret Fuller) or, if acknowledged (as in the case of Walt Whitman's reverence for Frances Wright), subsequently ignored or trivialized by historians and critics.

In addition, their influence has been neglected because of its very scope and diversity. The many interests and causes they espoused in their writings, their widespread travels, and their many social contacts meant that these two nineteenth century women would touch the lives of thousands of their contemporaries, and do so in different ways and at different stages of their own intellectual and political development. For this reason, the subsequent chapters will discuss only a few of the most well-known of the writers and thinkers they affected. Even so, the result is an eclectic grouping of names which normally would not appear together in the same study: Elizabeth Cady Stanton and Elizabeth Gaskell, for instance; or Walt Whitman and Anthony Trollope; or, yet again, Ernestine Rose and Charles Dickens—poets, fiction writers, and political reformers of both genders on two continents.

Most importantly, of course, we have ignored the influence of Frances Wright and Frances Trollope on the thinking of their age because we stereotyped and belittled their characters and careers. In denying them their rightful places in history and in literature, we have denied them also their pivotal stances in the literary and historical movements of their own times and of those that were to follow. In the next two chapters I will trace patterns of the intricate social and literary fabric which they helped to fashion and of which they were very much a part.

Chapter Seven
Wright, the American Suffragists, Mill, and Whitman

Rejected by the majority, Frances Wright's ideas nevertheless came to affect every level of American society. Those who have focused attention on her career have agreed on the paradox of her life, its electricity and color reduced to seeming paralysis and invisibility before her death. Yet her ideas would have impact on the mainstream of American culture. In 1924 William Randall Waterman concluded his study of Frances Wright with these words:

Just how deeply she influenced American thought it is difficult to say.... Probably it would be safe to say that through her lectures and editorials she did much to popularize and stimulate the demand for a more liberal religion, more liberal marriage laws, the protection of the property rights of married women, a more generous system of education, and the abolition of capital punishment and of imprisonment for debt. Slavery she opposed as irrational, and an obstacle to the progress of America.... Perhaps Miss Wright's greatest contribution was to the intellectual emancipation of women. A pioneer, she was scoffed at, hooted and reviled, but she showed what the feminine mind was capable of, and having blazed the way, other courageous women were not wanting to follow in her footsteps. (255-56)

While stressing that Wright's contributions were " 'broader' than the single issue of equal rights for women," Waterman could attest to Wright's continuing importance in one of the most significant movements of his own period: "At a moment when the women of the United States are rapidly bringing to a successful conclusion their long struggle for equal rights a study of the life of

Frances Wright seems most fitting, for Frances Wright was one of the foremost pioneers in the cause, although never a participant in the organized movement" (9).

Twenty years later, Merle Curti in *The Growth of American Thought* similarly stresses that the feminist movement in the United States "owed much to the clear logic and forceful argument by which this courageous crusader denounced the subjection of women by law and custom and pleaded for their emancipation on every level—economic, social, and cultural" (385). More recently, Eleanor Flexner in *Century of Struggle* comments on America's mistreatment of Frances Wright, asserting,

Yet her influence was enduring. No woman in the first half of the nineteenth century who challenged tradition escaped the effect of Frances Wright's leavening thought; nor was its impact limited to women alone. The lectures which she delivered in New York, Philadelphia, Baltimore, Boston, Cincinnati, Louisville, St. Louis, and elsewhere were largely before audiences of workingmen, who also read accounts of her addresses in the active labor press of the day; they helped to feed the rising popular demand for free education. (28)

Frances Wright's ideas appeared everywhere in American society—as did unrelenting attacks against her.

Naming Frances Wright as especially offensive, the Reverend Parsons Cooke justified the prohibition against woman's speaking, explaining, "Even if it were true, that some woman in an assembly had more talents than all the men present, the excess of her talents so far from making a reason why she should display them, would make it a still stronger case of usurping authority over the man" (9-10). Despite attacks from the pulpit, Frances Wright's brilliance was attracting a growing, loyal following among all classes of women as well as of men. Margaret Fuller was one of those who took advantage of the new paths Frances Wright was opening for women, even though she wished to do so at as much distance from the embattled Frances Wright as safety seemed to require.

Already carefully educated by her father and encouraged by him to believe "girls were the intellectual equals of boys" (Rosenthal v), Margaret Fuller must have been gratified to find women such as Frances Wright embarking on public careers to proclaim the rights of women and society's other oppressed groups. Marie Urbanski—agreeing with Fuller's earlier biographer, Madeline Stern—concludes that Margaret Fuller "undoubtedly had heard of Fanny Wright...since [Wright] lectured in Boston in August 1829, when Fuller was living in Cambridge and the Reverend Lyman Beecher in one of his sermons on political atheism complained that females of education and refinement were among her votaries..." (Urbanski 63).[1] Since Wright's views were being debated everywhere she had spoken, Margaret Fuller most certainly would have been aware of the controversy surrounding the Scottish reformer's appearances and editorials.

Nevertheless, Margaret Fuller's debt to Frances Wright must be inferred from the similarity of the views she expressed in *Woman in the Nineteenth Century* (1845) when compared to the public statements of Frances Wright more than a decade earlier. As Bernard Rosenthal has suggested, *Woman in the Nineteenth Century* "did not come from a political or social vacuum" (vi). Clearly Margaret Fuller is echoing Frances Wright's views when she asserts, "improvement in the daughters will best aid in the reformation of the sons of this age" (24); the American wife or mother "misses the education which should enlighten [her] influence [on her husband or children]" (72); "women are, indeed, the easy victims both of priestcraft and self-delusion; but this would not be, if the intellect was developed in proportion to the other powers" (105); and, finally, in effecting female "self-dependence, and a greater ...fulness of being" society must "look to the young; ...[for] action and conservation, not of old habits, but of a better nature, enlightened by hopes that daily grow brighter" (96). These words can barely be distinguished from those earlier pronouncements of Frances Wright on the same topics.

Had she lived longer, Fuller might have acknowledged the incendiary Wright's influence as she matured and became herself more and more actively involved in politics. Urbanski concludes, "Frances Wright's type of revolutionary fervor came to Margaret Fuller later in Europe as her ideas developed under the tutelage of Adam Mickiewicz and Guiseppe Mazzini" (65). Fuller's tragic death, in 1850 at the age of only 40, cut short her intellectual development and her influential career even before the elder Frances Wright's own death. We will never know if Margaret Fuller might have returned to the United States as politically committed and outspoken as she had been in Italy (immediately prior to her death) during the ferment of the Italian revolution.

In contrast, other leading women reformers of nineteenth century America went out of their way to recognize and praise Frances Wright's pioneering efforts for human rights. The first of these followers would be Ernestine Rose, the Polish-born reformer, "whose path often crossed" Frances Wright's as she petitioned and spoke for women's causes in the United States during the 1830s and 1840s (Neidle 40). Although Cecyle Neidle contends that Rose worked with Frances Wright (37), I can find no existing record of personal meetings or interchanges between them. However, Ernestine Rose openly and often expressed the bond of sympathy and respect she felt for Frances Wright.

Coming to the United States in 1836 after rejecting a marriage arranged by her father, suing him in the Polish courts for control of her inheritance (then returning it to her father after she had won her suit against him), supporting herself in Europe and in England before her marriage to the British Owenite, William Rose, Ernestine Rose already had proven her own political acumen and her commitment to women's independence at a young age. Nevertheless, she expressed gratitude for the work Frances Wright had begun in America as she followed in her footsteps to address the same issues: the injustices of slavery and child labor; the mistreatment of working people; the inadequacies of existing public education; as well as the need for married women's property rights, woman's suffrage, and more liberal divorce laws. Ernestine Rose insisted, as had Wright, that American rhetoric must parallel American legal practices. She demanded, "Carry out the republican principle of universal suffrage, or strike it from your banners and substitute 'Freedom and Power to one half of society, and Submission and Slavery to the other.' Give women the elective franchise. Let married women have the same right to property that their husbands have...." (Stanton *et al.* 1: 258).

Rose often directly expressed her admiration for Frances Wright. In Waverly, New York, at a Friends of Progress social-reform convention, a woman paid tribute to Ernestine Rose by asking Rose to name her newborn baby. According to Rose's biographer, Yuri Suhl, Rose responded by publicly and permanently linking herself to her Scottish-born predecessor, declaring " 'Then I name her Ernestine Frances Lyons'...The Frances was for Frances Wright" (121).

In 1860, at the Tenth National Woman's Rights Convention at the Cooper Institute in New York, Ernestine Rose once more commemorated Frances Wright's heroic life struggle for justice in the United States, saying

Frances Wright was the first woman in this country who spoke on the equality of the sexes. She had indeed a hard task before her. The elements were entirely unprepared. She had to break up the time-hardened soil of conservatism; and her reward was sure— the same reward that is always bestowed upon those who are in the vanguard of any great movement. She was subjected to public odium, slander, and persecution. But these were not the only things that she received. Oh, she had her reward!—...the eternal reward of knowing that she had done her duty; the reward springing from the consciousness of rights, of endeavoring to benefit unborn generations. How delightful to see the molding of the minds around you, the infusing of your thoughts and aspirations into others, until one by one they stand by your side, without knowing how they came there! That reward she had. It has been her glory, it is the glory of her memory; and the time will come when society will have outgrown its old prejudices, and stepped with one foot, at least, upon the elevated platform on which she took her position. (Stanton *et al.* 1: 692)

It was Frances Wright's example, Rose explained, which had given her strength when she campaigned for married women's property rights in New York, obtaining five signatures in five months, working on for 12 long years for final passage of the Married Women's Property Bill in the New York State legislature in 1848.²

Rose knew well how it felt to be ridiculed and slandered for expressing her convictions both as a contributer to the *Boston Investigator* and as a tireless public speaker whose "addresses were regarded as revolutionary. At times she came close to being tarred and feathered" (Neidle 40). But Ernestine Rose wrote and spoke as passionately as had Frances Wright on behalf of the "general reconstruction of American society" (Seller 256). For both women, Yuri Suhl concludes, "woman's rights [were] part of a larger struggle for human rights" (40), part of a "new form of society, based on the social philosophy of Owenism, [which they believed] would be the ultimate solution to mankind's ills" (42).

Rose's fellow suffragist, the Quaker reformer and abolitionist, Lucretia Mott, also paid on-going tribute to Frances Wright. Whether Mott actually had a personal relationship with Wright, as Perkins and Wolfson contended in their 1939 study, *Frances Wright Free Enquirer* (363), and Judith Nies more recently suggests, as well (*Seven Women* 121), she and her husband were both familiar with Wright's work and her philosophy from the beginning of Wright's public appearances. Both husband and wife had taken a courageous stand after Wright gave early lectures in Wilmington, Delaware, on knowledge and education. When Quakers who had attended Wright's lectures were disowned, and subsequently appealed their cases at the Philadelphia Yearly Meeting, the Motts, as Lucretia wrote friends, "came close to 'losing our place' by uttering our indignant protest against their intolerance" (Bacon 38).

Lucretia Mott not only defended Frances Wright's right to speak in public (and the rights of others to listen to Wright's ideas), Mott agreed with her and helped to disseminate Wright's views both within and beyond the Quaker community—most importantly to younger women such as Elizabeth Cady Stanton and Susan B. Anthony. Kathleen Barry recounts how Susan Anthony, while a student at Deborah Moulson's seminary, "listened to [Mott] with rapt attention" while Ellen DuBois relates Mott's critical role in Elizabeth Cady Stanton's intellectual development:

Meeting Lucretia Mott greatly accelerated Elizabeth Stanton's development as a feminist.... Despite [Mott's] Quakerism and her piety, Mott was familiar with and sympathetic to the traditions of secular radicalism.... Mott had read Wollstonecraft and Paine, knew Robert Owen the elder and, perhaps most important for Stanton's development, was acquainted with and sympathetic to the feminist ideas of Frances Wright. Mott cultivated Stanton's intellect and encouraged her feminism. She urged her to read Wollstonecraft, Wright, and the Grimkes' writings, which Stanton herself circulated in the early 1840s. (Barry 29; DuBois, *Elizabeth Cady Stanton* 11)

Mott spread Wright's views further as she spoke throughout the country.

In 1847, Mott addressed the yearly meeting of Hicksite Friends in Ohio, arguing for women's political equality and the need for comparable education for women (Melder 126). In 1848, she and Stanton organized the Seneca Falls Women's Rights Convention to put forth a series of resolutions, including woman's right to speak in public, her right to vote, her right to participate equally with men in the world, and her right to enter into occupations of all varieties (Melder 145-47). At the Rochester Women's Rights Convention in 1848, having elaborated on the plight of seamstresses and working women, Lucretia Mott noted that the oppressed, black or white, must demand their freedom. She advised her female audience no longer to be duped by "the flattery typically used to deceive women."[3] The following year, 1849, Mott defended the expansion of woman's role in a major speech in Philadelphia. After Frances Wright's death, Lucretia Mott lamented America's neglect of Wright's ideas, as of those of Robert Owen and Mary Wollstonecraft. Mott looked to the day when all three, Wright, Wollstonecraft, and Owen, would "have justice done them, and the denunciations of bigoted sectarianism [would] fall into merited contempt" (Hallowell 357).

With the elder suffragists, Lucretia Mott and Ernestine Rose, so insistent on Wright's importance to American society's political development, and so respectful of her personal courage and wisdom, it is little wonder, then, to find Susan B. Anthony and Elizabeth Cady Stanton commemorating Frances Wright throughout their careers. Along with Matilda Joslyn Gage, editors Stanton and Anthony made Wright's picture the frontispiece for their massive *History of Woman Suffrage* (1881) and wrote this dedication:

These volumes are Affectionately Inscribed To The Memory of Mary Wollstonecraft, Frances Wright, Lucretia Mott, Harriet Martineau, Lydia Maria Child, Margaret Fuller, Sarah and Angela Grimke, Josephine S. Griffing, Martha C. Wright, Harriot K. Hunt, M.D., Marianna W. Johnson, Alice and Phebe Carey, Ann Preston, M.D., Paulina Wright Davis, Whose Earnest Lives and Fearless Words, in Demanding Political Rights for Women, have been in the Preparation of these Pages, a Constant Inspiration to the Editors.

In the *History of Woman Suffrage*, the editors "identified three precipitating factors [for the Seneca Falls Convention of 1848]: the radical ideas of Wright and Rose on religion and democracy; the initial reforms in women's property law in the 1830s and 1840s; and...women's experiences in the antislavery movement" (DuBois, *Elizabeth Cady Stanton* 8-9). They honored Frances Wright's contributions to women's causes, and to the advancement of American women in the field of journalism through her editorship of the *Free Enquirer*, "the first periodical established in the United States for the purpose of fearless and unbiased inquiry on all subjects" (Stanton *et al.* 1: 44-45). Wright's "able

The Hall of Science, drawn by A.J. Davis, after a painting by C. Burton, in *The Free Enquirer* (1830). (Courtesy of the New-York Historical Society, N.Y.C.)

lectures...on political, religious, and social questions" they deemed vital to the growth of American thought—with Ernestine Rose following "to deepen and perpetuate the impression Frances Wright had made on the minds of unprejudiced hearers" (Stanton *et al.* 1: 51).

The editors of the *History of Woman Suffrage* further decried the way Wright's reputation had been degraded and her character attacked throughout her lifetime. They tried to reinterpret Frances Wright for the American public, concluding that Wright was

a person of extraordinary powers of mind,...the first woman who gave lectures on political subjects in America..... Her ideas on theology, slavery and the social degradation of woman, now generally accepted by the best minds of the age, were then denounced by both press and pulpit, and maintained by her at the risk of her life. Although the Government of the United States was framed on the basis of entire separation of Church and State, yet from an early day the theological spirit had striven to unite the two, in order to strengthen the Church by its union with the civil power.... The clergy at once became her most bitter opponents...though her work was of vital importance to the country and undertaken from the purest philanthropy. (1: 35-36)

Stanton and Anthony shared concern with Frances Wright's causes and an empathy created by their own experiences for the way Wright had been publicly degraded.

In their *History*, Stanton, Anthony, and Gage also included a long, commemorative speech on Frances Wright given by Chair Paulina W. Davis at the twentieth anniversary Woman's Rights Convention in Apollo Hall, New York. Recounting Wright's political career, Davis celebrated "this heroic woman," reminding her audience that "[Wright] pitied and endured the scoffs and jeers of the multitude and fearlessly continued to utter her rebukes against oppression, ignorance and bigotry. Women joined in the hue and cry against her, little thinking that men were building the gallows and making them the executioners. Women have crucified in all ages the redeemers of their own sex, and men mocked them with the fact" (Stanton *et al.*, *History* 1: 430). Similarly, Elizabeth Cady Stanton had recalled Frances Wright's career when writing Lucretia Mott about the debate over Victoria Woodhull's morality,

We have had women enough sacrificed to this sentimental, hypocritical prating about purity. This is one of man's most effective engines for our division and subjugation. He creates the public sentiment, builds the gallows, and then makes us hangmen for our own sex. Women have crucified the Mary Wollstonecrafts, the Fanny Wrights, the George Sands, the Fanny Kembles, the Lucretia Motts of all ages, and now men mock us with the fact, and say we are ever cruel to each other. Let us end this ignoble record and henceforth stand by womanhood. (Lutz 218)

Again Susan B. Anthony defended Wright in May 1860, at the New York City Women's Rights meeting at the Cooper Institute, demanding to know, "who of our literary women...has yet ventured one word of praise or recognition of the heroic enunciators of the great idea of woman's equality—of Mary Wollstonecraft, Frances Wright, Ernestine L. Rose, Lucretia Mott, Elizabeth Cady Stanton?" (Suhl 138). Attempting to remove the stains from Frances Wright's reputation, Stanton and Anthony revived both her memory and her ideas in American political thought.

Keeping Frances Wright's picture on the wall of her study, Susan B. Anthony read Wright's *A Few Days in Athens* in 1855 and published articles on Wright and Wright's writings in *The Revolution.*[4] Continuing in the tradition of Frances Wright's *Free Enquirer*, Stanton and Anthony—along with fellow editor of *The Revolution*, Parker Pillsbury—addressed numerous ills of American society. They "wrote and reprinted articles on prostitution, infanticide, the need for sex education, cooperative housekeeping, and the monogamous practices of Oneida communitarians and Utah Mormons. They published the writings of Frances Wright and Mary Wollstonecraft and discovered a feminist heritage that was many centuries old" (DuBois, *Feminism* 104). In 1868 in *The Revolution* they argued for "educated suffrage, irrespective of sex or color, equal pay for equal work, eight hours labor, abolition of standing armies and party despotisms." They cried, "Down with the Politicians—Up with the People" (Burnett 170).

In addition to Stanton's editorials on women's rights topics, *The Revolution* "pioneered fearlessly...as it pointed out labor's valuable contribution to the development of the country. It also called attention to the vicious contrasts in large cities, where many lived in tumble-down tenements in abject poverty while the few, with more wealth than they knew what to do with, spent lavishly and built themselves palaces...The Chicago *Workingman's Advocate* observed, 'We have no doubt [*The Revolution*] will prove an able ally of the labor reform movement' " (Lutz, *Susan B. Anthony* 142-43). The progressive causes espoused by *The Revolution* from 1868 to 1870 were, for the most part, ones that Frances Wright had spearheaded several decades earlier on behalf of working men and women, blacks, the impoverished, the disenfranchised, uneducated, and mistreated throughout the United States.

As Susan B. Anthony and Elizabeth Cady Stanton grew older, they became as politically and philosophically at odds with American culture as Frances Wright had been. This was particularly true of Stanton. When Dr. W. W. Patton of Howard University in 1885 preached in Washington's Congregational Church on the topic of "Woman and Skepticism," warning that "freedom for woman led to skepticism and immorality, he illustrated his position by pointing to Hypatia, Mary Wollstonecraft, Frances Wright, George Eliot" and others; it was said that at the close of the sermon [Anthony and Stanton] went directly up to Dr. Patton to remonstrate with him. "Doctor," ejaculated Susan with cutting bluntness, "Your mother, if you have one, should lay you across her knee and give you a good spanking for that sermon." (Stanton, *Eighty Years* 382)

"Oh no," interposed Elizabeth..."allow me to congratulate you. I have been trying for years to make women understand that the worst enemy they have is in the pulpit, and you have illustrated the truth of it." (Lutz, *Created Equal* 274)

Stanton followed Frances Wright in battling the American clergy throughout her life.

Stanton's *Woman's Bible*, published in 1898 when she was 80, no doubt was an inevitable outgrowth of her disagreement with institutionalized Christianity in the United States and her early sympathy with the anti-clerical humanism of Frances Wright. With the publication of the *Woman's Bible*, Stanton

was repudiated by the very organization she had helped to found. In her efforts to challenge religious teachings, which relentlessly preached women's inferiority, she stirred up the clergy, caused libraries to refuse to circulate the book, and fostered a storm of criticism in various newspapers. (Nies 91)

Stanton came to know the same kinds of attacks from clergy as those made against Frances Wright, yet, unlike Wright, Stanton had the comfort of Wright's pioneering efforts in America to help strengthen her resolve, as well as a long life in which, as she comments in her autobiography, she witnessed one "mistake" after another become recognized as "a step in progress." At 80 and "still considered a dangerous radical," Stanton felt she had gained

confidence in my judgment and patience with the oppostion of my coadjutors, with whom on so many points I disagree. It requires no courage now to demand the right of suffrage, temperance legislation, liberal divorce laws, or for women to fill church offices—these battles have been fought and won. But it still requires courage to question the divine inspiration of the Hebrew Writings as to the position of woman. Why should the myths, fables, and allegories of the Hebrews be held more sacred than those of the Assyrians and Egyptians from whose literature most of them were derived? Seeing that the religious superstitions of women perpetuate their bondage more than all other adverse influences, I feel impelled to reiterate my demands for justice, liberty and equality in the Church as well as in the State. (*Eighty Years and More* 467-68)

Stanton's adamant stance against institutionalized Christianity in the United

States became as unacceptable as had Frances Wright's.

In fact, in her last decade of life, Elizabeth Cady Stanton would advance her attacks on many American institutions. She "began to study socialism" to redress the labor issues which had arisen in America in the latter part of the nineteenth century. She warned, "although we forget and neglect [the masses'] interests and our duties, we do it at the peril of all...there must be a radical change in the relations of capital and labor" (Nies 91). In 1894, writing about the railroad strikes in Chicago, she announced, "My sympathies are with [Debs and his strikers]" (Nies 91) and, three years before her death, she wrote in 1898 in the *New York Journal*,

We have a higher duty than the demand for suffrage....We see that the right of suffrage avails nothing for the masses in competition with the wealthy classes, and, worse still, with each other....Agitation of the broader question of philosophical socialism is now in order. (Nies 62)

For Elizabeth Cady Stanton, as for Susan B. Anthony, Lucretia Mott, Ernestine Rose, and Frances Wright, women's rights were seen as part of a larger social picture. All envisioned a more compassionate, feminized, and "generous" society—and had lectured throughout the United States and written in numerous publications to achieve that end.

Frances Wright's ideas were viewed with equal sympathy in England by one of the leading social theorists of the nineteenth century. It was not so much that John Stuart Mill had been influenced by Frances Wright as that both had, in their youth, been influenced by the same individuals. Mill first had become acquainted with Wright when she was entertained in his home, along with his parents' fellow guests, Jeremy Bentham and Joseph Hume (Eckhardt, *Fanny Wright* 63). Mill at the time was studying with his father under an intensive curriculum designed by Jeremy Bentham—while Wright, then in her early twenties, had become Bentham's disciple for several years following the publication of her *Views of Society and Manners in America*. In addition, both Frances Wright and John Stuart Mill would come to know well the person and philosophy of the elder Robert Owen.

From Bentham and Owen, Frances Wright and John Stuart Mill would learn a philosophy of social reform—that society's ills could, and should, be addressed through political and institutional change. As with Wright, Mill too would develop an early, messianic ambition—as Mill expressed it, "to be a reformer of the world" (Stillinger 112). To this end, Wright and Mill both dedicated their lives, attempting to improve human society and human life through their efforts, the former in America and the latter in Britain, primarily. As F.W. Garforth writes of Mill,

His dominant purpose was clearly "the improvement of mankind," and if Mill may be said to have had *an* educational aim inclusive of all others, this was it. In one phrasing or another the idea of human improvement, of human well-being in its widest possible extension, occurs repeatedly in his writings. (*Educative Democracy* 2)

As we have seen, the same was true of Frances Wright. Buoyed up by a shared faith in human progress, by the promise of science, and by the seeming mutability (and improveability) both of individuals and of governments, Wright and Mill continued throughout their lives to believe in the principles learned in their youths. As we have already seen with Wright, and as F.W. Garforth says of Mill, "Later in life, after the disappointment of his early enthusiasms, he came to accept that the improvement must be gradual; but that it is possible he never doubted" (*Theory of Education* 36; *Educative Democracy* 97).

It is little wonder, then, as George Jacob Holyoake reported, that John Stuart Mill "held [Frances Wright] in regard as one of the most important women of her day, and pointed this out to the present writer on her last visit to England" (380). The similarity of their writings and their views reflects a common philosophy and common influences. Mill, however, would never know the humiliation and degradation experienced by Frances Wright in America. He could argue, as had she, for a socialist society and, in "The Utility of Religion," for a "religion of humanity" to replace Christianity, without inviting assaults on his person or on his character (Garforth, *Educative Democracy* 2). Mill had been born into his father's challenging circle of prestigious philosophers and associates—and would continue to be recognized as a leading figure in Britain's intellectual history, one of the

few Englishmen who have given themselves so unreservedly…to the task of improving the intellectual, moral, political, economic, and cultural life of his own country, especially among the "labouring classes." (Garforth, *Educative Democracy* 3)

Wright would not enjoy such continuing veneration and historical prominence in either the Britain she had fled or the America she embraced.

In addition to sharing with Frances Wright continuous efforts to improve the lives of the working classes, Mill agreed with her in opposing slavery and capital punishment, promoting birth control, advancing the rights of women, and repudiating the social and legal inequities of traditional marriage (although Mill favored reforming marriage, not—as with Wright—abandoning it— agreeing with her, however, on the need for more liberal divorce laws). In each case a dedication to education acted as a common thread binding together many of their social reform efforts.

Mill and Wright both believed that, as Garforth says of Mill, "people must be educated into democracy…as an on-going process which continually expands and enriches the possibilities of their communal experience" (*Educative Democracy* 52). While more concerned from the outset about the effects of democracy than Wright, the need "to protect against [democracy's] dangers—mediocrity, the commercial spirit, and the diminution of individuality"—Mill nevertheless argued in *On Liberty* (as had Wright in speeches given in the United States) for institutionalizing

the peculiar training of a citizen, the practical part of the political education of a free people, taking them out of the narrow circle of personal and family selfishness and accustoming them to the comprehension of joint interests, the management of joint concerns...which unite instead of isolating them from one another. (Garforth, *Educative Democracy* 52; Mill, *On Liberty* 134)

This was, of course, as both Mill and Wright understood, particularly necessary for women.

In a speech on female suffrage given in 1867, more than a decade after Frances Wright's death, Mill echoes the earlier reformer's American speeches, arguing,

We continually hear that the most important part of national education is that of mothers, because they educate the future men. Is this importance really attached to it? Are there many fathers who care as much, or are willing to expend as much for the education of their daughters as of their sons? Where are the Universities, where the high schools, or the schools of any description, for them? If it be said that girls are better educated at home, where are the training-schools for governesses? (Garforth, *Educative Democracy* 130).

In "The Enfranchisement of Women" (1851) and *The Subjection of Women* (1869) Mill would also urge improved education for women,

pointing to the injustice of socially approved male domination; to the moral influence of women both in the family—wives on husbands, mothers on children—and in society at large; to the competitive stimulus educated women would exercise on men; to the need for a greater national reserve of intellectual power; to the degradation of the marriage relationship by the existing inequality between man and wife; to the enormous gain in personal happiness and liberation of potential that would come from offering women equality of opportunity with men. (Garforth, *Educative Democracy* 132)

Wright had made these same arguments on behalf of education for women in speeches throughout the United States in the 1820s and 1830s. While Harriet Taylor has taken the blame for many of her husband's advanced views on women's rights, it is clear that many of these ideas had already been implanted in Mill, as in Wright, early on through the influence of Robert Owen and of Jeremy Bentham.

Mill's personal courage in his relationship with Harriet Taylor would prove his one area of public vulnerability during a long and much-respected career. Drawing up an agreement with Harriet Taylor prior to their marriage in 1851, he "put on record a formal protest against the existing law of marriage...and [gave] a solemn promise never in any case or under any circumstances to use [the legal powers marriage conferred upon the male over the female]." Further, he made clear his views that his future wife should have "the same absolute freedom of action and freedom of disposal of herself and of all that does or may at any time belong to her, as if no such marriage had taken place" (*Letters of John Stuart Mill* 58). (Frances Wright, of course, had not been granted such freedom in her own marriage.)

While Phyllis Rose in *Parallel Lives: Five Victorian Marriages* perpetuates the myth of Mill's subjugation to his wife (positing Mill's need to subordinate himself to a stronger personality, found first in his father and then in Harriet Taylor), Rose explains well the difficulty Mill was confronting:

The Mills were embarked upon a great experiment, something new in the history of relations between men and women—a true marriage of equals. But so unusual was the situation that for Harriet to be anywhere near equal she had to be "more than equal."...

Mill intended both the fact and the written portrait of their friendship—and later of their marriage—to be an *acte provocateur*. However, in attempting to perform a revolutionary act, setting up woman as ruler, he was tracing an ancient pattern more accessible to ordinary minds, the man besotted by love into yielding his rule to a woman, Hercules with a distaff, a figure of fun for centuries. What Mill saw as a daring political gesture seemed to others no more than a grievous case of uxoriousness. (136)

Mill's integrity demanded that he do more than pay lip-service to equality for women; at some cost to himself, he practiced his philosophy through his marriage to Harriet Taylor and the respect he paid her life and memory.

The Subjection of Women (1869) is Mill's lasting tribute to the philosophical and relational harmony he experienced with his wife—and his contribution to the nineteenth century's political struggle for women's rights.[5] Again, the work recalls Wright's earlier speeches and writings on similar subjects, as well as points made in her last work, *England, the Civilizer*. For instance, Mill concludes, as did Wright, that historically, "The moral education of mankind has hitherto emanated chiefly from the law of force, and is adapted almost solely to the relations which force creates" (*Subjection* 79). He rues, as did Wright, the way in which, "...by the mere fact of being born a male [man] is by right the superior of all and every one of an entire half of the human race....What must be the effect on his character, of this lesson?" (*Subjection* 149). He asserts, "But so long as the right of the strong to power over the weak rules in the very heart of society, the attempt to make the equal rights of the weak the principle of its outward actions will always be an uphill struggle...." (*Subjection* 153). Thus Mill followed Wright in calling for an end to "the legal subordination of one sex to the other—...wrong in itself, and now one of the chief hindrances to human improvement," advising that it "be replaced by a principle of perfect equality, admitting no power or privilege on the one side, no disability on the other" (*Subjection* 1).

Acknowledging the consequences of having divided human qualities up by gender, Mill agrees with Wright that men have become too abstract in their thinking, able to "lose sight of the legitimate purpose of speculation altogether," while "a woman seldom runs wild after an abstracton...her more lively interest in the present feelings of persons...makes her consider, first of all...in what manner persons will be affected by [ideas]" (*Subjection* 108-09). Therefore, Mill concludes that, "Women's thoughts are thus as useful in giving reality to those of thinking men, as men's thoughts [are] in giving width and largeness to those of women" (*Subjection* 109). Mill and Wright both believed that men and women must come together, through equal education and equal relationships, to join their strengths and work together for the betterment of society. He knew, from the personal experience of his own marriage, that "when the two persons both care for great objects, and are a help and encouragement to each other in whatever regards these...each can enjoy the luxury of looking up to the other, and can have alternately the pleasure of leading and of being led in the path of development" (*Subjection* 174; 177). The result of such sexual equality, Mill agreed with Wright, would be the personal betterment of individuals and the advancement of civilization.

After reading Mill's *The Subjection of Women* in 1869, Elizabeth Cady Stanton reflected:

I lay the book down with a peace and joy I never felt before, for it is the first response from any man to show he is capable of seeing and feeling all the nice shades and degrees of woman's wrongs and the central points of her weakness and degradation. (Lutz, *Created Equal* 171-72)

She was not quite so enthusiastic about Wright's most important male sympathizer—and Mill's contemporary—Walt Whitman. Betsy Erkkila reports that, after reading in Whitman's *Leaves of Grass* (1856),

I am stern, acrid, large, undissuadable—but I love you,
I do not hurt you any more than is necessary for you,
I pour the stuff to start sons and daughters fit

for These States—I press with slow rude muscle,
I brace myself effectually—I listen to no entreaties,
I dare not withdraw till I deposit what has so
long accumulated in me, (241-42)

Stanton wrote in her diary in 1883, "He speaks as if the female must be forced to the creative act apparently ignorant of the great natural fact that a healthy woman has as much passion as a man, that she needs nothing stronger than the law of attraction to draw her to the male" (Erkkila 137-138).

Whitman, in fact, while ambivalent about female sexuality, never deviated from his belief in the need for a powerful female influence on American society. So strong were Whitman's portraits of American women, so open was he in depicting their bodies (including, at times, their erotic desires), in addition to venerating their spirits, that "by 1882 the female body of Whitman's poems was deemed dangerous to the public morality. Not only was *Leaves of Grass* banned in Boston, but those who attempted to publish his offending poems were persecuted" (Erkkila 310).[6] In spite of these attacks on Whitman's portraits of women (his love poems to men ironically passed unnoticed), "women readers loved him and defended him passionately in letters and reviews...[he had beckoned] women readers out of domestic confinement toward an open road of equality and comradeship with men. To Eliza Farnham in her study *Woman and Her Era* (1864), Whitman was one of the pioneering feminists of his age. . . ." (Erkkila 311, 315).

Frances Wright's influence on Whitman's view of women, as well as on his understanding of religion, history, and society, cannot be overestimated. She was, as he told Horace Traubel, one of the three individuals (Elias Hicks and Thomas Paine being the other two) who were "the superber characters of my day or America's early days" (Traubel 2: 206), individuals he desired to remember and commemorate in his writing. While there are those who contend that Frances Wright was less formative than Whitman himself believed,[7] the evidence seems very much to the contrary. Whitman, of course, would tell Horace Traubel that *A Few Days in Athens*, Frances Wright's "book about Epicurus was daily food to me" as he was growing up—reading, as well, her editorials in the *Free Enquirer* to which his father subscribed (Traubel 2: 445). Still later, as a young journalist in New York attending Wright's lectures in Tammany Hall, he "read over and over again [Wright's] little Socratic dialogue"; once more, as late as "...the spring of 1851, [when his] friends invited him to lecture at the newly formed Brooklyn Art Union, on Fuller Street...[he spoke about] the reading [he] was doing at the time: Emerson's *Nature* and 'Divinity School Address,' Carlyle's *Sartor Resartus*, Epictetus, Frances Wright's *A Few Days in Athens*" (Asselineau, 45-46; Zewig 128). From his youth on into his thirties, Whitman tells us that he had continued to read and reread *A Few Days in Athens*. It is not surprising, then, that, as David Goodale revealed in 1938, Whitman had been so influenced by Wright's *A Few Days in Athens* that he echoed many of its words and phrases, especially in his poem "Pictures."[8]

More important than Whitman's direct quotes and paraphrasings of *A Few Days in Athens*, however, are Whitman's other borrowings from Wright's work. Gay Wilson Allen explains that Metrodorus's lesson about the eternity of all things in *A Few Days in Athens* became central to Whitman's concept of *Leaves of Grass*. Other teachings in *A Few Days in Athens*—about the need for harmony between the body and the soul, as about the naturalness of death—also had a formative influence on Whitman's thinking (Allen, *The Solitary Singer* 139-40).[9] Whitman incorporates into "Song of Myself" the respect for all forms of life Frances Wright had expressed in *A Few Days in Athens*, the sense "that everything that exists is equally wonderful." Similarly, he follows Wright in expressing his loathing for theologies which inculcate fear and guilt instead of self-love and love of humanity in their followers (Allen, *Reader's Guide* 22; 21).[10] In addition, as Henry Seidel Canby speculates, Whitman absorbed from *A Few Days in Athens* a desire "to appear an Epicurus of his own times, since, like Epicurus, he believed virtue could be learned through pleasure, and that life was to be lived, not shrunk from" (Canby 160). Certainly, Whitman would succeed in embodying for and advocating to the nineteenth century American public Epicurus's message of sensuality and pleasure in living.

In the person of Frances Wright herself, as well as that of her character Epicurus in *A Few Days in Athens*, Walt Whitman found much to emulate. As Newton Arvin explains, in the 1830s Whitman "had gone repeatedly to her public lectures and received from them a profoundly personal and intellectual impression which nothing was ever to efface..." (Arvin 163). David Goodale theorized in 1938 that "it may well have been that Whitman's admiration for Frances Wright as a lecturer motivated his own early ambition to become a public speaker" (Goodale 207), a desire he continued to hold as late as 1879, when, "after his lecture on Lincoln in New York City...he wrote in his diary: 'I intend to go up and down the land (in moderation,) seeking whom I may devour with lectures' " (Goodale 207). As a young man, he had been "devoured" by Frances Wright's rhetoric, gaining from her a sense of the power of words, the power of ideas, the power of one individual to move audiences. He no doubt drew on his memories of Frances Wright when he pictured "the orator advancing...ascend[ing] the platform, silent, rapid, stern, almost fierce—and deliver[ing] an oration of liberty—up-braiding, full of invective—with enthusiasm" (Furness 74).

David Goodale compares Frances Wright's picture of the orator in *Views of Society and Manners in America* with Whitman's poem about oratory, showing the similarities of word choice and concepts between the two works

(207). Whitman evokes "the orator's joys":

To inflate the chest, to roll the thunder of the voice
out from the ribs and throat,
To make the people rage, weep, hate, desire, with
yourself,...
To speak with a full and sonorous voice out of a broad
chest...
(Holloway, *Leaves* 152-53)

while Frances Wright recommended that successful orators evince:

animation, energy, high moral feeling, ardent patriotism, a sublime love of liberty, a
rapid flow of ideas and of language, a happy vein of irony, an action at once vehement
and dignified, and a voice full, sonorous, distinct, and flexible; exquisitely adapted to all
the varieties of passion or argument. (*Views of Society* 374)

Frances Wright's words about public speaking, as well her example as a
lecturer, had moved Whitman to imitate her very phrases as well as many of her
ideas and goals.

In the persona of his poems, as Betsy Erkkila points out, Whitman would
continue to emulate the orator, seeking "to project the sense of personal
presence and magnetism he admired in such orators as Elias Hicks and George
Fox...the egalitarian and millennial language...the rhetorical tinges of the
proletarian, anticapitalist appeals of Frances Wright and William Leggett" (4;
48). His sense of mission, to move his readers to action, was that of the orator.
Whitman insisted

on the reader's creative role...[as] part of his revolutionary strategy, his attempt to
collapse the traditionally authoritarian relation between poet and audience, text and
reader by transferring the ultimate power of creation to the reader. "A great poem is no
finish to a man or woman but rather a beginning," he said in the 1855 preface [of *Leaves
of Grass*]....'The touch of [the great poet] tells in action." (Erkkila 91)

To move his audience to action, Whitman created a sense of personal self for
the reader, not only through placing pictures of himself as the democratic poet
at the beginning of successive editions of *Leaves of Grass*, but also, as David
Simpson argues, by

turn[ing] writing into speech, the absent into the present...[through] the vocatic markers
and incantory rhythms of the text, which thus seeks constantly to express itself as
voice.... Everything possible is done to create...a sense of the incarnate presence of the
poet's voice and body. (179)

Whitman's rhetorical rhythms, David Goodale argues, bear witness to Frances Wright as a source of "his characteristic poetic idiom" (213).

Most importantly, it can be shown that Frances Wright profoundly influenced Whitman's ideas, from his earliest writings to his last. If, as David Goodale contends, "clues to the secret of Whitman's prose style and his early ideas of reform, especially in such of his writings as 'The Eighteenth Presidency' may be found in Frances Wright's political writings" (207), these same signifiers remain in evidence throughout Whitman's life works. His "vision of a harmonious society of artisans, farmers, and laborers owning homesteads in fee simple, his association of virtue with the laboring classes, and his emphasis on the interactive values of independence and cooperation, freedom and community," had been Frances Wright's before him, conveyed to Whitman in his youth through her *Free Enquirer* editorials, her speeches to New York workers in the 1830s, and her prose writings (from *Views of Society and Manners in America* and *A Few Days in Athens*, to her final *England, the Civilizer*) (Erkkila 27).

As editor of the *Aurora* (a New York penny paper for workers) in the early 1840s, as editor of the *Brooklyn Daily Eagle* (1846-48), and as author of his early "proletarian" tales, as well as of later works of prose and poetry, Whitman continued to emphasize recurring themes inculcated in him by Frances Wright:

reform in the relation of labor and capital, urging improvements in the factory system, wages, working conditions, and the treatment of women laborers. He agitated against the slave trade and the extension of slavery. He urged reforms in education and the prison system, and he spoke out against corporal punishment and capital punishment. (Erkkila 27-32; 34)

In the final passages of "Song of Myself," Whitman voiced once more his on-going sympathy with working-class people, with those on "a plain public road" (Cowley, *Leaves* 80), battling injustices, expressing his democratic feeling for the

Many sweating and ploughing and thrashing, and then the
chaff for payment receiving,
A few idly owning, and they the wheat continually
claiming. (Cowley, *Leaves* 73)

While as disillusioned by the events of his lifetime as Frances Wright came to be in her final years, Walt Whitman would continue to share Wright's persistent, republican dream, expressing in *Democratic Vistas* his hope for a post-Civil War America which would learn to balance "self-interest with social love, matter with spirit, science with religion, money with soul" (Erkkila 254). Betsy Erkkila argues that Whitman divorced himself from the individualism Emerson and Thoreau advocated, offering instead "a form of freedom that exists not in an isolated self or a romanticized state of nature but in relation to others...he was moving closer to the socialist concept of the individual finding her or his greatest freedom within a political community" (255). In other words, Whitman had kept alive in himself, and alive in his readers, Frances Wright's belief in the union of the individual with the community, the selfish with the generous human principle, the male with the female, a dream of a cooperative community, through his "grammar of reconciliation and union [in response] to a world of rupture and dislocation" (Erkkila 11). He maintained this dream to the last, as had Frances Wright in *England, the Civilizer*.

In expressing his vision, Whitman felt that he must transcend the restrictions of gender. As Justin Kaplan explains, "The 'I' of *Leaves of Grass* is almost as often a woman as a man, and the book is a supremely passionate argument for the androgynous union of strength and tenderness, sagicity and impulse" (63). Whitman had always "accept[ed]...genuine intellectuality in women"—in Frances Wright, George Sand, and Margaret Fuller, among others (Killingsworth 246-47). And Whitman had always celebrated women's strengths, as Frances Wright had done before him. David Goodale shows that Frances Wright, in *Views of Society and Manners in America*, advocated the teaching of American women (in words that Whitman would later echo), saying that they needed "in early youth to excel in the race, to hit a mark, to swim, and, in short, to use every exercise which would impart vigour to their frames and independence to their minds" (317). Whitman would turn Wright's hopes for American women into their accomplishments, praising them because, he said,

They know how to swim, row, ride, wrestle, shoot, run,
strike, retreat, advance, resist, defend
themselves. (Holloway, *Leaves* 87)

Whitman did more, however, than simply sing the praises of American women, advocate their causes, and promote both a public and a political role for them. He insisted, more and more, on the need for what his culture had defined as "female" values to predominate in society and in individuals.

Having insisted always on the equality of women, Whitman would come in the last part of his career to desire the supremacy of their traditional virtues over those of men. Betsy Erkkila explains that, "As America during the [Civil] war moved toward the traditionally masculine polarity of militarism, violence, and aggression, Whitman in his person and his writing moved toward the traditionally feminine polarity of nurturance, compassion, and love" (199). Having nursed the dying and wounded of both the North and the South, the black and white races, during the Civil War, Whitman subsequently, in *Democratic Vistas* and in his late poetry, "sought to remove motherhood from the private sphere and release the values of nurturance, love, generativity, and community into the culture at large" (Erkkila 259). Whitman's "democratic mother...came to symbolize the creative and democratizing force of history itself," Erkkila contends, a cultural pattern he sought to strengthen in order to counteract the "corporate, centralized, male-identified model of power" he saw threatening not only the future of America but humanity's future—the future of the world (262). Throughout his career, as a lecturer, editor, prose writer, and poet, Whitman heeded the early lessons he learned from reading and listening to Frances Wright. As his fear for the future increased, he became even more adamant in "challeng[ing] a political economy based on the separation of female and male, private and public, home and world, by placing the values of community, equality, creation, and love at the center rather than at the margins of democratic culture" (Erkkila 316).

Whitman never found any vision of society more moving or more just than the one Frances Wright had inspired in him as a young man. She had moved him to passion, called forth his idealism, and, most certainly, strengthened in him an individual sense of self-worth and personal creativity. In his seventies, he would continue to speak of the "majesty" of her character with awe and respect (Traubel 2: 499), for she had helped to give him passion, hope, a sense of career, and personal resolve to inspire in others the wonder and vision he had come to know through her. For Whitman, as for the American suffragists—Ernestine Rose, Lucretia Mott, Susan B. Anthony, and Elizabeth Cady Stanton—Frances Wright would be remembered always as a model and an inspiration. They agreed with John Stuart Mill's assessment of her. For each of these historic individuals, Frances Wright would remain one of the most important women of her era—a personal guide as well as a shaper of Anglo-American culture.

Chapter Eight
Trollope, Dickens, Gaskell, Stowe and A. Trollope

We will never know just how great an influence Frances Trollope's works came to have on her contemporaries. We know, of course, that she dominated British fiction in the 1830s and 1840s. Percy Fitzgerald, Charles Dickens's friend, biographer, and contributor to Dickens's *Journal*, remembers, "in the forties she was the one and only 'fashionable' story-teller to be read, and certainly her 'Widow Barnaby' and other jovial tales gave great entertainments, and was [sic] the pattern for a whole school of such things" (312). Not the least of the Widow Barnaby's imitations, as Helen Heineman points out, would be Thackeray's *Becky Sharp* a decade later (*The Triumphant* 158). In surveying the earnings of Dickens and his contemporaries, Robert Patten reports that Frances Trollope's works continued to sell steadily through the middle of the century (23) and that for many years the mother's income as an author quite exceeded that of her son Anthony (228-29). Charles Dickens, admittedly jealous early in his career of his literary rival Mrs. Trollope, nonetheless delighted in having her well-known name listed among the contributors to his *Bentley's Miscellany* in 1836 ("To Richard Bentley" 202). And, as her daughter-in-law Frances Eleanor Trollope reports, Mrs. Trollope's name continued to be used, and abused, in such claims as "written by Sir Francis Trollope," long after she had ceased writing (284). Five of her earlier novels were reissued for her reading public after her final novel was published in 1856 (Heineman, *The Triumphant* 233).

Frances Trollope's audience grew vast and loyal; her literary influence pervasive. In conveying a sense of that influence, I will concentrate on only a few works by some of her more prestigious contemporaries. I will look at Charles Dickens's *American Notes*, *Martin Chuzzlewit* and *Hard Times*; Elizabeth Gaskell's *Mary Barton* and *North and South*; Harriet Beecher Stowe's *Uncle Tom's Cabin*; and Anthony Trollope's *Barchester Towers*—all of which bear witness to the innovations of their literary predecessor Frances Trollope. What they found worth following in her pages we can still find in the best of Frances Trollope's works today: novel subject matter, vivid characterizations, and, especially, a frank and spirited authorial voice that seemed excitingly "modern."

So close are the connections between Dickens's *American Notes* and *Martin Chuzzlewit*, on the one hand, and Frances Trollope's *Domestic Manners of the Americans*, on the other, that Jerome Meckier in his recent book *Innocent Abroad* speaks of their "pronounced...intertextuality" (77). In fact, Meckier reveals how Dickens's *Martin Chuzzlewit* and his *American Notes* present a "conscientious rewriting of Mrs. Trollope's ideas and verdicts in order to promote his authenticity by detracting from hers" (102). Meckier convincingly argues that *American Notes* was intended to be a "structural parody of *Domestic Manners of the Americans*" (94). While Frances Trollope had denounced the American frontier as she left it behind, ending her *Domestic Manners of the Americans* with pleasant portraits of the relatively more sophisticated East, Dickens (and his alter-ego Martin Chuzzlewit) would travel further and further down the Mississippi, becoming (as Dickens felt structurally appropriate) more and more disillusioned as they receded into the American wilderness. Meckier comments on the paradox at the heart of Dickens's parody of *Domestic Manners of the Americans*: his desire to reveal Frances Trollope's journey as a "paler" version of his own "deconversion" while at the same time suggesting that hers was a female "overreaction" to the incidents she recounts (95). Dickens believed that women writers made "inferior social commentators," including fellow writers Harriet Martineau, Elizabeth Gaskell and George Eliot, along with Frances Trollope herself (Meckier 79). Meckier explains, "Not surprisingly, [Dickens's] most formidable rivals both in the travel-book battles and in the subsequent realism wars of the 1850s and 1860s were female" (79).

Insecurity caused Dickens to see Frances Trollope as a rival early on in his career. In Dickens's letters several years before his reworking of *Domestic Manners of the Americans*, we learn that he had declined an invitation to dine with Mrs. Trollope, admitting in his diary during this same period (in 1839) his anger that Frances Trollope's *The Life and Adventures of Michael Armstrong, the Factory Boy*, was being jointly advertised by the publisher Colburn along with his own *Pickwick Papers* and *Nicholas Nickleby* ("To Francis Trollope" 499). Dickens charged in his diary that *Michael Armstrong* was a reworking of *Nicholas Nickleby*—and not an "honest or responsible imitation of Nickleby, which it seems was 'unintentional'—of course" (House and Storey 640). In a letter to a friend, Dickens wrote with more bravado, and less rancour, "If Mrs. Trollope were even to adopt Ticholas Tickleby as being a better sounding name than Michael Armstrong, I don't think it would cost me a wink of sleep, or impair my appetite in the smallest degree"; however, he could not restrain himself from adding, "...I will express no fuller opinion of Mrs. Trollope, than that I think Mr. Trollope must have been an old dog and chosen his wife from the same species" ("To S. Laman Blanchard" 506-507).[1]

Mrs. Trollope's "borrowing" here could, at most, have been the idea of using a hard-working, young boy as her hero—although her Michael Armstrong was a child of the lower classes while Nicholas Nickleby, already a young man, was a gentleman whose family had fallen on hard times after his father's death. With the centrality of a young male hero in both novels, all comparisons between the two works disappear. Michael Armstrong endures the horrors of a factory system Dickens would neither investigate nor write about until more than a decade later; Nicholas Nickleby, on the other hand, confronts the deplorable Yorkshire schools not as a schoolboy himself but as a young instructor attempting to earn his living and provide for his mother and sister—a plot Frances Trollope did not rework into any of her own writings. Dickens must have worried that the boy's adventure by the better known author might draw readers away from a narrative pattern he considered his own, one for which he would soon become internationally famous.

Sensitive as Dickens appeared to be about other authors reading and borrowing from his own works, he apparently felt that he himself was immune to influence from his fellow writers. In 1841, only two years after his outbursts over Michael Armstrong, Charles Dickens sat down in his study to pour over his fellow authors' travel books on America—including Frances Trollope's *Domestic Manners of the Americans*—in preparation for his forthcoming journey and his own prospective book on the New World (Johnson 360). At this time, he would write Andrew Bell on the latter's travel book on America, saying, "I think you are rather hard on the Americans and that your dedication like Mrs. Troloppe's [sic] preface seems to denote a foregone conclusion" (402). Dickens believed that his own judgment of America would be a positive one—and, certainly, whatever its exact nature, that it would be more astute and more persuasive than those he had been studying by fellow writers on the subject. However, he seems to have underestimated the effect of his preparatory reading on his personal vision of the New World—especially underestimating the power of Mrs. Trollope's prose on his own sensibility.

So influenced was he by Frances Trollope's portrait of America that he would find it difficult to see with eyes other than her own. Most of the subjects he came to write about in *American Notes*—Americans' tobacco chewing and spitting, their vulgar table manners, the greed and profiteering of American businessmen, the hypocrisy of American "freedoms" coupled with American slavery, the electioneering and violence of American politics, to name a few—were, in fact, already familiar from the pages of Frances Trollope's *Domestic Manners of the Americans*. Dickens found himself trapped since, according to Jerome Meckier, "for Dickens especially, writing about America entailed writing about all of the best-known previous guidebooks" (76). When he found that he was in essential agreement with what he had read in Frances Trollope's *Domestic Manners of the Americans*, Dickens could only insist that his "deconversion" was "unique…one of a kind" (Meckier 76), more valid because more "male, moderate, and realistic" (Meckier 122) than Mrs. Trollope's, without coming to an assessment distinctively different from her own. In fact, he would take Mrs. Trollope's protests about the female frailty of her pen at face value, suggesting that, because she had *said* she could not draw political conclusions about the American society she had so effectively analyzed, that she had not, in fact, come to an insight essentially the same as his own: that America's social practices and its larger public policies were very much interrelated (Meckier 99). To separate her vision from his, Dickens would also distort Frances Trollope's philosophy, stereotyping her conclusions as more conservative than his own and as more of an argument for retaining the status quo than they actually had been (Meckier 78; 100-102; 122).

When he drew his fictional portrait of America in *Martin Chuzzlewit*, Dickens once more turned to the works of his older colleague Frances Trollope. This time the "intertextuality" goes beyond the careful reworking of *Domestic Manners of the Americans* which Jerome Meckier has discussed so well. In 1832 Frances Trollope had published not only her famous travel book on

America but also her first novel on the New World, *The Refugee in America* (1832). Elements of that work—and her later *The Barnabys in America; or, Adventures of the Widow Wedded* (1843), just completed in monthly installments the same year Charles Dickens was writing *Martin Chuzzlewit* (Heineman, *The Triumphant* 209)—are also rewoven into the pages of Dickens's more famous novel.

The most striking comparison between Trollope's *Refugee in America* and Dickens's *Martin Chuzzlewit* appears in the dystopias central to both novels. While it is true, as Meckier contends, that the Eden Land Corporation of *Martin Chuzzlewit* is based both on the Nashoba settlement Dickens read about in *Domestic Manners of the Americans* and "the dismal Cairo" Dickens had himself seen on his own trip to America (Meckier 95), it also recalls Trollope's "Perfect Bliss" in *Refugee in America*. In that work, Madame de Clairville explains that her husband has died in the utopian society of "Perfect Bliss," exhausted by overwork and heartbroken with disillusionment within a year (Trollope, *Refugee* 1: 213). So, too, would many of the settlers of Dickens's "Eden" in *Martin Chuzzlewit*, written 11 years later. Trollope in *Refugee* had lamented the demise of "the poor Frenchman [de Clairville], whose visions had been of scientific lectures, amateur concerts, private theatricals, and universal philanthropy" (1: 210), while in *Chuzzlewit* Dickens would also commiserate with a young Martin shocked to find that "national poets, the theatre, literature, and the arts" (274) have no toe-hold in America, from the mob-filled streets of New York to the barren frontier communities of Eden or New Thermopylae.

Other parallels between *Refugee in America* (1832) and *Martin Chuzzlewit* (1843) abound. Trollope's Mr. Conway, who befriends the English travelers (Mr. Gordon and his daughter Caroline), is portrayed as a unique American in *Refugee*, a kindly patriot, one of the very few who is thoughtful, and most importantly, not involved in the habitual "money-getting" of American businessmen. Similarly, Dickens's Mr. Bevan acts as Martin's benign American benefactor and also as an apologist for the barbarous nature of New World society.

Both novels depict the American character in great detail. To Trollope, American citizens seemed a "transient people" (*Refugee* 1: 197), living in a country where Dickens found "men...constantly changing their residences...and moving further off" (*Chuzzlewit* 230). Always in a rush from one place to another, Americans are portrayed in each work as eating in the same way. British visitors in both novels express their horror of American mealtimes. Trollope reports that diners "feed with ravenous rapidity, and imperturbable gravity of countenance" with "no other object in sitting down to dinner than to swallow their food" (1: 142). Dickens laments, "It was a solemn and an awful thing to see. Dyspeptic individuals bolted their food in wedges.... Spare men...came out unsatisfied from the destruction of heavy dishes, and glared with watchful eyes upon the pastry" (271). In *Refugee in America* and *Martin Chuzzlewit*, we see wives and landladies rushing back and forth constantly waiting on tables, until Dickens is provoked to admit, "What Mrs. Pawlish felt each day at dinner time is hidden from all human knowledge. But she had one comfort. It was soon over" (272).

Other than "in seeking and bringing whatever [food] the party required," American women are shown languishing in the background of each plot (*Refugee* 1: 61). Dickens comments that American women

were strangely devoid of individual traits of character, insomuch that any one of them might have changed minds with the others, and nobody would have found it out. [They]...were the only members of the party who did not appear to be among the most remarkable people in the country. (*Chuzzlewit* 272)

When Dickens's American women leave a room, their men react "as if a great weight had been taken off their minds by the withdrawal of the other sex" (*Chuzzlewit* 273). In *Refugee*, Caroline Gordon complains to her father that all American women "talk of nothing but 'helps,' and the 'last sermon' " (2: 105); when Caroline asks an American patriot, "how you manage to reconcile your theory of freedom, with the condition of your negroes? or your treatment of the Indians, with your doctrine of equal rights," Mr. Warner replies, "these subjects are considerable much beyond the scope of the female" (1: 161). On another occasion, when Mr. Gordon brings his daughter Caroline and Madame de Clairville to join a party of American men in conversation, Trollope reports that "he found their whole manner changed, and it was perfectly evident that the presence of ladies rendered it impossible in their opinion, to continue the conversation in the same strain...as to bringing any intellect into a discourse with ladies, that was quite out of the question" (3: 94-95).

In both novels America's male-dominated society seems overrun with colonels, squires, congressmen and other "important" figures. In *Martin Chuzzlewit*, "Martin found that there were no fewer than four majors present, two colonels, one general, and a captain, so that he could not help thinking how strongly officered the American militia must be" (272). These distinguished individuals pontificate to their British guests on American virtues and American values. After Martin joins the Eden Land Corporation, the "General" tells him, "You air now, sir, a denizen of the most powerful and highly-civilized do-minion that has ever graced the world; a do-minion, sir, where man is bound in one vast bond of equal love and truth. May you, sir, be worthy of your a-dopted country!" (358). In *The Refugee in America*, Squire Burns tells the Gordons, "...what a glory of a paradise they [English visitors] find here...we ask no more of a man, let him come from what country he will, than just to own that we are first and foremost; and after that, we grant him freedom to keep the rest of his thoughts to himself" (1: 61).

This New World paradise that such men as Trollope's Squire Burns and Colonel Smith, or Dickens's Colonel Diver and Major Pawkins, proudly defend as the epitome of freedom and equality embraces a problematic, yet thriving, institution—slavery. In *Refugee* Caroline Gordon is confronted with slavery's brutality as she learns that Colonel Smith cannot meet with herself and her father until he finishes "flogging Becky" (3: 166). Caroline hears a powerful legislator explain that the subject of slavery is no more fit for congressional debate than she had earlier found it to be for discussion in the drawing room, "The question of negro slavery," a career-minded Congressman explains, "is one which none but a set of associational fanatics can blunder upon..." (3: 86). So, too, in *Martin Chuzzlewit*, Mark Tapley is bewildered to talk to a slave who has had to buy his own freedom and now is working to buy that of his daughter; Mark comments to Martin that people are "so fond of Liberty in this part of the globe, that they buy her and sell her and carry her to market with 'em. They've such a passion for Liberty, that they can't help taking liberties with her" (283). Mark and Martin also witness the refusal of American government to end the abuses of slavery; in fact, they see a constitutional Judge commended for having

laid down from the Bench the noble principle that it was lawful for any white mob to murder any black man...[and for] aiding the enforcement of those free and equal laws, which render it incalculably more criminal and dangerous to teach a negro to read and write than to roast him alive in a public city. (362)

The subject of slavery in the United States is one that Frances Trollope had confronted directly and fully in *Jonathan Jefferson Whitlaw* (1836) seven years before *Martin Chuzzlewit*'s publication. Lynch law, slave uprisings, mob violence, the criminality of reading on the part of a slave, or teaching a slave to read or write on the part of whites, all had been vividly dramatized in Trollope's popular work, the first British or American novel to protest American slavery (Heineman, *The Triumphant* 143). In *The Barnabys in America; or, Adventures of the Widow Wedded* (1843), Frances Trollope would continue to confront the brutality of this American institution, as well as many of the other problems she had found in the United States in the early 1830s. It is this novel, *The Barnabys in America*, that Frances Trollope had just finished publishing in monthly installments as Dickens was issuing his *Martin Chuzzlewit*, also in monthly parts. Helen Heineman speculates that "the success of [Mrs. Trollope's novel] perhaps set Dickens to thinking when his *Chuzzlewit* sales began to drop. Hoping to spark interest and increase sales, he, like Mrs. Trollope before him, sent the hero on his travels to America" (Heineman, *The Triumphant* 209). Again, Mrs. Trollope's distinctive vision of America finds many echoes in Dickens's *Chuzzlewit*.

Upon the Barnabys' arrival in the New World, they find Americans to be "everyone of them...cheats" and "vain peacocks," (*Barnabys in America* 2: 25), just as Martin Chuzzlewit finds every American (except Mr. Bevan) to be "greed personified...ambitious to outwit his fellows" (Meckier 57). The adventurous Mrs. Barnaby, like the inquisitive Mark Tapley, formulates polite but probing questions to provoke the responses of her American hosts, the intended readers of her forthcoming travel book on American society. She mischievously asks them to compare theory with practice in their democracy by setting before them this series of questions:

In what manner does the republican form of government appear to affect the social habits of the people?

How far does the absence of a national form of worship produce the results anticipated from it?
At what degree of elevation may the education of the ladies of the Union be considered to stand, when compared to that received by the females of other countries?
In what manner was slavery originally instituted?
And what are its real effects both on the black and the white population? (*Barnabys in America* 2: 32)

Predictably, Trollope's Wedded Widow receives braggadocio, not analysis, in answer to her questions. The Barnabys listen to Colonel Wingrove, a member of the American Congress, not merely defend but praise "the elegant luxury of owning a score of slaves" (*Barnabys in America* 2: 47). While Trollope's Louisiana plantation owners are shocked by the slave uprising which concludes the Barnabys' trip to America, that enterprising couple and the other British visitors in this novel are not at all surprised when they hear: "He [Colonel Beauchamp] has been dead this hour,...' returned the negro, casting down his eyes, but very nearly smiling at the same moment; 'and Judge Johnson,' he added, in the same respectful tone, 'has been done for longer still' " (*Barnabys in America* 3: 302). Nor is Mark Tapley in *Martin Chuzzlewit* shocked to hear a freed slave in New York tell the story of his "second master having his head cut open with a hatchet by another slave" (283). Both authors clearly sympathize with the rebelling slaves, as they do with the dismayed British visitors who escape back to the Old World in these novels, much in the same way as their disillusioned creators, Frances Trollope and Charles Dickens, did before them.

Frances Trollope had taken the lead not only in traveling to America and voicing her dismay with the "utopia" she had found there, but also in correcting what Charles Dickens would distort as her "English smugness" in favoring Britain over America (Meckier 100-01). Upon returning to England in 1832, Mrs. Trollope immediately began a career satirizing British society—as Dickens did, as well—including English evangelism in her novel *The Vicar of Wrexhill* (1837), British pretentiousness and social climbing in *Charles Chesterfield* (1840) and *The Blue Belles of England* (1840), as well as the exploitative British factory system, among other early subjects. Frances Trollope's *Michael Armstrong, The Factory Boy* (1839)—which had so annoyed Charles Dickens when it was advertised as a companion to *Pickwick Papers* and *Nicholas Nickleby*—began a whole series of attacks on the British industrial system in the 1840s and 1850s. The most famous of these industrial reform novels would include Dickens's own *Hard Times* (1854), 15 years after the publication of *Michael Armstrong*, along with Elizabeth Gaskell's *North and South* (1855) the next year and *Mary Barton* (1848) several years earlier (nine years after Trollope's *Michael Armstrong*). Frances Trollope once more had set a precedent in her choice of subject matter as well as in many of the particulars of her critique.

Frances Trollope's *Michael Armstrong* begins the pattern of the fictional heroine visiting the home of a laborer, understanding that the problems of working class drunkenness, demoralization and poverty are created by an inhumane system, not an inferior, slothful class of people. The heroine then serves to communicate a realistic and at the same time compassionate view of working conditions and industrial pollution in the novel—a paradigm which Dickens's *Hard Times* and Gaskell's *North and South* would later repeat. With Trollope's *Michael Armstrong* appears the romance of what Rosemarie Bodenheimer calls the "female knights errant," the story of a heroine who both nurtures and rescues (or attempts to do so) the working poor (even if she fails to reform the factory system itself) (Bodenheimer 25).

Mary Brotherton in *Michael Armstrong* visits the Armstrong home, is shocked at the family's poverty, and becomes emotionally entangled in their working-class lives. When Michael disappears, to be apprenticed in a cruelly inhumane Deep Valley mill, Mary takes a more adventurous, public course of action. She becomes involved in the Reverend Mr. Bell's Ten Hour Reform movement; searches widely for the unfortunate Michael; eventually rescues his co-worker Fanny Fletcher from Deep Valley; finds the escaped hero; moves Michael's crippled brother Edward, Michael Armstrong himself, and the happy Fanny Fletcher with her to the continent; educates them there; and, finally, marries Edward and lives out her married life under the same roof (her own roof) as the now betrothed Fanny and Michael. Frances Trollope concludes,

> Circumstances...had rendered her own country less dear to her than it is to most others; she therefore not only determined to plant herself elsewhere, but to do so in such a manner as would enable her to make her new abode her home, in the best sense of the word, and this could only be done by...mak[ing] it the home of others, also. (386)

Thus, the wealthy Mary Brotherton changes completely the lives and social status of three working class children. But what of the hundreds of other workers she has left behind her in the factories of England?

The plots of Dickens and Gaskell show a similar ambivalence. In Dickens's *Hard Times*, Sissy Jupe becomes, according to Walter Allen, "the moral center of the novel, the custodian of Dickens's values" (Allen xvii). Sissy, too, is a rescuer, confronting Louisa's seducer Harthouse, saving the unhappy Louisa Bounderby from disgrace at his hands, and helping Louisa's brother, Tom Gradgrind, avoid prosecution for robbery by arranging Tom's escape from England. Louisa, as well, plays her own female knights-errant role in the novel—visiting the laboring Stephen Blackpool's home in Coketown and consoling him as he lies injured, near death, after a fall down the Old Hell Shaft. But Blackpool dies, Coketown thrives, and the greedy mill-master Bounderby leaves behind him a will which continues his line through twenty-five clones who will live off his estate and carry on his selfish traditions: "the same precious will was to begin its long career of quibble, plunder, false pretences, vile example, little service and much law" (Dickens, *Hard Times* 282).

This authorial ambivalence towards the plight of workers continues in Gaskell's *North and South*. Margaret Hale befriends the family of Bessy and Nicholas Higgins, standing up to the proud mill owner Mr. Thornton on their behalf and on behalf of other workers, asking, "You consider all who are unsuccessful in raising themselves in the world, from whatever cause, as your enemies, then...?" to which Thornton replies, "As their own enemies, certainly..." (84). After protecting Thornton from rioters at his own mill, shielding him from a stone aimed at him, and being injured herself, Margaret Hale persists in arguing for greater compassion for his workers, eventually bringing Mr. Thornton together with one bright, independent worker, Nicholas Higgins, and uniting employer and employee in a closer working relationship. Finally, Margaret saves Mr. Thornton's factory itself by becoming its primary investor and agrees to marry (and continue her influence upon) the lovelorn millowner himself. Margaret has played an active, public role in befriending a working class family, converting a millowner, saving the mill from ruin, and creating within its doors a model of cooperation between labor and management. One mill has been modified and its workers' lives improved—as happens, as well, in Gaskell's earlier *Mary Barton* where millowner Mr. Carson learns compassion for Chartist union member John Barton—after widespread unemployment, poverty and disease have led Barton to intense hatred and to murder, eventually, of Carson's own son. *Mary Barton* concludes, as did *Michael Armstrong*, with Mary's emigration, this time to Canada rather than Mary Brotherton's Germany, away from the desperate streets and industrial misery of Britain to live out her life in exile with her family.

In all of these works, while a few are saved, the factory system grinds on, largely unchanged, with male owners remaining in control of their factories and their workers' lives. Critics primarily debate the degree to which these authors remained "patriarchal" despite their criticism of the factory system and the men who run it. P. J. Keating, in *The Working Classes in Victorian Fiction*, contends that British reform writers were

demanding a revolution in class relationships without any alteration in the balance of power. By personalyzing class conflict and placing blame on the human failings of individual employers and employees, sympathy is aroused for the workers' appalling conditions without this being taken to imply that there is anything fundamentally wrong with the social structure as a whole. (227-28)

Nancy Armstrong agrees, arguing that both Gaskell and Dickens (and she would no doubt add, Frances Trollope) actually worked to suppress political resistance while touting the domestic antidote of personal love and caring relationships (163; 48). Rosemarie Bodenheimer speaks of Gaskell and Trollope's "romance of the female paternalist" (22) while David Roberts, in *Paternalism in Early Victorian England*, argues that "[they] fall back on the tradition of paternalism.... For Mrs. Trollope that better scheme was a paternalist one, a position Mrs. Gaskell also came to, but more reluctantly..." (90).

To conclude that these writers remain essentially "paternalistic," however, is to distort much of their fictional critique. All three writers clearly were disillusioned with patriarchy. What seems most obvious in the works of each is a world of failed fathers. In *Hard Times*, Sissy Jupe's father has disappeared; Louisa Gradgrind's father, on the other hand, has been all too present, too controlling, schooling his children to destroy their sensitive, creative imaginations in favor of "hard" facts. Mr. Bounderby has given birth not to natural children but to 25 most unnatural facsimiles who will spread his contamination even further in the world. In *Mary Barton*, John Barton ignores his daughter and grows more and more angry, more vengeful, after the death of his wife and the loss of her soothing influence. Mr. Carson, too, fails his family, indirectly bringing about the death of his own son by ignoring the plight of the laid-off workers in his mill. In *North and South*, as well, Mr. Hale fails to father his family properly, resigning his ministry because of doubt in the authority of God (the ultimate Father); abandoning responsibility for the move of his household from Helstone to Milton; and, more importantly, neglecting his responsibility for the emotional welfare of his wife in this time of family turmoil—leaving everything in the care of his 18-year-old daughter Margaret.[2] In Milton, Mr. Hale's failure is compounded by that of Mr. Thornton, who does not properly value and care for his workers any more than does Mr. Carson in *Mary Barton*.

Mr. Thornton's transgressions, however, do not begin to compare with those of another millowner, Martha Dowling's father, in Frances Trollope's *Michael Armstrong*. It is Sir Matthew Dowling's cruelty to the young Michael which first causes his loving daughter Martha to feel pain—and enables her to be converted by another abusive millowner's daughter, Mary Brotherton. Both daughters come to understand that the insensitivity and human cruelty of their own fathers (although Mary Brotherton's father is now deceased) symbolize that of the factory system at large.

Indeed, in all these works, fathers fail their families and their societies—largely by having eliminated the female, the nurturing and compassionate, sides of their own personalities. Gradgrind insists on "hard facts"; Sir Dowling is actively cruel to Michael Armstrong and to the many children who work in his factory; Bounderby lies about and rejects his own mother to make his greedy way up in the world; Mr. Hale and Mr. Thornton falter from goodness by emphasizing the rational, the orderly and the male in the lessons and conversations they share; John Barton shuts himself off from tenderness and love after his wife's death. Ironically, fathers are seen to fail because they have become too masculine—too cut off from their female qualities, their female partners and counterparts—just as are the millowners from their workers. The separate spheres of the sexes parallel the separation of the rich from the poor, the employer from the employee, the north from the south, those "unholy division[s]" of industrial Britain lamented by Mary Brotherton in *Michael Armstrong* (137).

Thus, all of these writers *do* critique the patriarchy, placing value on the lost feminine in the industrial world order. However, Dickens, who perhaps most valued the power of the (female) imagination over (male) reason and most longed for a female balance to be restored to a heartless world, could least afford to fantasize alternatives to patriarchy. Part of his claim to importance as a social critic in a field dominated by women, as Jerome Meckier has pointed out, depended on his gender—his being male, logical, unemotional, superior in his talents and in his vision of the world (122).

Hard Times, not surprisingly, becomes the most despairing of all the works here considered. No lasting change is affected (or even attempted) in Bounderby's factory through the events of the novel. Parliament maintains its bureaucratic function as "the national cinder-heap," with "national dustmen" (195) continuing to "entertain one another with a great many noisy little fights among themselves" (204). Mr. Gradgrind has repented the way in which he has schooled his own, and other, children—Stephen has become a thief; Louisa is separated from her husband—but his teaching lives on, most notably in the enterprising young Bitzer who has learned all too well that "the whole social system is a question of self-interest" (273).

Further, Nancy Armstrong suggests that Dickens's conclusion to *Hard Times* actually participates in further containing the female as an active force in the world. She believes that Dickens's resolution "subjugat[es] the female...[he] returns Louisa to her father in a state of infantile dependency...exalting the passive woman and ridding the world of all active female desire" (Armstrong 55). Louisa may be an emotional catalyst for other characters in *Hard Times*, but she is to remain isolated and unfulfilled under her father's roof. Sissy, whom Walter Allen calls the novel's "moral center," is given a little more liberty—but that freedom is contained fully within the traditional female sphere (Allen xvii). Unlike Louisa, Sissy will have children; she will love them and teach them to think

no innocent and pretty fancy ever to be despised; trying hard to know her humbler fellow-creatures, and to beautify their lives of machinery and reality with those imaginative graces and delights without which the heart of infancy will wither up, the sturdiest physical manhood will be morally stark death, and the plainest national prosperity figures can show will be the Writing on the Wall. (283-84)

Sissy would help her family and her fellow townspeople endure (but not change) life's miseries and the squalor of Coketown. As with her creator, the imaginative Dickens himself, Sissy can brighten and decorate lives; she cannot alter them.

In Dickens's *Hard Times*, the emphasis of the novel remains on the world of the fathers, failed fathers though they may be—on the Bounderbys and on the Gradgrinds, their grand schemes and the ruination they bring to others. In Frances Trollope's *Michael Armstrong*, as Susan Morgan has said of Elizabeth Gaskell's *Mary Barton* and *North and South*, the world of the failed fathers has been replaced by that of the daughters (Morgan 101). In the three industrial novels of Gaskell and Trollope, all the fathers die—John Barton, Mr. Hale, Sir Matthew Dowling and Mr. Brotherton. In contrast, Trollope's and Gaskell's daughters persist and thrive at the end of these works. Mary Barton acts as a benign influence on millowner Carson before leaving to raise her own family in Canada, far from the injustices of England. Margaret Hale has inherited Mr.

Bell's money and become the largest investor in Mr. Thornton's factory—more powerful, by far, than her father had ever been. And Mary Brotherton has accomplished the rescue of workers Michael, Edward and Fanny, creating with her companions an alternative world on the continent. Mary Brotherton has learned first from the Reverend Mr. Bell (Gaskell would repeat the name of Trollope's Reverend Mr. Bell and, as Donald Stone points out [138], of Mr. Thornton in *North and South*—the name of the kindly master Michael Armstrong works for after he leaves Deep Valley) (Trollope, *Michael Armstrong* 203), and later Mary learned from her own experiences, the essential lesson that unfortunate circumstances and a lack of education are all that separate the lower from the upper classes. Mary alters both the circumstances and the education of Michael, Edward, and Fanny.

Thus, Gaskell's and Trollope's daughters act to alleviate social injustices and to find or create alternative communities. As they do so, they seek to change the relationship between the sexes as they have wished to alter that between the classes, between employers and employees, in their novels. Each heroine of *Mary Barton*, *North and South* and *Michael Armstrong* has married (except the secondary heroine Martha Dowling in *Michael Armstrong*), but each has also rescued her husband: Jem from the hands of the law in *Mary Barton*; Mr. Thornton from the loss of his factory in *North and South*; and Edward Armstrong from working class poverty and ignorance in *Michael Armstrong*. In each case, then, a balance of power has been achieved in the relationship between the sexes. Each heroine has led as active, independent, and courageous a life as has her husband—and Mary Brotherton and Margaret Hale have the further advantage of their wealth to counterbalance their husbands' gender privilege.

Elizabeth Gaskell's novels generally have been seen as more realistic and more willing to engage with the problems of industrial reform than either Dickens's or Trollope's. Critic Angus Easson argues that Mrs. Trollope tended to ignore the "larger issues of capital and labour, of adult workers, or the real complications of the system" (66). While favoring violence as a solution no more than Dickens or Trollope, Gaskell at least has scenes of worker gatherings, union organizing, and physical confrontations between employees and employers. Further, she suggests that women can come to play an active role in the operation of factories, first through economic investment, and secondly and most importantly, as the not-so-silent partners who stand in front of, not behind, their husbands, sons, or brothers to further labor negotiations and humane factory practices. The role of Gaskell's heroines here is to help promote "the process of accommodation and...[the] avoidance of the fervor of revolt. For here there is no fantasy of rebellion, subversion, or a separated woman's world; she imagines a negotiated settlement that asserts a power of choice even in the acceptance of dependence" (Bodenheimer 63). It is not that Gaskell had no such fantasies; her separate female sphere had already been worked out beautifully elsewhere, in Miss Matty's gentle world of *Cranford* (1853).

Gaskell, then, "feminizes" the industrial worlds of *Mary Barton* and *North and South* through accommodation, accepting female and/or worker dependence on male husbands or millowners. Not so in Frances Trollope's *Michael Armstrong*. The resolution of Trollope's novel, seen at times as "paternalistic" and as the most ineffectual of all these works' conclusions, may, in fact, be the most radical of all. It is true of *Michael Armstrong* that Trollope's "dramatically staged female subversions finally fail to engage with the novel's emphatically male structures of power," but accommodation is not their intent (Bodenheimer 35). Mary Brotherton does leave behind her an enlightened heroine, Martha Dowling; a practical reform movement which both Mary and Michael Armstrong have worked to further (the Ten Hour Law movement—one which Charles Dickens had never supported) (Brantlinger 44); and the more humane mill of WOOD AND WALKER as a model of industrial practice (Trollope, *Michael Armstrong* 221). Yet Trollope did not share Gaskell's desire to moderate the existing system, a solution she found personally unsatisfying. By the time she published *Michael Armstrong*, she was, after all, 60 years old— and the process Gaskell advocates in *North and South* would necessitate a long and difficult—perhaps impossible—course of action.

Instead, Trollope's Mary Brotherton abandons her decadent and corrupt homeland as a place she can no longer hold "dear" (*Michael Armstrong* 386). In Germany, Mary creates a new "home," away from the world of failed fathers, a separate, feminized sphere—at once the most fantastic and escapist, as well as the most radical, plot of all. In setting up her own home on the continent, creating her own family, and nurturing its members through her "ample heart...[and] ample purse," Mary Brotherton attempts not merely to escape her society's injustices, in the manner of Gaskell's Mary Barton, but to create a model culture (*Michael Armstrong* 386). Her utopian community—one where she has, at times, been seen as playing out "the romance of the female paternalist" who is now at the helm herself, determining the lives of her grateful, converted workers (Bodenheimer 22)—seems curiously detached from the political revolts and disputes erupting everywhere on the continent at that time. We know only one thing about her world—something so difficult to comprehend that the narrator merely intimates its occurrence for fear that it will "provoke incredulity" in the reader (*Michael Armstrong* 386). In this world of possibility, Mary Brotherton has fashioned a permanent solution to the divided British nations of rich and poor. She has intermarried the two classes and, in this lasting way, altered forever the relationship between them. Further, she has provided her workers with the education which she finds can alone elevate and empower them as individuals in the world.

Nor is the resolution to *Michael Armstrong* pure fantasy on the author's part. As we have seen in their industrial reform novels, Dickens relegated women to a minor political role, while Gaskell attempted to modify the traditional, female role to allow women a secondary partnership with men. But Frances Trollope gave her heroine Mary Brotherton the same personal independence, social autonomy, and political vision she would come to enjoy herself. Frances Trollope would leave England for the continent. She would establish a home there, with separate living quarters within its walls for her son Tom and his family (as Mary and Edward include Michael and Fanny), and she would do so with her own money—money earned from novels such as *Michael Armstrong*, rather than from inherited wealth, such as Mary Brotherton's. The Trollope home in Florence, Italy, would be at once a sphere as separate as Mary Brotherton's German "paradise" (*Michael Armstrong* 386) from industrial injustices and social revolutions fermenting on all sides and, at the same time, a world as richly shared with others—with the British artists and writers of many nationalities, and, much to Elizabeth Barrett Browning's dismay (although she and her husband came to find Mrs. Trollope herself "very agreeable, and kind, and good-natured"), a world shared with all sorts of people, "the full flood and flow of Florentine society" (Browning, "To Mrs. Martin" [1851] 475-76).

Nor was Frances Trollope herself a "female paternalist" who delighted in wielding power over her dependents or in enslaving them into her service. Her son Thomas Adolphus Trollope remembered his life with his mother as richly full, a life which was very much as he wanted it to be, "very happy—I fear I may say...exceptionally happy" (*What I Remember* 248). Frances Trollope's influence on her companion son was as freeing and as enriching as Mary Brotherton's is intended to be on her former dependents, now her friends, relatives, and social equals, at the end of *Michael Armstrong*. Both Mary Brotherton and her creator designed "feminized" worlds where value is placed on the female, on art and on culture, on love shared between men and women. As Thomas Trollope remembered of his mother,

> She was, I think, to an exceptional degree surrounded by very many friends, mostly women, but including many men, at every period of her life. She was, during all her life, full of, and fond of, fun; had an exquisite sense of humor; and at all times valued her friends and acquaintances more exclusively, I think, than most people do, for their intrinsic qualities, mainly those of the heart, and not so much perhaps intellect...as brightness. (*What I Remember* 490)

After first imagining her model social structure at the end of *Michael Armstrong*, Frances Trollope fled England to bring about her own new world in Florence, Italy.

Harriet Beecher Stowe, who was welcomed to Frances Trollope's home in Florence in 1860, would become another important author of the period—an American author—who would create a "feminized" world similar to those of Gaskell and Trollope (Wilson 451). Stowe's novel, *Uncle Tom's Cabin*, not only shares an emphasis on human feeling and human justice with Frances Trollope's writings but much more that would suggest the possibility of direct inspiration from that older, influential writer. The very year Harriet Beecher Stowe moved to Cincinnati, 1832, seems significant. As one Stowe biographer reports, "Mrs. Frances Trollope was Cincinnati's obsession in 1832. In the spring she had brought out her *Domestic Manners of the Americans*" criticizing the city of Cincinnati itself (Wilson 103). As a new arrival to the more rough and crude Midwest from her childhood East, Harriet Beecher Stowe might have appreciated many of Trollope's views of Cincinnati life. Harold H. Scudder would later comment that, four years afterwards, by the time Frances Trollope wrote her anti-slavery novel *Jonathan Jefferson Whitlaw* in 1836, she was "probably better known in America, than any other woman in England" (46).

Thus, it would have been very difficult for as knowledgeable and alert a social critic as Harriet Beecher Stowe would prove herself to be, to have remained totally ignorant of Frances Trollope's name, her response to America's overtly masculine, violent society, as well as her early anti-slavery writings in *Domestic Manners of the Americans, Refugee in America*, as well as the later *Jonathan Jefferson Whitlaw*. If literary critic Harold Scudder found it difficult in 1944 to understand why Mrs. Stowe had made no mention of Frances Trollope's *Jonathan Jefferson Whitlaw* in her letters and other writings, he found it even more remarkable that her biographers would accomplish the "rather difficult achievement" of ignoring the many obvious connnections between Frances Trollope's earlier novel and Stowe's *Uncle Tom's Cabin* published 15 years later (46). Today he would still find it difficult to comprehend the continued silence on the subject by subsequent biographers and critics of Harriet Beecher Stowe.

In 1944 Scudder instanced 11 different correlaries between Trollope's *Jonathan Jefferson Whitlaw* and Stowe's *Uncle Tom's Cabin*. Among the most important of these were the two cruel slave overseers, Jonathan Jefferson Whitlaw and Simon Legree; the escaped young slave women, Phebe and Emmeline; the powerful, older slave women, the *"deae ex machinae"* of the novels' resolutions, both of whom play upon the superstitions and fears of their white masters; the sons of bankrupt Kentucky slaveowners who search for their fathers' former slaves (George Shelby for Uncle Tom, Edward Bligh for Phebe); and the emigration of Stowe's ex-slaves to Canada, France, and then Africa, and of Trollope's to Germany (Scudder 46-68).

To examine just one of the similarities Scudder has noted is to understand the close relationship of Trollope's and Stowe's works. Frances Trollope's Juno, now an elderly woman, had been born into a French Creole family where she was taught to read and did so widely, through the New Orleans lending library. Because "dancing and music masters luckily both declared that they could by no means consent to such unwanted degredation [as to teach a Creole child]....Juno escaped the danger of becoming 'elegantly accomplished' " (*Jonathan Jefferson Whitlaw* 2: 4). Juno's remarkable powers of mind, then, were the result of her extensive reading and her close observation of human nature. The narrator of *Jonathan Jefferson Whitlaw* comments, "if all who undertook to rule their fellows studied the ins and outs of human feelings as patiently as old Juno, power as gigantic as Napolean's might perhaps be seen to sweep over the earth oftener than once in half a dozen centuries" (2: 2-3). Since slaves were forbidden to read and write, Juno gained a reputation for extraordinary, mystical powers—a reputation she encouraged in order to frighten Colonel Dart and outmaneuver his cruel overseer Jonathan Jefferson Whitlaw. When Baron Steinmark expresses his dismay at Juno's deceitful ways, she replies,

"And I would to heaven master...that the same freedom of spirit, and that power which the white man has of doing his will openly, belonged to me, as it does to you! then old Juno would leave off her tricks, and never again try to seem other than the poor old cripple she is. But it would not do, master; Juno would lose all her power of doing good." (2: 169)

And so Juno uses her cunning to aid runaway slaves, helping Phebe and Caesar in their flight. However, after Jonathan Jefferson Whitlaw has caused her granddaughter Selina Croft to commit suicide and helped to hang Edward Bligh, Juno seeks revenge. She tries to get Edward's black Christian followers to rebel against Whitlaw—but to no avail. Finally, Juno outwits Whitlaw, coaxes him into her trap, and has four willing male slaves carry out his murder.

In *Uncle Tom's Cabin* Stowe's Cassy, too, is a murderer. She has killed her infant son rather than see him go through the torture of family separation and abuse experienced by her first two children. Stowe tells us Cassy would murder again if she could, "...Cassy had often resolved in her soul an hour of retribution, when her hand should avenge on her oppressor all the injustice and cruelty to which she had been witness, or which she had in her own person suffered" (398). When, aged and wrinkled, Cassy tries to encourage Uncle Tom to kill Simon Legree for her—"I'd a done it myself, only my arms are so weak"—he refuses to betray his Christian beliefs (398). Cassy finds she must use her head, and not her hands, as her weapon of revenge—as Trollope's Juno discovered before her. Like Juno, too, Cassy had been "a woman delicately bred," the daughter of a white slave master and a black woman who had raised her "in luxury...learn[ing] music, French and embroidery" (363). Simon Legree has come to fear Cassy's intelligence and her cunning—a fear she heightens by warning him, "I've got the devil in me!" (371). As Stowe explains, "No one is so thoroughly superstitious as the godless man"—and Legree becomes easy prey, as was the godless Whitlaw for Trollope's Juno (403).Through "the game that Cassy played with Legree...he would sooner have put his head into a lion's mouth than to have explored the garret" where Cassy and Emmeline would go to hide (406). Thus, Cassy skillfully outwits Legree and enables the innocent Emmeline and herself to escape his cruelty forever.

Harold Scudder also noted other, lesser parallels between *Uncle Tom's Cabin* and its predecessor *Jonathan Jefferson Whitlaw*. He discussed similar scenes (the wilderness wood-fueling stations and the New Orleans milieu of each work); the rescue of Caesar by the German Steinmark family and of George Harris by the Dutchman Van Trompe; the near-white Eliza and her counterpart Selina Croft who both "pass" as white in their respective novels; as well as New Orleans brawl scenes in which Trollope's Whitlaw is threatened and Stowe's St. Clare is stabbed to death. More importantly, Scudder remarked on the presence of a martyr figure in each work, the white Edward Bligh in *Jonathan Jefferson Whitlaw* and the black Tom in *Uncle Tom's Cabin*—men who give up their lives in order to reveal the higher order of their Christian principles and the earthly injustices of the cruel slave system, despite their fates.

Critic Helen Heineman contrasts Trollope's novels with Stowe's in one important area. Trollope as a novelist, she says, was more "interested in this earth, not in the kingdom of heaven" (*Frances Trollope* 68). Heineman suggests that

Frances Trollope would have had no use for Mrs. Stowe's Uncle Tom who dies forgiving his tormentor, with the author's obvious approbation. Mrs. Trollope's principal slave [Juno] fights back, and with four helpers she recruited from among those not persuaded by Christian teachings, ambushes Whitlaw, and brutally assassinates him. (*The Triumphant* 147)

Frances Trollope's anti-slavery novel ends with a violent slave uprising and the successful murder of the novel's unjust slave overseer.

Yet, *Jonathan Jefferson Whitlaw* is, first and foremost, Heineman contends, a "woman's book [in which] a black woman avenges a terrible injustice, and a white woman [Clio Whitlaw] has the opportunity to set things right again. Was ever wish-fulfillment more graphically rendered?" (*The Triumphant* 148). Frances Trollope's novel denounces Colonel Dart's Paradise Plantation, where 500 slaves are overseen by Jonathan Jefferson Whitlaw. Trollope contrasts Paradise Plantation with a true utopian community,

Reichland, property of the German Baron Steinmark and family, worked by its non slave-owning proprietors. There family members share labor, and the resulting scene— prosperous, green, and flourishing —is the book's real paradise. (*The Triumphant* 145)

Eventually, Trollope's ideal society must be transported from American soil back to Germany, incorporating into its midst the slave couple Phebe and Caesar, just as *Michael Armstrong*'s Mary Brotherton must also establish her own egalitarian community in Germany, away from Britain's enslaving industrial and class system, in Trollope's other well-known social justice novel of the period. In both of these works, altruistic women (Clio Whitlaw in *Jonathan Jefferson Whitlaw* and Martha Dowling in *Michael Armstrong*) are left behind to plant the seeds of human kindness and to encourage feminine nurturing on soil traditionally unreceptive to the spirit of cooperation and community. Meanwhile, Frances Trollope establishes fully harmonious, egalitatian societies, embracing both sexes, contrasting social classes, and differing races, to flourish outside the English-speaking world.

Similarly, in *Uncle Tom's Cabin*, Harriet Beecher Stowe created her own woman's novel emphasizing a utopian, female-centered world. According to Elizabeth Ammons, in *Uncle Tom's Cabin* Stowe sought

to convert those in power—white men (and the women with influence on them)—away from the partriarchal institution, slavery, which she associated with the devil, toward a new social ideal, one associated with the mother-Christ and manifest miraculously in the little girl Eva, the black man Tom, and the strong Quaker mother Rachel Halliday. (170)

Ammons suggests that Uncle Tom is characterized in Stowe's novel "as a stereotypical Victorian heroine: pious, home-centered, self-sacrificing, non-violent"—values that are further manifest in the serene kitchen of the Quaker Rachel Halliday (167-68). Ellen Moers and Gillian Brown agree on the important role Rachel Halliday plays in the novel—and the importance of her world of "mother-rule...and domestic economy" to Stowe's philosophy (Brown 522).[3]

Trollope's Juno looks on while male slaves murder Whitlaw in *Jonathan Jefferson Whitlaw* (1836).

Harriet Beecher Stowe counterbalances the unjust rule of the fathers in American society with the petticoat politics of her home-centered women, as when Mrs. Bird challenges Senator Bird after Congress has passed the Fugitive Slave Act of 1850:

"...is it true that you have been passing a law forbidding people to give meat and drink to those poor colored folks that come along?....You ought to be ashamed, John. Poor, homeless, houseless creatures. It's a shameful, wicked, abominable law, and I'll break it, for one, the first time I get a chance; and I hope I *still* have a chance, I do. Things have got to a pretty pass, if a woman can't give a warm supper and a bed to poor, starving creatures, just because they are slaves, and have been abused and oppressed all their lives, poor things...I tell you, folks don't run away when they are happy; and when they do run, poor creatures! they suffer enough with cold and hunger and fear, without everybody's turning against them, and law or no law, I never will, so help me God!" (*Uncle Tom's Cabin* 81-83)

Female rebellion against institutionalized injustice lies at the heart of Stowe's authorship and at the heart of her most famous piece of fiction, as well.

In *Uncle Tom's Cabin,* Stowe's world of failed fathers is reformed by assertive wives and mothers who refuse to accept that inhumanity could be legitimate or legal. Dorothy Berkson argues that Stowe's vision in *Uncle Tom's Cabin* is of a "new society that will result from this wedding of Christian and feminine virtures....[a society that will be] communal, anti-materialistic, non-competitive, racially tolerant, and essentially classless. It will be a society governed by the same principles that govern the loving, well-ordered family" (245). Harriet Beecher Stowe and Frances Trollope before her both argue in their anti-slavery novels that "the domestic model projects a political model of nationhood" (Sundquist 23). Stowe's Mrs. Shelby, Rachel Halliday, Eva, Lucy, Eliza Harris, Cassy, Mrs. Bird, and others in a fictional world Ellen Moers has characterized as richly filled with memorable females, "show that what women are, what women do in their 'merely' domestic lives will affect the great struggle for abolition" (22). In both *Uncle Tom's Cabin* and *Jonathan Jefferson Whitlaw*, the private world becomes public, and the domestic, political. The world of failed fathers once more is indicted for not valuing the female, for not being more feminine, for not becoming fully human. Alike in so many particulars of their plots, *Jonathan Jefferson Whitlaw* and its successor 15 years later, *Uncle Tom's Cabin*, essentially agree that the values left at home in the care of women must be restored to the halls of government and the stalls of the marketplace—and that women must take the lead if true community is ever to be established there.

When we come to the last author to be considered, Anthony Trollope, it should not be strange to find, then, certain familiar features which would distinguish his writing from other male authors of the period: "In [his] delightfully topsy-turvy world women are by far the stronger sex," according to U. C. Knoepflmacher, and not at all "those delicate self-effacing creatures we associate with Victorian womanhood" (35). Knoepflmacher argues that Anthony Trollope owed this vision of woman to the personality of "his formidable mother" (111). What is surprising is the way in which Knoepflmacher and other critics have ignored the literary connections between the writings of Frances Trollope and those of her son Anthony (while dwelling on the familial ones). Very few critics have discussed the similarities of the two authors' fictional worlds (most seem unaware even of the existence of Frances Trollope's novels) and seldom have these connections been examined in any depth.

As we found earlier, critics who deal with Frances Trollope's relationship to her son usually tend to do so in order to place the blame upon her for Anthony's childhood suffering. In 1971 James Pope Hennessy voiced many of these criticisms in his study, *Anthony Trollope*, repeating the suggestion that Frances Trollope had abandoned Anthony when she came to America, that later in life she made her eldest son Tom into her "substitute husband" (51), that she had been a "warm-hearted, illogical, and impetuous [wife while her husband Mr. Trollope] was chilling and rational, cold and phlegmatic" (36). Hennessy believes that Anthony "admired but had had little opportunity to love" (59) his mother—a woman he feels most failed her son by being "a restless rather than a restful mother" (36).

Although we can never know exactly what Anthony Trollope felt about his mother (undoubtedly it was a complex mix of emotions), we do know that she very much affected the course of his life in a positive way. She obtained for him his lifelong job with the post office; employed him as an emissary between herself and her publisher Bentley for several years; and helped him get his first novel published—although the publisher "tried to pass off this unknown writer's novel as a new book from the pen of Anthony's mother, the well-established and popular Mrs. Trollope herself" (Skelton 1).

It is almost certain that, in this period of his early twenties, Anthony read his mother's novels as well as the letters (with their impressive publishing facts and figures) as he carried them back and forth between his mother and the Bentley offices.[4] In his *Autobiography*, Anthony would acknowledge that he came to belong "to the [literary] guild through my mother" (76); however, he would find her profession a difficult one. As he admitted:

I know how utterly I should have failed myself had my bread not been earned elsewhere while I was making my efforts. During ten years of work, which I commenced with some aid from the fact that others of my family were in the same profession, I did not earn enough to buy me the pens, ink, and paper which I was using. (193-94)

Far from being aloof from her youngest son's literary ambitions, Frances Trollope seemed quite concerned about his well-being and sensitive to his aspirations for success in a profession she, too (despite her prominence), had found very cruel. The result, according to Helen Heineman, was "the bitterest satire she was ever to write" (*The Triumphant* 199).

Frances Trollope's *Charles Chesterfield: or the Adventures of a Youth of Genius* and *The Blue Belles of England* (1840-41) comprise a fictional transformation of her fears about Anthony....She knew that her son too dreamed of being "a writer of novels" and felt himself "destined to immortalize himself by his pen" (*CC* 1: 88). These two books are as much a sign of her maternal concern for her youngest son as were the hours spent at his bedside [during his puzzling illness in the summer of 1840] during their months of composition. (*The Triumphant* 199)

Anthony Trollope clearly desired to follow in his mother's footsteps; her influence upon his life was immense.

So, too, was his mother's influence upon his writing. While only a few critics have noted similarities between Frances Trollope's works and those of her son, most frequent have been the comparisons between Anthony's travel book on American society, *North America*, and his mother's *Domestic Manners of the Americans*. Anthony Trollope, like Charles Dickens, had come to America expecting to be more favorably impressed by the country than his mother had been, prepared to "correct" her "emotional" attacks and err on the side of logic and generosity. Instead, as James Pope Hennessy aptly notes, Frances Trollope's criticisms became "elegant arrow-shafts" next to the "thundering broadsides" of her own son (222). Comparisons of the two writers' novels, however, have been far less frequent. Robert Lee Wolff has noted that both Frances Trollope and her son caricatured living clergy in their works— Mrs. Trollope, J.W. Cunningham, Vicar of Harrow, in *The Vicar of Wrexhill* (1837) and, in *The Warden*, Anthony portrays three "well-known contemporary bishops, each with the same first name as the bishops whose attitudes and behavior he is intended to satirize" (Wolff 7-8).[5] Wolff further suggests that it is Mrs. Trollope's Cartwright in *The Vicar of Wrexhill* who became

the forerunner of all the hypocritical and untrustworthy Low-Clergymen of Victorian fiction, notably including Mrs. Trollope's own son Anthony's Obadiah Slope in *Barchester Towers* (1853) [sic]: they usually have Old Testament first names (Cartwright's is Jacob); they are not gentlemen socially; they are often repulsive physically. But women...fall in love with their amiable and oily manners. (Wolff 208)

Another critic has pointed out specific parallels between the works of mother and son. Helen Heineman has discussed the way in which the Widow Barnaby became a forerunner of her son's Mrs. Proudie (as well as Thackeray's Becky Sharp); Mrs. Sherbourne in *Charles Chesterfield* (1840-41) the model for Lady Carbury in *The Way We Live Now* (1875); Mrs. Gardiner-Stewart in *The Blue Belles* (1840-41) the predecessor of Signora Neroni in *Barchester Towers* (1857); Mrs. Trollope's sympathetic fortune hunters in *Blue Belles* the prototypes of Arabella Trefoil in *The American Senator* (1877); and Mr. Wentworth of *One Fault* (1839) the precursor of Louis Trevelyan of *He Knew He Was Right* (1869)—both works studies of the "obsessive temperament" known so well to Frances in her husband and to Anthony in his father (*The Triumphant* 158-89; 201; 192).

It is especially, as Helen Heineman has noted, Anthony's female characters who have been influenced by his mother's portrayals:

Alone among the great male writers of his century, Anthony produced vibrant, robust, and complex female characters—one has only to recall Lady Carbury, Madame Max Goesler, Mrs. Winifred Hurtle, Arabella Trefoil, Violet Effingham, and of course, the great Lady Glencora. What has escaped attention is the degree to which he drew his inspiration for these ladies from his own indomitable mother and the triumphant females with whom she populated her many novels. (*The Triumphant* 201)

One recent study of Anthony Trollope's female characters, Deborah Denenholz Morse's *Women in Trollope's Palliser Novels* (1987), makes no mention at all of Frances Trollope, her fiction, or her heroines. Jane Nardin's *He Knew She Was Right: The Independent Woman in the Novels of Anthony Trollope* (1989) is more sensitive to the importance of this remarkable mother-son relationship, noting Anthony's "unresolved ambivalence" towards women, his "return repeatedly to the frustration of ambitious women trapped by the very views of feminine nature he sometimes defends" (11). Nardin believes that, while Anthony in his own conformist marriage attempted to revise the ending to his parents' traditional marriage to make it turn out properly, it was "through his mother [that] he learned to look beneath the conventional surface a woman presents to the world for some hidden, unfeminine talent or desire" (14; 12-13). Anthony's mother had certainly presented the world, and her youngest son, with an enigma—a woman at once absorbed and happy surrounded by her family (in whatever part of the world she happened to be) and a spirited writer whose courage, talent and drive had enabled her to establish a successful career in the latter part of her life, entertaining the British reading public for several decades. Anthony could look to his mother, if not to his father, for guidance in persevering and succeeding in a career, providing for a family, and maintaining two separate roles at one time. As Helen Heineman has maintained, "Beyond her heroic breadwinning, Anthony owed his mother a three-fold debt: his rigorous and disciplined writing habits, his prevalent realism, and his understanding of the multi-faceted female character" (*The Triumphant* 201). I believe Anthony's debt to his mother extends even further than Heineman has suggested.

When we look at their fictional worlds, we often find a similar struggle being played out through the plots of both mother and son. In *Barchester Towers*, as U.C. Knoepflmacher suggests, "the real battle fought in Barchester is not the short-lived struggle between 'Proudieism' and 'Grantlyism' but rather the more elementary contest waged between men and women" (35). The comic potential of the battle of the sexes had been explored joyfully, as well, in the fiction of Frances Trollope—especially through her favorite creation, the Widow Barnaby, forerunner of Mrs. Proudie herself. As the Widow prepares for her second marriage, the author of *The Widow Barnaby* explains that

both parties [the Widow Barnaby and Mr. O'Donagough] were determined to inform themselves very particularly of the worldly condition of the other, before they advanced one step farther towards matrimony, for which state, though the gentleman had spoken with rapture, and the lady had listened with softness, both had too proper a respect to think of entering upon it unadvisedly. (3: 201-02)

After a quarrel with her third husband in *The Widow Married* (1840), the pragmatic Widow Barnaby

luckily...remembered the weakness of a divided bundle of fagots, and at the same instant, determined at once to swallow whatever her spouse in his wisdom, thought it convenient to administer; and moreover, to the very best of her power, to make all others swallow it likewise. (1:70)

However, the Widow's husband, Major Allen, is victorious here to his own cost (as Dr. Proudie will find, as well).

Careful as always to keep her "settlement" in her own hands, rather than in her husband's, Mrs. Barnaby is likewise as skillful as her successor, Mrs. Proudie, in the other arts of "managing" a husband. Commiserating with her daughter Patty over the lodgings Major Allen has chosen for them—"but men will be men, Patty, all the world over, worse luck!"—she undermines her husband's authority as does her son's Mrs. Proudie: "The evening passed, as such evenings generally do. A family group, placed in lodgings of which the females greatly disapprove, but which being chosen by the male, must be endured, seldom manifest any striking symptoms of hilarity" (2: 216; 216-17). While Major Allen gets his way from time to time, and has proven himself successful in devising plans of his own, he lovingly concedes to the master judgment of the Widow Barnaby:

"I hope I shall never be such a fool, wife, as to fix downright upon any thing without first taking your judgment upon it," said the major, with energy. "You most decidedly are what our admirable [American] friends have called first-rate." (*The Barnabys in America* 2: 278)

The Widow Barnaby appeared in several novels in succession, Frances Trollope confessing to her readers, "with all her faults, and she has *some*, I love her dearly; I owe her many mirthful moments, and the deeper pleasure still of believing that she has brought mirthful moments to others also" (*The Barnabys in America* 1: 3).

Mrs. Proudie would not serve Anthony as the same kind of alter-ego the Widow Barnaby provided his mother—another widowed woman who could "go on as I have done, from the very first almost, that I remember any thing, always getting on, and on, and on" (*The Barnabys in America* 2: 29), a model of survival and joviality Frances Trollope would both create in her fiction and emulate in her life.

However, in his *Autobiography*, Anthony Trollope confesses his love for his recurring character, Mrs. Proudie, and his pain in killing her off in order to gratify one disgruntled reader:

I have sometimes regretted the deed, so great was my delight in writing about Mrs. Proudie, so thorough was my knowledge of all the little shades of her character. It was not only that she was a tyrant, a bully, a would-be priestess, a very vulgar woman, and one who would send headlong to the nethermost pit all who disagreed with her; but that at the same time she was conscientious, by no means a hypocrite, really believing in the brimstone which she threatened, and anxious to save the souls around her from its horrors. And as her tyranny increased so did the bitterness of the moment of her repentance increase, in that she knew herself to be a tyrant—till that bitterness killed her....I have never dissevered myself from Mrs. Proudie, and still live much in company with her ghost. (252-53)

No tyrant, Mrs. Proudie's forerunner, the Widow Barnaby, was, nonetheless, a strong-willed, ambitious, ill-bred woman—yet an endearing, stalwart, good-humored presence who could comfort and encourage her creator Frances Trollope.

His mother's multi-faceted Widow Barnaby no doubt helped to influence what Alice Green Fredman characterizes as Anthony Trollope's distinctive "modernism":

He was, in fact, both a representative Victorian in some of his choices of characters and forms, and one of the most unrepresentative and most modern of the great nineteenth-century English novelists. In this latter role, he not only introduced atypical and distressing characters, whose psyches he plumbed with compassion and completeness; he also presented uneasy studies in moral relativism, describing strangely disconcerting situations and problems. (5)

Mrs. Proudie represents only one instance of a remarkable number of erring characters who are drawn most sympathetically. Signora Neroni in *Barchester Towers* and Lizzie Eustace of *The Eustace Diamonds* (1873) were other such female figures whose blend of the admirable and the deplorable, the sensitive and the selfish, the adventurous and the willful, render them complex and provocative women.

So, too, with many of Anthony Trollope's male characters, as well. Fredman shows that Anthony Trollope treats "self-deception...usually...with sympathy....one is hard put to find any traditionally heroic hero, young or old, in Trollope's novels" (Fredman 12). Frances Trollope's faltering young Charles Chesterfield—or her older Mr. Gordon in *The Refugee in America*, a man who pays tribute to the female gender (Lady Darcy, his daughter Caroline, and "the heroic Emily")—suggest the gentle, "feminized," nature of Anthony Trollope's major male figures (*Refugee* 3: 298). The kindly widower Mr. Harding in *Barchester Towers*—who clings to his bachelor independence, as does also Frances Trollope's compassionate Unlce Walter in her novel of the same name (1852)—"had that nice appreciation of the feelings of others which belongs of right exclusively to women" (A. Trollope, *Barchester Towers* 503). The nurturing Mr. Harding displays the ultimate heroism of an ordinary man living his life with extraordinary gentleness and care:

He does such duties as fall to his lot well and conscientiously, and is thankful that he has never been tempted to assume others for which he might be less fitted.
The Author now leaves him in the hands of his readers; not as a hero, not as a man to be admired and talked of, not as a man who should be toasted at public dinners and spoken

of with conventional absurdity as a perfect divine, but as a good man without guile, believing humbly in the religion which he has striven to teach, and guided by the precepts which he has striven to learn. (A. Trollope, *Barchester Towers* 508)

Such are Anthony Trollope's heroes, men of both private and public compassion and decency, as they were his mother's, as well.

Those men who see themselves as separate from women, who use women but cannot share in their feelings, become the villains in the novels of both mother and son. Mrs. Trollope's Mr. Cartwright, in *The Vicar of Wrexhill*, desires "to touch, to influence, to lead, to rule, to tyrannize over the hearts and souls of all he approaches....[he] rest[s] all his hopes of fame, wealth, and station on the power he can obtain over women..." (127). Her distinguished Reverend Henry Harrington of *Uncle Walter* marries the wealthy Lady Augusta Withers, careful as he always is to follow "that profound far-sighted and ever-present perception of the side on which his bread would ultimately be found to be buttered" (1: 17). So, too, Anthony's Mr. Slope in *Barchester Towers* "went about his work zealously, flattering such as would listen to his flattery, whispering religious twaddle into the ears of foolish women, ingratiating himself with the few clergy who would receive him..." (57). When Mr. Slope suffers a setback, "He did not lie prostrate under this blow, or give himself up to vain lamentations; he did not henceforward despair of life, and call upon gods above and gods below to carry him off" (491). Instead, we learn,

It is well known that the family of the Slopes never starve: they always fall on their feet like cats, and let them fall where they will, they live on the fat of the land. Our Mr. Slope did so. On his return to town he found that the sugar-refiner had died, and that his widow was inconsolable: or, in other words, in want of consolation. Mr. Slope consoled her, and soon found himself settled with much comfort in the house in Baker Street. (496)

Occasionally, however, such predators upon women do meet their match, as does Mr. Emilius upon marrying the ingenious Lizzie Eustace at the end of *The Eustace Diamonds* (1893).

Most important of all comparisons between the fiction of mother and son, however, may be the similar authorial voices they cultivated in their works. Frances Trollope approached her relationship with her reader much as she felt a parent should approach family members:

It would be nearly impossible to convey in words an adequate idea of the difference which exists in a household where the parents make a secret of all things of important interest, and where they do not....Without this easy, natural, spontaneous confidence, the family union is like a rope of sand, that will fall to pieces and disappear at the first threat of any thing that can attract and draw off it loose and unbound particles.... Let no parent believe that affection can be perfect without it; let no mother fancy that the heart of her girl can be open to her if it find not an open heart in return....It is not in the nature of things that confidence should exist on one side only: it must be mutual. (*The Vicar of Wrexhill* 82-83)

Frances Trollope's voice is an intimate one.

By confiding in her reader, she creates an air of mutual, shared interest between herself and her audience. In one of many such direct addresses in her fiction, in a passage from *Uncle Walter*, she turns to whisper in her public's ear:

It will probably be now expected that we should present the Lady Augusta Harrington [to the reader]; and this I believe would be doing things in the proper order, and it cannot be denied that etiquette ought to have great weight in all things appertaining to No. 5, Vale Street; but nevertheless I cannot resist the temptation which the course of the narrative seems to offer of introducing my favourite Kate.... (*Uncle Walter* 1: 32)

Impetuous and warm-hearted in sharing her creations with her readers, she is also anxious, as a woman of the world, to share her many observations with them. She alerts her audience to hypocrisy and callousness lurking beneath the surface of the utmost social respectability: "The words of very decent, well-behaved people, like the Doctor [Harrington], often require translating into plain English, in order to be fully intelligible even to their own hearts" (*Uncle Walter* 1: 132). She points out society's madness:

The world would have denied that the mind of Lady Juliana was in a state to deserve the appellation of *insane*, but a large portion of it would have admitted that it was *unsound*. Walter did not sufficiently recognise the difference between tweedledum and tweedledee; yet it lawfully divides the inmates of a mad-house from those who put them there. (*Uncle Walter* 1: 155)

She advises her reader to beware of bright young men such as the Reverend James Harrington, "a man with a good deal of learning, though marvellously little information. Men of this stamp are by no means very uncommon" (*Uncle Walter* 2: 221). She is an author who delights in sharing with her audience what she knows of the world and knows of human nature.

Frances Trollope not only trusts her readers with her confidences and her observations on society, but enjoys such an intimacy with them that she can afford to be playful at her own expense. At the outset of *The Barnabys in America*, she delights in jesting about herself, trusting in her loyal audience's familiarity with her *Domestic Manners of the Americans* written a decade earlier. She will, she says, send the Widow Barnaby abroad on "an expedition, too, that was to lead her to a land which all the world knows I cherish in my memory with peculiar delight" (*Barnabys in America* 1: 3). Later, in the same work, she alludes, as well, to *Jonathan Jefferson Whitlaw*, although once more not by name, saying only, in an amusingly understated reference to her one-time villain's horrible demise,

Some circumstances relating to the nephew, and to the manner in which he both obtained and bequeathed his fortune, became the subject of a narrative published in England some few years ago; but of this notoriety Mrs. Clio Whitlaw was herself wholly unconscious; and so great was the humble simplicity of her character, that she would have thought it greatly more probable that her dog Watch should have been put into a book than herself.

(*Barnabys in America* 2: 184)

Frances Trollope enjoys mixing the reality of her creations' lives with the reality of her own life—blending the heroic adventures and narrative plots of the two together into an inseparable whole.

In addition, from her first work to her last, she reminds readers that her fiction is an artifice, one that is primarily concerned with fulfilling their wishes for just and pleasurable entertainment while, at the same time, satisfying her own. She concludes her first novel *The Refugee in America* (1832) by admitting that the task of merging her readers' desires with her own at times proves difficult:

But little more remains to be said. Notwithstanding the absurdity which most young people saw in such a marriage, Mr. Gordon and Lady Darcy were united a very few weeks after they had attended Emily to the altar. But if this was ridiculous, what will be said to the narrative being brought to its conclusion, and the lovely Caroline still free? Is it that I have forgotten my favourite? Far from it. But after such a banishment, I have a peculiar pleasure in leaving her to taste the enjoyment of one full unfettered season of English grace and splendour. May she not for one year be adored by a thousand, instead of one? (3: 300-01)

Far more reluctant than her son to rush her heroines into matrimony—often doing so only after arranging for their economic independence—Frances Trollope would have had some reservations about *Barchester Tower*'s Eleanor Bold who rejoices to "give up the heavy burden of her independence, and once more assume the position of a woman, and the duties of a trusting and loving wife" (479).

Nonetheless, mother and son share a remarkably similar authorial presence. When Alice Fredman characterizes Anthony's voice, she could be talking about Frances Trollope herself:

Trollope's novels bear ample testimony to these assertions that he has always regarded his characters as real people whom he had lived with and argued with and worried with as he described them. This is probably one of the reasons he never cared much about the formal requirements of plot, preferring to rest his claims on the independent existences of his men and women....Acting as an invisible character in its own right, Trollope's authorial voice is gossipy, mundane, often discursive. It is this presence which both connects and makes acceptable and responsible the assorted shifts in place, pace, and mood. (33)

Fredman explains that Anthony's fiction "requires that the listener trust the narrator...that author and reader should move along together in full confidence with each other...he has persuaded us to put our faith in the personality behind the authorial voice" (39-40). So, too, did Frances Trollope develop an illusion of closeness with her readers. Anthony Trollope followed suit, sharing many confidences with his audience. In *Barchester Towers* he confesses,

My readers will guess from what I have written that I myself do not like Mr. Slope; but I am constrained to admit that he is a man of parts. He knows how to say a soft word in the proper place; he knows how to adapt his flattery to the ears of his hearers; he knows the wiles of the serpent, and he uses them. Could Mr. Slope have adapted his manners to men as well as to women, could he ever have learnt the ways of a gentleman, he might have risen to great things. (58)

Again, Anthony promotes gentleness in his truly manly men.

Not only does Anthony share his values with his readers, but also the difficulties of his craft. As with his mother before him, Anthony anguishes from time to time over how to please both himself and his readers:

The sorrows of our heroes and heroines, they are your delight, oh public! their sorrows, or their sins, or their absurdities; not their virtues, good sense, and consequent rewards....When we become dull we offend your intellect; and we must become dull or we should offend your taste. (*Barchester Towers* 490)

Struggling to bring his imaginary world to its proper conclusion, Trollope despairs even further:

And who can apportion out and dovetail his incidents, dialogues, characters, and descriptive morsels, so as to fit them all exactly into 439 pages, without either compressing them unnaturally, or extending them artificially at the end of his labour? Do I not myself know that I am at this moment in want of a dozen pages, and that I am sick with cudgelling my brains to find them? (490)

When the work is finished, he knows what Frances Trollope would also lament in *Charles Chesterfield*, that

the kindest-hearted critic of them all invariably twits us with the incompetency and lameness of our conclusion. We have either become idle and neglected it, or tedious and over-laboured it. It is insipid or unnatural, over-strained or imbecile. It means nothing, or attempts too much....I can only say that if some critic, who thoroughly knows his work, and has laboured on it till experience has made him perfect, will write the last fifty pages of a novel in the way they should be written, I, for one, will in future do my best to copy the example. Guided by my own lights only, I confess that I despair of success. (490-91)

Characteristically, Anthony Trollope deprecates his own astonishing powers of creativity, as he would in *An Autobiography*, as well:

I do not think it probable that my name will remain among those who in the next century will be known as the authors of English prose fiction;—but if it does, that permanence of success will probably rest on the character of Plantagenet Palliser, Lady Glencora, and the Reverend Mr. Crawley. (330)

So, too, had his mother downplayed her talents, from *Domestic Manners of the Americans*, at the beginning, to *Fashionable Life; or Paris and London* (1856) at the end of her career.

Frances Trollope and her son Anthony agreed in many of their philosophies of life and literature, as well. Anthony called his fiction "realistic," carrying on a tradition his mother had been faulted for, before him (A. Trollope, *An Autobiography* 206). Both believed that a novel should both entertain and direct the reader, at the same time, with Anthony explaining:

A novel should give a picture of common life enlivened by humour and sweetened by pathos...the canvas should be crowded with real portraits, not of individuals known to the world or to the author, but of created personages impregnated with traits of character which are known.... (*An Autobiography* 116)

Anthony prided himself that his fiction was moral:

I do believe that no girl has risen from the reading of my pages less modest than she was before, and that some may have learned from them that modesty is a charm well worth preserving. I think that no youth has been taught that in falseness and flashness is to be found the road to manliness; but some may perhaps have learned from me that it is to be found in truth and a high and gentle spirit. (*An Autobiography* 134-35)

Frances Trollope would have been pleased to think that her novels had served as moral guides—although her works would stress the "modesty" of women far less than their independent spirits.

Both writers, considering themselves "Conservative-Liberals," admired genteel, gracious, middle and upper class behavior while asking their readers to penetrate the surface of society and "read" human relationships in new ways (A. Trollope, *An Autobiography* 266). Anthony would argue against the double standard by which the sexes were judged in *An Autobiography*, lamenting that, "In regard to a sin common to the two sexes, almost all the punishment and all the disgrace is heaped upon the one who in nine cases out of ten has been the least sinful....But for our erring sons we find pardon easily enough" (304-05). While both would treat the plight of the fallen woman in their fiction, Frances Trollope used her writing as a vehicle to raise public consciousness about the abuses of slavery, child labor, evangelical liberties, and marriage laws, about social abuses and the institutions that perpetrate them, far more than would her son. While Donald D. Stone suggests that Anthony Trollope's "protagonists often reconcile themselves to the faulty ways of the world" (58), Trollope as a narrator, explains Alice Green Fredman, "demonstrates that peculiarly Trollopean fairness and compassion which endows even his depictions of villains with a curious, persuasive sympathy" (37). Trollope did carry on his mother's compassion and her passion for justice, but by insisting on a close analysis of individuals more than of institutions. In his treatment of his characters we find

pity and justness [through] a kind of reiteration which has been frequently misunderstood as redundancy. It results from his method of portraying a character through direct statement, action, dialogue, and indirect discourse until he is satisfied that justice has been done and that all points of view have been heard from. The device of what is almost incremental repetition is a hallmark of Trollope's style: he starts with the single sentence and works his way out through direct and indirect discourse and paragraph to dual or multiple plots and structures to the great superstructures of the Barsetshire and the Parliamentary series....it enables Trollope to achieve an effect of fullness, of total accountability. (Fredman 37-38)

As Anthony Trollope examines his creations from every angle, he gives his characters their full expression. He seeks to know their weaknesses and their strengths, their good and their bad qualities—and to enable his readers to do so, as well. His aim is justice—a justice which would encourage a responsible and thorough assessment rather than a hasty stereotyping by others. In the writings of both mother and son we find an extraordinary care for individual life and good-humored, authorial companions to guide us on our life journeys.

Frances Trollope's literary influence, as we have seen, was pervasive. Certainly, her inspiration extended beyond the few writers we have discussed here, yet in their works—the works of the great writers, Dickens, Gaskell, Stowe, and Anthony Trollope, all of whom learned from, built on, and, in some ways, surpassed their predecessor—we see her legacy. She helped to open doors and legitimize subjects for each of them. She created popular, influential character types they would carry on developing in their respective works—as would other authors, as well. And Frances Trollope passed on a literary vision—a dream of affecting the institutions and altering the shape of societies to come. They would respond to, imitate, and refine upon her fantasies in their own ways. Frances Trollope's authorial voice, much beloved by the British public, never really died out. Though her name was soon forgotten, her voice carried on in the works of other reform novelists, women authors, and, especially, in the frank and familiar, warming tones of her son Anthony. His authorship would become at once his own remarkable gift to literature and a telling tribute to his spirited mother. In such ways, Frances Trollope would leave her mark on her family, on literature, and on the age she helped to inspire.

Chapter Nine
Conclusions

And yet, despite their considerable literary and political influence, Frances Wright and Frances Trollope had known much failure. Their friendship had been dashed on the rocks of personal differences. The experiments in cooperative living at New Harmony and Nashoba which had kindled their imaginations had failed, as well—damaging Frances Wright's health and reputation, young Henry Trollope's health, and Frances Trollope's New World hopes, all at once. Moreover, few of the goals to which they had dedicated their lives were realized in their own lifetimes. Both had died before the Civil War brought an end to slavery in the United States. The evangelical excesses they deplored continued on despite their efforts. The fight for women's property rights and education, both in the United States and in Great Britain, persisted beyond their deaths. A free and comprehensive public system of education, from elementary school to college, for women as well as for men, would not come about in America until decades after Frances Wright gave her pioneering speeches on knowledge and education.[1] Nor would the two writers see much effect beyond the passage of the Ten Hour Labor Law from their efforts to encourage humanitarian and cooperative action and to discourage the greed and selfishness of nineteenth century industrial capitalism. Nevertheless, Frances Trollope and Frances Wright did affect the gradual process of social change they had advocated. Theirs was an active role in the great movements, the great changes, of their ages in the United States and in Great Britain. Addressing countless individuals through their writing—and Frances Wright in her lecture audiences—they played a significant role over several decades in helping to change social attitudes: towards slavery in the United States; towards child labor and wage slavery in both America and in England; towards the education of women and other oppressed classes and peoples in both countries; towards the imprisonment and callous treatment of the poor in England and in the United States; towards married women's property rights and equality for women within and without the institution of marriage; and towards public roles for women (not in the least through their own actions as popular writers, businesswomen, social reformers, world travelers, and, in the case of Frances Wright, as a newspaper editor and as a public speaker, as well). The swift and angry character assassinations heaped upon them bear witness to the fear they had aroused as their audiences grew, their ideas became known, and their views gained gradual acceptance. While they died largely ignored and forgotten by the public to whom they had appealed—the one with her wicked, satiric exposures, the other with her hopeful, utopian visions—they had influenced thousands of readers and listeners over the years—among them the important individuals we have considered who carried on facets of their work and their ideas in the years to come: Charles Dickens, Elizabeth Gaskell, John Stuart Mill, Lucretia Mott, Elizabeth Cady Stanton, Harriet Beecher Stowe, Anthony Trollope and Walt Whitman, among others. The dream Wright and Trollope shared, of a more cooperative, generous, feminized future, is one they had passed on to inspire others beyond their own lifetimes.

Their lives illustrate a pattern pointed to by contemporary political scientists and social analysts such as Garry Wills, who explains, "change is initiated by the principled few, not the compromising many" (Wills, *Confessions* 162). Further, Wills states, these initiators

must pay a terrible price. They are resented, since they ask for change, and people find change hard. They are put off as long as they can be, dismissed, treated at first as invisible and then as affronts. Such "fanatics" are mocked, threatened, jailed, beat up, shot at....[Political change] begins with individual risk and heroism...[with persons who] make a claim because it is right, not because it is wanted, even by its putative beneficiaries normally it is not wanted. (165)

Frances Trollope and Frances Wright persisted in arguing until their deaths for causes of social justice. They saw too clearly the basic inhumanity underlying the social rationalizations for slavery, child labor, and denial of married women's property rights, among other issues, to endure knowledge of these injustices for long in silence. They also believed that their fellow human beings were persons like themselves, persons who could not long harbor such knowledge without eventually acting to bring about reform. Despite both the immediate outrage and the on-going criticism, humiliation, and rejection their careers provoked, they remained outspoken and deeply committed to helping bring about a more perfect civilization through non-violent, gradual, political change.

Both were dedicated to the goal of elevating humanity to a higher plane of social interaction, mental development, political responsibility, and moral commitment. They believed in individual generosity and interpersonal cooperation—despite all the evidence to the contrary they saw around them—and, through their words and actions, strove to encourage the highest form of behavior and to set forth models of community and society to inspire others. Because they realized the commonality and interdependency of the races and sexes, they argued that all must act together to maintain "the conservation, care, and happiness of the species" (Wright, *England the Civilizer* 11). Human decency, fair play, good manners, a sense of justice, compassion for the ill, the

Photograph of Frances Wright toward the end of her life. (Courtesy of the Cincinnati Historical Society.)

aged, the infant—these were the qualities of "true civilization" (Wright, *England the Civilizer* 383) which Trollope and Wright insisted were possible of realization.

In this goal of affecting social change, Frances Trollope and Frances Wright were "radical." They challenged the system in their opposition to slavery and their insistence on marriage reform. They believed that captialism had to be altered and that scientists could use their knowledge to help in bringing about a better world. Yet they saw that new processes, new machinery, new inventions were not in themselves the answer; these, too, as they pointed out, both had and would become tools of injustice and cruelty in the modern industrial world. Thus, Frances Trollope and Frances Wright argued for education for workers and other ignorant, "exploitable" peoples, new laws to protect laborers from the insatiable greed of company owners, and cooperative factory systems to recognize and to strengthen the reciprocal bond which must exist between employers and employees for their mutual benefit. Frances Wright could point to Robert Owen's New Lanark in Scotland to illustrate how factory owners could create community feeling and interaction through worker education, fair wages, cooperative store ownership, and other innovations. Frances Trollope in *Michael Armstrong* could point to the mills of MESSRS. WOOD AND WALKER, at Bradford, where, as the Reverend Mr. Bell explains to Mary Brotherton:

"The high-minded owners of yonder factory are losing thousands every year by their efforts to purify this traffic of its enormities—and some thousand small still voices call down blessings on them for it. But while it costs them ten shillings to produce what their neighbors can bring into the market for nine, they will only be pointed at as pitiably unwise in their generation by all the great family of Mammon which surrounds them. Few, alas! will think of following the example! All they can do therefore is in fact but to carry on a system of private charity on an enormous scale—but till they are supported by law, even their vast efforts, and most noble sacrifices can do nothing towards the general redemption of our poor northern people from the state of slavery into which they have fallen." (211)

Social justice could never be too costly, both Frances Trollope and Frances Wright were to argue; for each, the basic measure and value of a civilization would always remain its essential human decency.

Thus, both writers were "radical" in advocating social and political reform. At the same time, they adhered to an essential "conservatism," defined recently as "the sense that one belongs to some continuing, and pre-existing, social order" (Scruton 21), a concern for "the cohesion and continuity of society—what makes people band together and remain together with some satisfaction" (Wills, *Confessions* 213). Their radicalism co-existed with concern for the conservation of valuable social and cultural traditions—a concern that humanity as a whole must learn to practice "conservation" of the community and of the species, a role increasingly parcelled out to women alone. As we have seen, in her final novel, *Fashionable Life in Paris and London* (1856), Frances Trollope portrays a simple, practical community of women as a model of what is possible in humane society, just as Frances Wright's last work,

England, the Civilizer (1848), outlines what Wright believes are the essentials for social cohesion.

Their ideological complexity identifies them as part of a pattern scholars have found in "figures in nineteenth century Europe whose special uses of the moral, esthetic, technological and political pasts make it difficult to place them as traditionalists or radicals" (Nisbet 109). Such figures as John Stuart Mill, according to Frank S. Meyer, illustrate how erroneous the "bifurcated" Western tradition of "conservatism" versus "liberalism" has been (28). M. Stanton Evans insists that conservatism and liberalism are not "disparate elements" but have been "unnatural[ly] separat[ed]...because of the way we have been taught our intellectual history" (125-26). Frances Trollope and Frances Wright reveal what some have called a "natural and necessary unity" (Evans 125) between conservative and liberal ideologies—not just in their conservative concern for maintaining "the cohesion and continuity of society" (Wills, *Confessions* 213), but also in the conservative battles they fought against the forces of blind progress and materialism in their day.

If "conservatives" are those who can be characterized as "hav[ing] steeled themselves against the *mystique* of the new, the prevailing prejudice that only innovation is valuable, that salvation arises from innovation" (Meyer 459), then Frances Wright and Frances Trollope must be seen as "conservative" in their struggle against many of the effects and goals of nineteenth century capitalism. They understood at the outset of the industrial age what Garry Wills points out today in *Reagan's America: Innocents at Home*, that "capitalism is an instrument for change, for expansion, driven toward ever new resources, products, markets....It literally remakes lives in order to have new customers for new models....There is nothing less conservative than capitalism, so itchy for the new" (381-82). In the nineteenth century Frances Trollope illustrates in *Michael Armstrong* how capitalism had changed the relationship between the sexes, had altered the relationship between parents and children, had transformed the shape of society (as Wills points out it is still doing in our own time: "We are a different people when we have made movies on the scale that we have, and televisions and jet airplanes. We become a different people when we have made nuclear weapons on the scale that we have.") (*Reagan's America* 382).[2] In pleading for humane rather than material values and for the preservation of a cultural heritage representing the best from the past, Frances Trollope and Frances Wright may be seen as fighting a conservative battle against the strengthening forces of innovative, "radical," nineteenth century industry and commerce.

Their battle, of course, is still being continued as the struggle for the survival of life on this planet goes on amid depleted natural resources, industrial waste and pollution reaching life-threatening levels, and an "advanced" technology which has given us the nightmare possibility of nuclear holocaust.

Those individuals who strive worldwide to bring us back from the brink of planetary disaster, often known as "radicals," are engaged in fighting some very "conservative" battles for the continuity and preservation of the species and of the basic constructs of civilization.

In studying the lives of Frances Trollope and Frances Wright, we can discover the distortion and damage which result from labeling and stereotyping individuals in an "either/or" fashion. As we have seen, the term "conservative" when applied to Frances Trollope must embrace many of the most radical movements of the nineteenth century. The term "radical" when applied to Frances Wright must ignore some of the fundamental tenets of her philosophy—her emphasis on gradual political process rather that on social revolution, her resistance to many of the elements of "progress" represented by nineteenth century industrial capitalism, and her insistence on conservation, on a union between the selfish "male" forces for the "propagation, the conservation, and the enjoyment of the individual" with the more generous "female" forces for the "cooperation, care, and happiness of the species" (Wright, *England, The Civilizer* 11). Neither writer wanted change that would coarsen human interaction; both were dedicated, always, to the promotion of rational, humane, orderly and gracious behavior.

Both "conservative" and "liberal," propelling society forward towards reform, as well as reweaving the threads of continuity and interrelationship that would allow for the maintenance of human life and civilization on earth, Frances Trollope and Frances Wright have been diminished by the brief footnotes and simplistic labels that categorize them in the annals of history and literature. Their lives and works merit greater recognition for their many efforts and their contributions to the advancement of blacks, of women, of workers, and of humanity as a whole. Their persistence in furthering these causes provides illustration for Doris Lessing's point in *Prisons We Choose to Live Inside*, "that it is always the individual, in the long run, who will set the tone, provide the real development in a society....It is individuals who change societies, give birth to ideas, who, standing out against tides of opinion, change them" (72-73). While public indifference and oblivion befell Frances Trollope and Frances Wright by the end of their lives, they continued to stand firm in their beliefs and to work steadfastly for the benefit of society until their deaths. While both the stereotyping and the indifference of the nineteenth century have continued to deny them stature in the present day, the record of their strong commitments remains preserved both in their own volumes and in the literary and political legacies they have left behind.

Thus, Frances Trollope and Frances Wright belong in the company of those few "who advance humanity as a whole" (Lessing, *Prisons* 74), individuals who were to leave a mark on their historical period because of their refusal to give up and be silenced. Heroic in their determination, they persisted in advocating unpopular causes until, eventually, those causes could no longer be ignored and, at last, gained acceptance from a majority in their society. Today, their writings remain as interesting and as instructive as their lives.

Frances Wright calls upon our humanity, urging women, in particular, to take their place in history by dedicating themselves to restoring cooperative interaction and to off-setting the emphasis on the individual and on the selfish which has resulted from male dominance in society. It is up to women, Wright explains, to help men find, and women maintain and restore in themselves, the necessary balance between the generous and the selfish, the cooperative and the individual, in their lives and in the greater society. Frances Wright's voice still insists:

[all] must be wholesomely housed and suitably provided for. All the wretched must be comforted, fed, clothed, lodged. Cities must be relieved of their multitudes. The breath of heaven, and the green fields, and the fresh earth restored to man, and, with these, wholesome exercise, and occupation, and recreation. Age and childhood must be seen to. The work of duty and of love must be accomplished, if we would open in a right spirit a new era. Society has been so long driven by the selfish principle singly, that it may be hard for her to receive inspiration from the generous...the outstanding generation has grown up, and lived, in the service of *self* only; and felt nothing for, and known nothing of the collective species....Woman must give the tone in this; and place herself everywhere on the side of humanity, union, order, right reason, and right feeling. (*England, the Civilizer* 468)

Frances Wright would be dismayed to find twentieth century "liberated" women rushing to emulate men rather than modulating capitalism's selfishness through female leadership in cooperation and nurturance.

Frances Trollope, too, speaking through the voice of the Reverend Mr. Bell to guide Mary Brotherton in *Michael Armstrong*, decries "the bloated wealth" which "has enriched a few, [while] prov[ing] a source of utter destruction to the many," cautioning that we "MUST listen to [the lengthy accounts of social enormities by society's critics], and that soon, or [society] may mourn her negligence when it is too late to repair it" (202-03). At the same time, Mr. Bell advises,

"It is not the acquisition of any natural power, principle, or faculty, that we should deplore; all such, on the contrary, should be hailed as part and parcel of our magnificent birthright, and each new use we learn to make of the still much-unknown creation around us, ought to be welcomed with a shout of praise....It is not from increased, or increasing science that we have any thing to dread, it is only from a fearfully culpable neglect of the moral power that should rule and regulate its uses, that it can be other than one of God's best gifts." (205)

Photograph of Frances Trollope in old age. (Courtesy of the Trustees of the Boston Public Library.)

Frances Trollope's young heroines provide the moral vision necessary to reawaken a sense of community responsibility and to bring about reform in her works, countering individual greed and selfishness with compassion and communion. This moral direction provides the only path Frances Trollope envisions for the future well-being of society.

Despite the erosion of their personal friendship, Frances Trollope and Frances Wright continued to believe in women's cooperative action as necessary for the advance of civilization. Despite the further deterioration of their own marriages, they recognized and called for a more perfect union between the sexes and for a restored balance between male and female as necessary for the survival of the species. As Frances Wright stated, "[our] effective power in the moral world must be the result of the two human instincts acting conjointly and in unison. This can only be when the two persons in human kind—man and woman—shall exert equal influences in a state of equal independence. The result of this will be justice" (*England, the Civilizer* 22).

Undismayed by their individual failures of relationship and community, they continued their work hopeful for the gradual improvement of society and for a more cooperative future. The victims themselves of unfair stereotyping, they sought to avoid what Doris Lessing calls "the tendency of the human mind to see things in pairs—either/or, black/white, I/you, we/you, good/bad, the forces of good/the forces of evil...of seeing ourselves as in the right, them as wrong, our ideas as correct, theirs as nonsense, if not as downright evil" (Lessing, *Prisons* 15-16). Striking out neither at each other, the opposite sex, nor their public humiliators and attackers, both continued to work steadily, Frances Trollope with her irrepressible sense of humor, Frances Wright with her quiet dignity and seriousness, to move civilization forward to a less selfish, exploitative, and cruel age. In their courageous work, as Frances Wright expressed it, to "elevate ever higher and higher the standard of human excellence" (*England, the Civilizer* 470), they have left us a legacy we can continue to ignore only at the price of personal diminishment and cultural peril. If it is true, as Susan Morgan despairingly acknowledges in *Sisters in Time*, that "the values of individualism and competition and aggression, won, that what actually lay ahead...was the Boer Wars, the Great War, and the continuous aggressions we live in now" (110), it is also true that Frances Trollope and Frances Wright, by persisting in their struggle, left us a legacy of uplifting influence on both individuals and on the course of social history. Rather than dream of escaping a reality we cannot bear (as Ariel Dorfman reveals so many doing in contemporary society), how much better to share the dream of Frances Trollope and Frances Wright—a dream not of escaping reality but of improving it, instead (5).

Notes

Preface

[1]See Helen Heineman, *Frances Trollope* (Boston: Twayne, 1984); *Mrs. Trollope: The Triumphant Feminine in the Nineteenth Century* (Athens, OH: Ohio UP, 1979); *Restless Angels: The Friendship of Six Victorian Women* (Athens, OH; Ohio UP, 1983); and Celia Eckhardt, *Fanny Wright: Rebel in America* (Cambridge, MA: Harvard UP, 1984).

[2]See, for instance, the most well-known of recent women's literary anthologies, eds. Sandra M. Gilbert and Susan Gubar, The *Norton Anthology of Literature By Women: The Tradition in English*. (New York: W.W. Norton & Co., 1985). See also a representative historical anthology, Joyce D. Goodfriend and Claudia M. Christie, eds, *Lives of American Women: A History of Documents* (Boston: Little, Brown & Co., 1981). One other text, Virginia Sapiro, *Women in American Society: An Introduction to Women's Studies* (Palo Alto, CA: Mayfield Publishing Co., 1981) gives typically brief mention (one sentence) to Frances Wright as publisher of the *Free Enquirer*, erroneously calling that New Harmony-born publication which Frances Wright co-edited with Robert Dale Owen, "the first reform periodical published solely by women" (194-95). Frances Trollope, never to become an American citizen (as would Frances Wright), is not mentioned at all—understandable, perhaps, although she wrote more perceptively about the lives of early nineteenth century American women in both *Domestic Manners of the Americans* and several of her novels than most of her contemporaries and would have provided readers with an excellent source for further reading.

[3]See Eileen Bigland's portrayal of Frances Trollope in *The Indomitable Mrs. Trollope* (Philadelphia: J.B. Lippincott Co., 1954).

[4]See Celia Eckhardt, "Of Fanny and Camilla Wright: Their Sisterly Love," *The Sister Bond: A Feminist View of a Timesless Connection*." Ed. Toni A. McNaron. (New York: Pergamon, 1985) 39.

Chapter Two

[1]See, for instance, C.P. Snow, *Trollope: His Life and Art* (New York: Scribner's Sons, 1975) 25, and Michael Sadleir, *Trollope: A Commentary*. 1927. (New York: Octagon Books: A Division of Farrar, Straus & Giroux, 1975) 70-71.

[2]See Heineman, *Frances Trollope* 63, 75, 80, 138.

[3]Deborah Morse in *Women in Trollope's Palliser Novels* (Ann Arbor: U of Michigan RP, 1987) points out that Trollope's fiction reveals "tension...[an] ambivalent response to the Victorian ideals for womanhood that lay at the heart of the 'Woman Question' controversy" (137). Interestingly enough, however, Morse never once refers to

Frances Trollope in her study, even while discussing Trollope's views on egalitarian marriages, female activism and rebelliousness in the mid-nineteenth century, and possible sources for his ambivalence.

Chapter Five

[1]Walt Whitman, *Democratic Vistas*, in *Prose Works*, 1892, Vol. 2, ed. Floyd Stovall (New York: New York UP, 1964) 425: "Not the book needs so much to be the complete thing, but the reader of the book does. That were to make a nation of supple and athletic minds, well train'd, intuitive, used to depend on themselves, and not on a few coteries of writers."

[2]Walt Whitman, *Democratic Vistas*, in *Prose Works*, 1892, Vol. 2, ed. Floyd Stovall (New York: New York UP, 1964) 373-74, 383, 391; Whitman speaks of "individualism, which isolates. There is another half, which is adhesivenesss or love, that fuses, ties and aggregates, making the races comrades, and fraternizing all" (381) and a future America with "more universal ownership of property, general homesteads, general comfort—a vast, intertwining reticulation of wealth" (383); Wright, *England, The Civilizer* 455.

Chapter Six

[1]Frances Trollope, *The Life and Adventures of Michael Armstrong, the Factory Boy* (London: Henry Colburn, publ., 1839 in three volumes; 1840 in the one volume edition to which all references in this text will be made) 204.

[2]Lecky argued that Puritanism stressed the male character of religion, denying the significance of the Virgin Mary. Frances Wright, in *England, the Civilizer*, associated the militant male principle with Cromwell and Puritanism, as well, contrasting it with the Roman Catholic Church of the period, "a church peaceable, willing to live, and let live" (105, 214).

[3]See Sandra M. Gilbert and Susan Gubar, *The Madwoman in the Attic: The Woman Writer and the Nineteenth-Century Literary Imagination* (New Haven: Yale P, 1979; 1980) 125-26. Katherine M. Rogers and William McCarthy, eds., *The Meridian Anthology of Early Woman Writers: British Literary Women from Aphra Behn to Maria Edgeworth*, 1660-1800 (NY and Scarborogh, Ontario: New American Library, 1987) also note that the authors they include in their anthology seldom mention their mothers while "express[ing] gratitude and devotion to supportive fathers" (xviii).

[4]See Carolyn Heilbrun, *Reinventing Womanhood* (New York: Norton, 1979), 107-24, and Ursula Owen, ed., *Fathers: Reflections By Daughters* (New York: Pantheon, 1985).

[5]In *Reinventing Womanhood*, Heilbrun argues further that, "women writers...have failed to imagine autonomous women characters. With remarkably few exceptions, women writers do not imagine women characters with even the autonomy they themselves have achieved" (71).

[6]See Christopher Lasch, *Haven in a Heartless World: the Family Beseiged* (New

York: Basic Book, Inc., 1979).

Chapter Seven

¹See also Madeline B. Stern, *The Life of Margaret Fuller* (New York: E.P. Dutton and Co., Inc., 1942).

²See Cecyle S. Neidle, *America's Immigrant Women* (Boston: Twayne Publ., 1975) 37-9; Yuri Suhl, *Eloquent Crusader: Ernestine Rose* (New York: Julian Messner, 1970) 139.

³See Lucretia Mott, *Discourse on Woman, Delivered at the Assembly Building*, Dec. 17, 1849 (Philadelphia, 1850), 21, qtd. in Keith E. Melder, *Beginnings of Sisterhood: The American Women's Rights Movement, 1800-1850* (New York: Schoken Books, 1977) 126; qtd. in Melder, 148.

⁴See Ida Husted Harper, *Life and Work of Susan B. Anthony*, Vol. 2, 1898 (Salem, New Hampshire: Ayer Co. Publ., Inc., 1983) 935; Alma Lutz, *Susan B. Anthony: Rebel, Crusader, Humanitarian* (Boston: Beacon, 1959) 52, 142; Ellen Carol DuBois, *Feminism and Suffrage: The Emergence of an Independent Women's Movement in America: 1848-1869* (Ithaca: Cornell P, 1978) 104.

⁵See Alice Rossi's study of the respective contributions of each partner to *The Subjection of Women* in *Essays on Sex and Equality: John Stuart Mill and Harriet Taylor Mill* (Chicago: U of Chicago P, 1970).

⁶For differing perspectives on Whitman's attitude toward female sexuality and women's roles see Harold Aspiz, *Walt Whitman and the Body Beautiful* (Urbana: U of Illinois P, 1980) 218-48; Roger Asselineau, *The Evolution of Walt Whitman: The Creation of a Book* (Cambridge, MA: The Belknap P of Harvard UP, 1962) 159-61; Myrth Jimmie Killingsworth, "Whitman and Motherhood: A Historical View" (1982), in Edwin H. Cady and Louis J. Budd, *On Whitman: The Best From American Literature* (Durham, NC: Duke UP, 1987) 245-61; Merle Curti, *Human Nature in American Thought: A History* (Madison: U of Wisconsin P, 1980) 161; and Floyd Stovall, *The Foreground of Leaves of Grass* (Charlottesville: U of Virginia P, 1974) 22.

⁷See T.R. Rajasekharaiah, *The Roots of Whitman's Grass* (Rutherford: Farleigh Dickinson UP, 1970) 31.

⁸See David Goodale, "Some of Walt Whitman's Borrowings," *American Literature*, 10 (May 1938) 202-13.

⁹See also Erkkila, 18, for other of Whitman's thematic borrowings from Frances Wright.

¹⁰See also Asselineau, *The Evolution of Walt Whitman: The Creation of a Book* (Cambridge: The Belknap P of Harvard UP, 1962) 45-48, for a discussion of Whitman's anticlerical views, so similar to those he heard and read in Frances Wright.

Chapter Eight

¹Frances Trollope later would borrow from Dickens's *Pickwick Papers*, as Heineman reveals. See her discussion of Trollope's playful use of Sergeant Buzfuz by name and her mischievous creation of "Barnaby Papers" in *The Widow Barnaby* (1838)

in *The Triumphant Feminine*, 158-59. Patrick Brantlinger suggests that the idea of *Michael Armstrong* may have come from *Oliver Twist* (*The Spirit of Reform: British Literature and Politics*), 1832-1867 (Cambridge: Harvard UP, 1977), 44, but Heineman points out that, once more, the parallel seems a weak one (*The Triumphant*, 172).

[2]See Bodenheimer, *The Politics of Story in Victorian Social Fiction* (Ithaca: Cornell UP, 1988) 55-56.

[3]See also Ellen Moers, *Harriet Beecher Stowe and American Literature* (Hartford, CT: The Stowe-Day Foundation, 1978) 25.

[4]See J.A. Sutherland, *Victorian Novelists and Publishers* (Chicago, IL: U of Chicago P, 1976) 150.

[5]See also Arthur Pollard, *Anthony Trollope* (London: Routledge and Kegan Paul, 1978) 50.

Chapter Nine

[1]See Flexner, *Century of Struggle*, (28) on the long fight for female education in the United States.

[2]Mr. Bell in Trollope's *Michael Armstrong* opens Mary Brotherton's eyes to the effects of the factory system on the family (203, 204).

Works Cited

Allen, Gay Wilson. *A Reader's Guide to Walt Whitman*. New York: Octagon Books of Farrar, Straus and Giroux, 1981.

_____. *The Solitary Singer: A Critical Biography of Walt Whitman*. New York: The MacMillan Co., 1955.

Allen, Walter. Introduction to Charles Dickens's *Hard Times*. 1854. New York: Harper and Row, 1965.

Ammons, Elizabeth. "Stowe's Dream of the Mother-Savior: *Uncle Tom's Cabin* and American Women Writers Before the 1920's." *New Essays on Uncle Tom's Cabin*. Ed. Eric J. Sundquist. Cambridge: Cambridge UP, 1986.

Armstrong, Nancy. *Desire and Domestic Fiction: A Political History of the Novel*. New York: Oxford UP, 1987.

Arvin, Newton. *Whitman*. 1938. New York: Russell and Russell, 1969.

Aspiz, Harold. *Walt Whitman and the Body Beautiful*. Urbana: U of Illinois P, 1980.

Asselineau, Roger. *The Evolution of Walt Whitman: The Creation of a Book*. Cambridge: The Belknap P of Harvard UP, 1962.

Bacon, Margaret Hope. *Valiant Friend: The Life of Lucretia Mott*. New York: Walker and Co., 1980.

Baker, Paul, ed. Introduction. *Views of Society and Manners in America*. Cambridge: Belknap P of Harvard UP, 1963.

Barry, Kathleen. *Susan B. Anthony: A Biography of a Singular Feminist*. New York: New York UP, 1988.

Beecher, Catherine E. *Letters on the Difficulties of Religion*. Hartford, 1836.

Beecher, Lyman. *Lectures on Political Atheism*. Boston: Jewett, 1852.

Berkson, Dorothy. "Millennial Politics and the Feminine Fiction of Harriet Beecher Stowe." *Critical Essays on Harriet Beecher Stowe*. Ed. Elizabeth Ammons. Boston: G.K. Hall and Co., 1980.

Bigland, Eileen. *The Idomitable Mrs. Trollope*. Philadelphia: J.B. Lippincott Co., 1954.

Bodenheimer, Rosemarie. *The Politics of Story in Victorian Social Fiction*. Ithaca: Cornell UP, 1988.

Brantlinger, Patrick. *The Spirit of Reform*. Cambridge: Harvard UP, 1977.

Brown, Gillian. "Getting in the Kitchen with Dinah: Domestic Politics in *Uncle Tom's Cabin*." *American Quarterly*. 36.4 (Fall, 1984).

Brown, Joel. "Unpub. Memoir of Frances Wright." Library of Cincinnati and Hamilton County.

Browning, Elizabeth Barrett. *The Letters of Elizabeth Barrett Browning*. Vol. 1. Ed. Frederic G. Kenyon. New York: MacMillan, 1897.

_____. "To Mrs. Martin." 14 Dec. 1832. Letter in *The Letters of Elizabeth Barrett Browning*.

_____. "To Mrs. Martin." 30 Jan. 1851. Letter in*The Letters of Elizabeth Barrett Browning*.

Burnett, Constance Buel. *Five for Freedom.*. 1953. Westport CN: Greenwood, 1976.

Canby, Henry Seidel. *Walt Whitman: An American*. Boston: Houghton Mifflin Co., 1943.

Cooke, Parsons. "Female Preaching Unlawful and Inexpedient." Lynn, MA: 1837. In *Beginnings of Sisterhood: The American Woman's Rights Movement, 1800-1850*. Keith E. Melder. New York: Schocken Books, 1977.

Cooper, James Fenimore, ed. *The Correspondence of James Fenimore Cooper*. New Haven: Yale UP, 1922. Eckhardt*Fanny Wright*.

Curti, Merle. *Human Nature in American Thought: A History*. Madison: The U of Wisconsin P, 1980.

_____. *The Growth of American Thought*. New York: Harper and Brothers, Publ., 1943.

D'Arusmont, Frances S.G. "Memorial on Suffrage." 3 Feb. 1874. Eckhardt *Fanny Wright*.

Dickens, Charles. *Hard Times*. New York: Harper and Row, 1965.

_____. *The Life and Adventures of Martin Chuzzlewit*. 1844. Oxford: Oxford UP, 1981.

_____. "To Andrew Bell." 12 Oct. 1841. Letter in *Pilgrim Edition: The Letters of Charles Dickens*. Vol. I. (1820-1839). Ed. Madeline House and Graham Storey. Oxford: Clarendon P, 1965.

_____. "To Frances Trollope." 30 Jan. 1839. Letter in*Pilgrim Edition*.

_____. "To Richard Bentley." 30 Nov. 1836. Letter in *Pilgrim Edition*.

_____. "To S. Laman Blanchard." 9 Feb. 1839. Letter in *Pilgrim Edition*.

Dorfman, Ariel. *The Empire's Old Clothes: What the Lone Ranger, Babar, and Other Innocent Heroes Do to Our Minds*. New York: Pantheon, 1983.

DuBois, Ellen Carol, ed. *Elizabeth Cady Stanton and Susan B. Anthony: Correspondence, Writings, Speeches*. New York: Schocken Books, 1981.

_____. *Feminism and Suffrage: The Emergence of an Independent Women's Movement in America: 1848-1869*. Ithaca and London: Cornell UP, 1978.

Easson, Angus. *Elizabeth Gaskell*. London: Routledge and Kegan Paul, 1979.

Eckhardt, Celia. *Fanny Wright: Rebel in America*. Cambridge: Harvard UP, 1984.

_____. "Of Fanny and Camilla Wright: Their Sisterly Love." *The Sister Bond: A Feminist View of a Timeless Connection*. Ed. Toni A. McNaron. New York: Pergamon, 1985.

Erkkila, Betsy. *Whitman the Political Poet*. New York and Oxford: Oxford UP, 1989.

Evans, M. Stanton. "Toward A New Intellectual History." *Freedom and Virtue: The Conservative/Libertarian Debate*. Ed. George W. Carey. Lanham: UP of America, Inc., and The Intercollegiate Studies Institute, Inc., 1984.

Fitzgerald, Percy. *Memories of Charles Dickens*. Briston: J. W. Arrowsmith, 1913.

Flexner, Eleanor. *Century of Struggle: The Women's Rights Movement in the United*

States, rev. ed. Cambridge, MA: Belknap P of Harvard U, 1975.

Forster, Margaret. *Significant Sisters: The Grassroots of Active Feminism 1839-1939*. New York: Oxford UP, 1984, 1985.

Fredman, Alice Green. *Anthony Trollope*. New York: Columbia UP, 1971.

Fuller, Margaret. *Woman in the Nineteenth Century*. (1855). New York: W.W. Norton and Co., Inc., 1971.

Furness, Clifton Joseph, ed. *Walt Whitman's Workshop*. New York: Russell and Russell, 1964.

Garforth, F.W. *Educative Democracy: John Stuart Mill on Education in Society*. Oxford UP, 1980.

_____. *John Stuart Mill's Theory of Education*. New York: Barnes and Noble, 1979.

Garnett, Harriet. "To Julia Garnett Pertz." 26 Nov. 1831. Letter in Heineman *Restless Angels*.

_____. "To Julia Pertz." 12 Dec. 1847. Letter in Heineman *The Triumphant* .

_____. "To Julia Pertz." 29 Dec. 1851. Letter in Heineman *The Triumphant* .

Gaskell, Elizabeth. *North and South*. 1855. London: Oxford UP, 1973.

Gilbert, Amos. *Memoir of Frances Wright: The Pioneer Woman in the Cause of Human Rights*. Cincinnati, 1855. Public Library of Cincinnati and Hamilton County.

Gilbert, Sandra and Susan Gubar, eds. *The Madwoman in the Attic: The Woman Writer and The Nineteenth-Century Literary Imagination*. New Haven and London: Yale UP, 1979, 1980.

_____. *The Norton Anthology of Literature By Women: The Tradition in English*. New York: W.W. Norton & Co., 1985.

Goodale, David. "Some of Walt Whitman's Borrowings." *American Literature*. 10 May 1938.

Goodfriend, Joyce and Claudia M. Christie, eds. *Lives of American Women: A History of Documents*. Boston: Little, Brown & Co., 1981.

Hallowell, A.D., ed. *James and Lucretia Mott: Life and Letters*. Boston and New York: Houghton Mifflin and Co., 1884.

Harper, Ida Husted. *Life and Work of Susan B. Anthony*. Vol. 2. 1898. Salem, NH: Ayer Co. Publ., Inc., 1983.

Heilbrun, Carolyn. *Reinventing Womanhood*. New York: Norton, 1979.

Heineman, Helen. *Frances Trollope*. Boston: Twayne Publishers, 1984.

_____. *Mrs. Trollope: The Triumphant Feminine in the Nineteenth Century*. Athens: Ohio UP, 1979.

_____. *Restless Angels: The Friendship of Six Victorian Women*. Athens: Ohio UP, 1983.

Hennessy, James Pope. *Anthony Trollope*. Boston: Little, Brown and Co., 1971.

Holyoake, George Jacob. *The History of Co-operation in England: Its Literature and Its Advocates*. Vol. I. London: T.F. Unwin, 1908.

House, Madeline and Graham Storey, eds. Pilgrim Edition: *The Letters of Charles Dickens*, 1820-1839. Vol. I. Oxford: Clarendon P, 1965.

Johnson, Edgar. *Charles Dickens: His Tragedy and Triumph*. Vol. I. New York: Simon and Schuster, 1952.

Kaplan, Justin. *Walt Whitman: A Life*. New York: Simon and Schuster, 1980.

Keating, P.J. *The Working Classes in Victorian Fiction*. London: Routledge and Kegan Paul, 1971.

Kenyon, Frederic G., ed. *The Letters of Elizabeth Barrett Browning*. Vol. I. New York: MacMillan Co., 1897.

Killingsworth, Myrth J. "Whitman and Motherhood: A Historical View (1982)." In *On Whitman: The Best From American Literature*. Eds. Edwin H. Cady and Louis J. Budd. Durham, NC: Duke UP, 1987.

Knoepflmacher. U.C. *Laughter and Despair: Readings in Ten Novels of the Victorian Era*. Berkeley: U of California P, 1971.

Lafayette. "To Harriet Garnett." 14 June 1852. Letter in Heineman *The Triumphant Feminine*.

Lane, Margaret. *Frances Wright and the "Great Experiment."* Totowa, NJ: Manchester UP, 1972.

Lasch, Christopher. *Haven in a Heartless World: The Family Beseiged*. New York: Basic Book, Inc. 1979.

Lecky, W.E. *History of European Morals*. Vol. 2. 1869. London: 1913.

Lerner, Gerda, ed. *The Female Experience: An American Documentary*. Indianapolis: Bobbs Merrill, 1977.

Lessing, Doris. *Prisons We Choose to Live Inside*. New York: Harper and Row, 1987.

Lutz, Alma. *Created Equal: A Biography of Elizabeth Cady Stanton, 1815-1902*. 1940. New York: Farrar, Straus and Girouz, 1974.

_____. *Susan B. Anthony: Rebel, Crusader, Humanitarian*. Boston: Beacon, 1959.

Meckier, Jerome. *Innocent Abroad: Charles Dickens's American Engagements*. Lexington: The UP of Kentucky, 1990.

Melder, Keith E. *Beginnings of Sisterhood: The American Women's Rights Movement, 1800-1850* . New York: Schoken Books, 1977.

Meyer, Frank. *The Conservative Mainstream*. New Rochelle, NY: Arlington House, 1969.

Mill, John Stuart. *On Liberty*. Ed. M.G. Fawcett. Oxford: Oxford UP, 1912.

_____. *The Early Draft of John Stuart Mill's Autobiography*. Ed. J. Stillinger, Champaign: U of Illinois P, 1961.

_____. *The Letters of John Stuart Mill*. Vol. I. Ed. Hugh S. Elliot, 6 March 1851. London: Longmans, Green and Co., 1910. In ed. Alice S. Rossi. *Essays on Sex and Equality: John Stuart Mill and Harriet Taylor Mill*. Chicago: U of Chicago P, 1970.

_____. *The Subjection of Women*. 1869. New York: Source, 1970.

Moers, Ellen. *Harriet Beecher Stowe and American Literature*. Hartford: The Stowe-Day Foundation, 1978.

Morgan, Susan. *Sisters in Time: Imagining Gender in Nineteenth Century British*

Fiction. New York: Oxford UP, 1989.

Morse, Deborah D. *Women in Trollope's Palliser Novels*. Ann Arbor: U of Michican Research P, 1987.

Mullen, Richard, ed. Introduction. *Domestic Manners of the Americans*. Oxford: Oxford UP, 1984.

Mylne, James. "To Julia Garnett." 12 Aug. 1827. Letter in Eckhardt *Fanny Wright.*

Nardin, Jane. *He Knew She Was Right: The Independent Woman in the Novels of Anthony Trollope*. Carbondale: Southern Illinois UP, 1989.

Neidle, Cecyle S. *America's Immigrant Women*. Boston: Twayne Publ., 1975.

Nies, Judith. *Seven Women: Portraits from the American Radical Tradition*. New York: Viking, 1977.

Nisbet, Robert. *Conservativism: Dream and Reality*. Minneapolis: U of Minnesota P, 1986.

Owen, Robert Dale. "An Earnest Sewing of Wild Oats." *Atlantic Monthly*. July 1874.

_____. *Owen's Travel Journal*. 1827. Ed. Josephine M. Elliott, Indiana Hist. Soc.Pub., 25.4. Indianapolis: Indiana Historical Society, 1977.

_____. *Threading My Way*. 1874. New York: A.M. Kelley, 1967.

Owen, Ursula, ed. *Fathers: Reflections by Daughters*. New York: Pantheon, 1985.

Patten, Robert. *Charles Dickens and His Publishers*. Oxford: Clarendon P, 1978.

Perkins, H.J.G. and Theresa Wolfson. *Frances Wright Free Enquirer: The Study of a Temperament*. New York and London: Harper Brothers, Publ., 1939.

Pertz, Julia G. "To Sismondi." 3 Sept. 1827. Letter in *Restless Angels: The Friendship of Six Victorian Women*. Helen Heineman. Athens: Ohio UP, 1983.

Pollard, Arthur. *Anthony Trollope*. London: Routledge and Kegan Paul, 1978.

Rajasekharaiah, T.R. *The Roots of Whitman's Grass*. Rutherford: Farleigh Dickinson UP, 1970.

Roberts, David. *Paternalism in Early Victorian England*. New Brunswick: Rutgers UP, 1979.

Rogers, Katherine M. and William McCarthy, eds. *The Meridian Anthology of Early Women Writers: British Literary Women from Aphra Behn to Maria Edgeworth, 1660-1800*. New York: New American Library, 1987.

Rose, Phyllis. *Parallel Lives: Five Victorian Marriages*. New York: Vintage, 1983.

Rosenthal, Bernard, ed. Introduction. *Woman in the Nineteenth Century*. 1855. New York: W.W. Norton and Co., Inc., 1971.

Rossi, Alice S., ed. *Essays on Sex and Equality: John Stuart Mill and Harriet Taylor Mill*. Chicago: U of Chicage P, 1970.

Sadleir, Michael. *Trollope: A Commentary* . 1927. New York: Octagon Books: A Division of Farrar, Straus, and Giroux, 1975.

Sapiro, Virginia. *Women in American Society: An Introduction to Women's Studies*. Palo Alto, CA: Mayfield Publishing Co., 1981.

Scruton, Roger. *The Meaning of Conservativism*. 1980. New York: MacMillan, 1984.

Scudder, Harold H. "Mrs. Trollope and Slavery in America." *Notes and Queries*. Vol.

187. 29 July, 1944.

Seller, Maxine Schwartz, ed. *Immigrant Women*. Philadelphia: Temple UP, 1981.

Shelley, Mary. "To Frances Wright." 12 Sept. 1827. Letter in Eckhardt *Fanny Wright*.

Simpson, David. "Destiny Made Manifest: The Styles of Whitman's Poetry." *Nation and Narration*. Ed. Homi K. Bhabha. London: Routledge, 1990.

Skelton, David. *Anthony Trollope and His Contemporaries: Study in the Theory and Conventions of Mid-Victorian Fiction*. New York: St. Martin's, 1972.

Smalley, Donald, ed. Introduction, Notes, and Appendices. *Domestic Manners of the Americans*. New York: Vintage Books, 1949.

Snow, C.P. *Trollope: His Life and Art*. New York: Scribner's Sons, 1975.

Spacks, Patricia Meyer. *The Female Imagination*. New York: Avon, 1976.

Stanton, Elizabeth Cady. *Eighty Years and More (1815-1897); Reminiscences of Elizabeth Cady Stanton*. 1898. New York: Source, 1970.

_____. *Elizabeth Cady Stanton as Revealed In Her Letters, Diary and Reminiscences*. Vol. II. Ed. Theodore Stanton and Harriet Stanton Blatch. New York: Harper, 1902.

Stanton, Elizabeth Cady, Susan B. Anthony and Matilda Joslyn Gage, eds. *History of Woman Suffrage 1848-1861*. Vol. I. 1881. New York: Arno P and *The New York Times*, 1969.

_____. *History of Woman Suffrage 1861-1876* . Vol. II. 1882. New York: Arno P and *The New York Times*, 1969.

Stebbins, Lucy P. and Richard P. Stebbins. *The Trollopes: The Chronicle of a Writing Family*. 1945. New York: AMS, Inc., 1966.

Stern, Madeline B. *The Life of Margaret Fuller*. New York: E.P. Dutton and Co., Inc., 1942.

Stillinger, J. ed. *The Early Draft of John Stuart Mill's Autobiography*. Champaign: U of Illinois P, 1961.

Stone, Donald D. *The Romantic Impulse in Victorian Fiction*. Cambridge: Harvard UP, 1980.

Stovall, Floyd. *The Foreground of Leaves of Grass*. Charlottesvile, VA: UP of Virginia, 1974.

Stowe, Harriet Beecher. *Uncle Tom's Cabin, or, Life Among the Lowly*. 1852. New York: Harper and Row, 1965.

Suhl, Yuri. *Eloquent Crusader: Ernestine Rose*. New York: Julian Messner, 1970.

Sundquist, Eric R. Introduction. *New Essays on Uncle Tom's Cabin*. Ed Eric J. Sundquist. Cambridge, MA: Cambridge UP, 1986.

Sutherland, J.A. *Victorian Novelists and Publishers*. Chicago: U of Chicago P, 1976.

Taylor, Barbara. *Eve and The New Jerusalem: Socialism and Feminism in the Nineteenth Century*. New York: Pantheon Books, 1983.

Thackeray, William M. Review of *The Vicar of Wrexhill*. *Fraser's Magazine*. 17 (1838). Heineman *Mrs. Trollope*.

_____. Review of "St. Patrick Eve, Morning Chronicle." 3 Apr. 1845. Heineman *The*

Triumphant.

Traubel, Horace. *With Walt Whitman in Camden.* 2 vols. New York: Appleton, 1908.

Trollope, Anthony. *An Autobiography.* Eds. Michael Sadleir and Frederick Page. Oxford: Oxford UP, 1980.

_____. *Barchester Towers.* 1857. New York: Doubleday and Co., 1945.

_____. *North America,* Vol .I. New York: St. Martin's, 1986.

Trollope, Frances.

_____. *Charles Chesterfield: or, The Adventures of a Youth Genius.* Vol. 3. London: Henry Colburn, Pub., 1841.

_____. *Domestic Manners of the Americans.* Ed. Richard Mullen. Oxford: Oxford UP, 1984.

_____. *Fashionable Life; or, Paris and London.* 3 vols. London: Hurst and Blackett, 1856.

_____. *Life and Aventures of Jonathan Jefferson Whitlaw.* 3 vols. London: Richard Bentley, 1836.

_____. *Refugee in America: A Novel.* 3 vols. London: Whitaker, Treacher, and Co., 1832.

_____. *The Barnabys in America; or, Adventures of the Widow Wedded.* 3 vols. London: Henry Colburn, Publ., 1843.

_____. *The Life and Adventures of Michael Armstrong, the Factory Boy.* London: Henry Colburn, Publ., 1840.

_____. "The Rough Draft: An Unpublished Preface." *Domestic Manners of the Americans.* Ed. Donald Smalley. New York: Vintage Books, 1949.

_____. *The Vicar of Wrexhill.* 3 Vols. London: Bentley, 1837.

_____. *The Widow Barnaby.* 3 Vols. London: Bentley, 1839.

_____. *The Widow Married: A Sequel to the Widow Barnaby.* 3 Vols. London: Henry Colburn, Publ., 1840.

_____. *Uncle Walter: A Novel.* 3 Vols. London: Colburn and Co., 1852.

_____. "To Charles Wilkes." 14 Feb. 1828. Cincinnati Historical Society.

_____. "To Harriet Garnett." 7 Dec. 1828. Letter in Heineman *The Triumphant.*

_____. "To Julia Garnett Pertz." 7 Oct. 1827. Letter in Heineman *Restless Angels.*

_____. "To Julia Garnett Pertz." 26 Dec. 1827. Letter in Heineman *The Triumphant.*

_____. "To Julia Garnett Pertz." 27 Dec. 1827. Letter in Heineman *The Triumphant.*

_____. "To Julia Garnett Pertz." 12 March 1830. Letter in Eckhardt *Fanny Wright.*

_____. "To Julia Garnett Pertz." 22 Aug. 1831. Letter in Heineman*Restless Angels.*

_____. "To Lafayette." 23 Apr. 1829. Letter in Heineman *The Triumphant* .

_____. "To Thomas Adolphous Trollope." (1832). Letter in Heineman *The Triumphant.*

Trollope, Frances Eleanor. *Frances Trollope: Her Life and Literary Work from George III to Victoria.* Vol. 2. London: Richard Bentley and Son, 1895.

Trollope, Thomas A. *What I Remember.* New York: Harper and Brothers, 1888.

Urbanski, Marie Mitchell Olesen. *Margaret Fuller's Woman in the Nineteenth Century: A Literary Study.* Westport and London: Greenwood P, 1980.

Waterman, William Randall. *Frances Wright*. New York: Columbia UP, 1924.

Walsh, Robert. "To Phiquepal D'Arusmont." 12 Oct. 1850. Letter in Eckhardt *Fanny Wright*.

Welsh, Alexander. *The City of Dickens*. Cambridge: Harvard UP, 1986.

Wheeler, Anna. "The British Co-operator." April 1830. In *Eve and The New Jerusalem: Socialism and Feminism in the Nineteenth Century*. Barbara Taylor. New York: Pantheon Books, 1983.

Whitman, Walt. "Democratic Vistas." *Prose Works*, 1892. Vol. 2. Ed. Floyd Stovall. New York: New York UP, 1964.

_____. *Leaves of Grass: Facsimile of 1856 Edition*. Norwood, PA: Norwood, PA: Norwood Editions, 1976.

_____. *Leaves of Grass: Inclusive Edition*. Ed. Emory Holloway. New York: Doubleday, 1926.

_____. *Leaves of Grass: The First (1855) Edition*. Ed. Malcolm Cowley. New York: Viking, 1959.

Wilson, Forrest. *Crusader in Crinoline: The Life of Harriet Beecher Stowe*. Philadelphia: J.B. Lippincott, Co., 1941.

Wills, Garry. *Confessions of a Conservative*. Garden City: Doubleday, 1979.

_____. *Reagan's America: Innocents at Home*. Garden City: Doubleday, 1987.

Wolff, Robert L. *Gains and Losses: Novels of Faith and Doubt in Victorian England*. New York: Garland Publishing Co., Inc., 1977.

Wright, Camilla [Whitby]. "To Harriet Garnett." 20 Nov. 1828. Letter in Heineman *The Triumphant*.

_____. "To Julia Garnett." 10 Jan. 1826. Letter in Eckhardt "Of Fanny and Camilla Wright: Their Sisterly Love." Celia Eckhardt *The Sister Bond: A Feminist View of a Timeless Connection*. Ed. Toni A McNaron. New York: Pergamon, 1985.

Wright, Frances [Mme. D'Arusmont]. *A Few Days in Athens* (1850). New York: Arno, 1972.

_____. "Address I." *Wright Life, Letters, and Lectures*.

_____. "Address II." Wright *Life, Letters, and Lectures*.

_____. "Address III." Wright *Life, Letters, and Lectures*.

_____. "Address Containing a Review of the Times." Wright *Life, Letters, and Lectures*..

_____. "Address on the State of the Public Mind and the Measures Which It Calls For." Wright *Life, Letters, and Lectures*.

_____. "An Address to Young Mechanics." Wright *Life, Letters, and Lectures*.

_____. *Biography, Notes and Political Letters of Frances Wright D'Arusmont* (1844). Wright *Life, Letters, and Lectures*.

_____. "D'Arusmont vs. D'Arusmont and Others," *Western Law Journal* 8 (Oct. 1850-Oct. 1851). Eckhardt *Fanny Wright*.

_____. "Divisions of Knowledge." Wright *Life, Letters, and Lectures*.

_____. *England, The Civilizer: Her History Developed In Its Principles*. London: Simpkin, Marshall and Co., 1848.

_____. *Explanatory Notes* in *New Harmony Gazette.* 30 Jan., 6, 13 Feb. 1828.

_____. *Frances Wright, Life, Letters, and Lectures.* 1834-1844. New York: Arno, 1972.

_____. *Free Enquirer.* 29 April 1829. Eckhardt *Fanny Wright.*

_____. "Free Inquiry." Wright, *Life, Letters, and Lectures.*

_____. "Last Will and Testament." 13 Sept. 1852. Cincinnati Historical Society.

_____. Lecture V. Wright *Life, Letters, and Lectures.*

_____. Lecture VII. Wright *Life, Letters, and Lectures.*

_____. Letter III. Wright *Life, Letters, and Lectures.*

_____. Letter V. Wright *Life, Letters, and Lectures.*

_____. Letter VI. Wright *Life, Letters, and Lectures.*

_____. Letter VII. Wright *Life, Letters, and Lectures.*

_____. "Nature of Knowledge." Wright *Life, Letters, and Lectures.*

_____. "Of Existing Evils, and Their Remedy." Wright *Life, Letters, and Lectures.*

_____. "Parting Address." Wright *Life, Letters, and Lectures.*

_____. Preface. "Course of Popular Lectures" (1829). Wright *Life, Letters, and Lectures.*

_____. Preface. Wright *Life, Letters, and Lectures.*

_____. "To Harriet Garnett and Julia Garnett Pertz." Feb. 1828. Letter in Heineman *Restless Angels.*

_____. "To James Richardson." 18 Aug. 1827. Letter in Eckhardt *Fanny Wright.*

_____. To John M. Morgan, Esq.: London." 9 June 1833. Public Library of Cincinnati and Hamilton County.

_____. "To W.Y. Gholson: Covington, Kentucky." 13 Nov. 1851. Letter. Cincinnati Historical Society.

_____. "To W.Y. Gholson." 6 June 1852. Letter. Cincinnati Historical Society.

_____.*Views of Society and Manners in America.* Ed. Paul R. Baker. Cambridge: Belknap P of Harvard UP, 1963.

Zweig, Paul. *Walt Whitman: The Making of the Poet.* New York: Basic, 1984.

Index

169

www.ingramcontent.com/pod-product-compliance
Lightning Source LLC
Chambersburg PA
CBHW031843090426
42741CB00005B/335